MARRIAGE AND
DEATH NOTICES

FROM THE

𝕲𝖊𝖓𝖎𝖚𝖘 𝖔𝖋 𝕷𝖎𝖇𝖊𝖗𝖙𝖞

1817–1843

Marty Hiatt, Ann Hennings
and Patricia B. Duncan

HERITAGE BOOKS
2024

HERITAGE BOOKS

AN IMPRINT OF HERITAGE BOOKS, INC.

Books, CDs, and more—Worldwide

For our listing of thousands of titles see our website
at
www.HeritageBooks.com

A Facsimile Reprint
Published 2024 by
HERITAGE BOOKS, INC.
Publishing Division
5810 Ruatan Street
Berwyn Heights, MD 20740

Originally published in 2005
as a Special Issue of
Northern Virginia Genealogy

International Standard Book Number
Paperbound: 978-0-7884-2800-5

Introduction

The weekly newspaper, *Genius of Liberty* was published in Leesburg, Virginia from January 1817 through May 1843. The first owner, editor, and publisher was Samuel B. T. Caldwell. He was born 1789 in Hillsboro County, New Hampshire and settled in Leesburg about 1815. The printer was Cyrus R. Saunders. Other editors were Brook W. Sower and George Richards. From its beginning, brief announcements regarding deaths and marriages were published in the paper.

People who lived "in town," were more likely to be mentioned, but the coverage was actually very wide. It appears that Mr. Caldwell would publish any marriage or death notice that was supplied, so long as space was available. There are notices from as far away as Warren County, Virginia, and New York. Sometimes notices were copied from the Maryland or Washington, DC newspapers. Also, *Genius of Liberty* notices may request other newspapers copy, like "Ohio papers please copy," suggesting that the deceased had family connections elsewhere.

No matter where people lived, or how prominent they were, the announcement was usually brief. Data about extended family members was never included. Occasionally a column would be filled with 2 or 3 inches of complimentary comments about a deceased person. In those instances we have inserted [long obit] at the end of the announcement. This does not mean there was information about the family or cause of death. The few times that was included, it was copied exactly as printed. Two examples of long obituaries are printed on the last page of this book.

Several years ago, Don Francis visited Leesburg to meet with the current owner of the original copies of the *Genius of Liberty* who allowed Francis to extract any desired information. From this Francis compiled a list of marriage and death notices he found in the newspaper." He shared that list with Ann Hennings, who many years later provided it to *Northern Virginia Genealogy*. After Pat Duncan computerized the data, Mrs. Hennings and Marty Hiatt compared Mr. Francis' list to the original newspapers. We added a few notices that Mr. Francis had omitted, but not every announcement in the paper will be found in this book. There were too many humorous events, such as the marriage of Mr. Pink and Miss Purple, to include them all. The style of these entries is not consistent because we followed the way the notice was printed in the paper or abstracted by Mr. Francis. In the earlier years Mr. Francis also calculated the dates and added them to the text.

Only the first five years of this newspaper have been microfilmed. That film is available at Thomas Balch Library in Leesburg, Virginia. A few random copies are available throughout the United States, but it has not been possible to find another large collection. We hope by making this information available to the public, it will help break down a few of those old research "brick-walls."

Marty Hiatt, CGRS
January 2005

Dedication

This book is dedicated to the very gracious
and generous man who allowed us to spend
many hours in his home, reading his newspapers
and abstracting this information.

Thank you.

Genius of Liberty

Published by Samuel B. T. Caldwell

Vol. I, No. 1 – Saturday, January 11, 1817
John Follin and Mary Barker, both of Fairfax Co. m. Thursday, January 2, 1817 by Rev. Gilmore.
James Smarr and Nancy McCarty, of Loudoun Co. m. January 2, 1817 by Rev. Filmore [sic].
Charles Thornton and Sarah Sinclair, all of Loudoun Co. m. Thursday, January 9, 1817 by Rev. Gilmore.
John H. Cassaday and Jane Bennett, all of Loudoun Co. m. January 2, 1817 by Rev. Mines.
Miss Nancy Mathias of Leesburg, d. Friday, January 3, 1817.

Vol. I, No. 2 – Saturday, January 20, 1817
James Saunders of Loudoun and Priscilla Forman of Berkeley Co. m. January 2, 1817 by Rev. Boyleston.
Thomas Rollins and Elizabeth Ball, all of Loudoun m. [January 2, 1817] by Rev. John Littlejohn.
David Hamilton and Rebecca Reed, all of Loudoun m. [December 2, 1816 per Wertz] by Rev. John Littlejohn.
John Shalters and Ellen Dixon, all of Loudoun m. [December 13, 1816] by Rev. John Littlejohn.
Thomas Gore and Sarah Walker, all of Loudoun m. Thursday last [January 2, 1817] by Rev. John Littlejohn.

Vol. I, No. 3 – Saturday, January 27, 1817
Richard Roach and Anna Orrison m. Thursday, January 23, 1817 by Rev. John Littlejohn.
William Howell and Catharine Shepherd m. January 23, 1817 by Rev. John Littlejohn.

Vol. I, No. 4 – Saturday, February 4, 1817
Abel Orrison and Catharine Hough m. Thursday, January 30, 1817 by Rev. John Littlejohn.

Vol. I, No. 6 – Saturday, February 18, 1817
John B. Findley and Janett Findley m. Thursday, February 13, 1817 by Rev. John Littlejohn.
Samuel A. Tillett and Jane Tillett m. February 13, 1817 by Rev. John Littlejohn.
Nelson Hutchison and Lydia Burson, all of this county m. February 13, 1817 by Rev. Willis.

Vol. I, No. 10 – March 18, 1817
Robert Whitacre and Hannah Ewers m. Thursday, Feb 27, 1817 by Rev. Wm. Gilmore.
Stacey Lacey and Mahala Sandford m. Tuesday, March 4
Payton Triplett and Sarah Combs m. Wednesday, March 5, 1817.
Joseph Russel and Nancy Near m. Thursday, March 13, 1817 by Rev. John Littlejohn.

Timothy Taylor and Harriett Osburn m. Thursday, March 13, 1817 by Rev. Mines.

Vol. I, No. 13 – Tuesday, April 8, 1817
Miss Louisa Douglass, age 15 years, daughter of late Gen. Douglas, d. Saturday,
    April 5, 1817.
George Fortney, age 49 years of Leesburg, d. Friday, April 4, 1817.

Vol. I, No. 15 – Tuesday, April 22, 1817
Thursday last [April 17th], by Rev. John Littlejohn, Augustine G. Monroe and
    Bethany Saunders, both of this town.
A man by the name of Thomas Foreman was recently tried at Norfolk and
    convicted of passing counterfeit notes. Sentence – 3 years imprisonment in
    the common jail and $1000 fine.

Vol. I, No. 16 – April 29, 1817
Mr. Isreal Lacey and Ann Thompson, m. Sunday, April 20, 1817 by Wm. Gilmore.
Dr. Marcus C. Buck, of Frederick Co. Va., and Elizabeth P. Drake, of Leesburg,
    m. Tuesday, April 22, 1817 by Wm. Gilmore.
Benjamin Watson and Malitda [Matilda] Ball, m. Thursday, April 24, 1817.

Vol. I, No. 18 – May 13, 1817
On Thursday the 1st May at Dr. Charles Cocke's in Albermarle, Virginia by the
    Rev. Mr. Dunn of Loudoun, General Armistead T. Mason to Miss Charlotte
    Eliza Taylor, youngest daughter of the late John Taylor, Esq. of
    Southampton.

Vol. I, No. 26 – July 8, 1817
Charles Carpenter and Elizabeth Van Horn, all of Frederick Co., m. Thursday,
    July 3, 1817 by Rev. Thos. Littleton.
George L. Lackland, of Montgomery, Md., and Eliza E. Edwards, of Loudoun, m.
    Thursday, June 26, 1817 by Rev. John Littlejohn.
Samuel C. B. McClellan and Matilda Jacobs, m. Thursday, July 3, 1817.
John Saulton and Elizabeth Wolkard, of this place, m. Thursday, July 3, 1817 by
    Rev. John Littlejohn.
Died in this town Saturday evening last [July 5, 1817], William Wright.
Died on the 24th ult., Thomas M'Kean, Esqr., formerly Gov. of Pennsylvania.

Vol. I, No. 28 – July 22, 1817
Died on Thursday morning last [July 17], Mr. H. Glasgow, a respectable
    inhabitant of this place.

Vol. I, No. 34 – September 2, 1817
Died suddenly on the 29th ult. Mrs. A. T. Chichester.

Vol. I, No. 37 – September 23, 1817
Married on 7th inst. at Washington City, John S.Gallaher, printer and Catherine
    Shannon, both of that place.

Vol. I, No. 39 – October 7, 1817
John Williams and Nancy Brown, of this county, m. 2nd inst. [October 2] by Rev.
    Wm. Gilmore.
Jonathan McCarty and Isabella M. Farling m. Sunday, September 28, 1817 by
    Rev. Wm. Gilmore.

John Thompson and Ellin Tribby m. Sunday, September 28, 1817 by Rev. Wm.
Gilmore.
Died in this town on Tuesday last, of the billious fever, Doct. J. E. Veil late of
Richmond. He arrived here on Thurs. previous t his death with his family, for
the purpose of establishing himself in this place as a druggist.

Vol. I, No. 40 – October 14, 1817

Reuben Hut[ch]inson and Miss Leah Bayly m. Wednesday, October 8, 1817 by
Rev. Gilmore.
Jasper Thompson and Aminto [sic] Rivers, all of this county, m. Saturday,
October 11, 1817 by Gilmore.
In Alexandria, Robert Bentley of Leesburg, and Catherine Longdon of Alexandria,
m. Thursday, October 9, 1817 by Rev. Wilmer of Alexandria.

Vol. I, No. 41 – October 21, 1817

Died on October 14, J. E. Vail, age 7 years, eldest son of the late Dr. J. E. Vail.
Mr. Christopher Vail, of Richmond, thanks citizens of Leesburg ... for the
attention ... bestowed on the afflicted family of his son of whom together with
a grandson, it has pleased God to deprive him of in the short space of 15
days.

Vol. I, No. 43 – November 4, 1817

Died on Sunday morning last, Mrs. Mary Saunders, consort of Mr. Britton
Saunders, of this county.

Vol. I, No. 46 [sic] – November 18, 1817

In Harrisonburg, Rockingham Co., by Rev. Mr. Baker, Charles Douglas of this
place and Ann B. Waterman, m. October 30, 1817.

Vol. I, No. 47 – November 25, 1817

Thompson F. Mason of Alexandria and Elizabeth Price of Leesburg m.
November 20, 1817 by John Mines.

Vol. I, No. 51 – December 23, 1817

Rev. Littlejohn, on Thursday, December 18, 1817, m. Mr. Leonard T. Wheeler to
Miss Mary Ann Sopher.
On same day, Mr. Isaac Schell to Miss Margaret Dorson.
On same day, Mr. Josiah Hood to Miss Nancy Jones.

Vol. II, No. 3 – January 20, 1818

David Beatty and Martha Sears m. Thursday, December 25, 1817 by Wm.
Gilmore.
John Rine and Sarah Dailey m. Thursday, January 1, 1818 by Wm. Gilmore.
William Ballon [sic] and Nancy Davis m. Sunday, January 4, 1818 by Wm.
Gilmore.
John Bowling and Eliza Joice, all of Loudoun, m. Thursday, January 8, 1818 by
Wm. Gilmore.
Robert Deau, of Frederick, and Amelia Denny, of Fairfax, m. Thursday, January
8, 1818, by Littlejohn.
Isaac Lafferty, of Jefferson, and Anne A. Durham, of Loudoun Co., m. Tuesday,
January 14, 1818 by Littlejohn.
Samuel G. Hamilton and Anne H. Fox m. Thursday, January 16, 1818 by
Littlejohn.

William B. Shipley and Nancy L. Dykes m. Thursday, January 16, 1818 by
    Littlejohn.
Peter Feester and Susan Stoneburner, all of this county, m. Sunday, January 18,
    1818.

Vol. II, No. 4 – January 27, 1818

Moses Gulick and Martha Mudd, both of Loudoun, m. Thursday, January 22,
    1818 by Wm. Gilmore.
William Paxson Jr. and Diademia Lacey, m. January 22, 1818 by Rev. J.
    Littlejohn.
Dan'l. P. Conrad, merchant of of this place, and Mary Ann Richards, of
    Portsmouth, N. H., m. January 22, 1818 by Rev. J. Littlejohn.

Vol. II, No. 6 – February 17, 1818

James Lord and Penny Gardner, both of Fairfax Co., m. February 14th inst.

Vol. II, No. 14 – April 14, 1818

Joseph Eidson and Mahala McCarty m. Thursday, April 9, 1818 by Wm.
    Gillmore.
Hezekiah Ogden and Nancy Lynn m Thursday, April 9, 1818 by Wm. Gillmore.
George Shawen and Jane Hamilton m. 1st inst. by J. Littlejohn.
Died Wednesday the 1st inst., Mr. George Head Sr. of this town.

Vol. II, No. 15 – April 21, 1818

George Mason Chichester and Sally Elliott m. Tuesday, April 14, 1818 by John
    Mines.
Samuel A. Jackson and Sarah Nichols, all of this county, m. Thursday, April 16,
    1818 by John Littlejohn.

Vol. II, No. 17 – May 5, 1818

James F. Newton of Loudoun Co. and Eleanor S. Hansborough of Culpeper m.
    Thursday, April 23, 1818 by Rev. Mr. Woodville.
Died on Sunday, 3rd inst., Peter Boss, an old and respectable inhabitant of this
    town.

Vol. II, No. 18 – May 12, 1818

Died Saturday the 25th ult., Mrs. Elizabeth Brandon, 36 years of age, buried from
    Northfork Baptist Meeting House on Saturday, long time member.
Died Saturday the 25th ult. in her 36th year, Mrs. Sarah Brandon leaving a
    husband and 7 small children, one 4 days old. Buried North Fork Baptist
    Meeting House.

Vol. II, No. 22 – June 9, 1818

Wm. Clowe and Lucinda Wayatt [sic] m. Monday, May 25, 1818 by Wm. Gilmore.
John Ethell and Mrs. Mary Morel [sic] m. Sunday, May 31, 1818 by Wm. Gilmore.
John H. Holsclaw and Martha Beard m. Thursday, June 4, 1818 by Wm. Gilmore.

Vol. II, No. 24 – June 23, 1818

John Johnson and Sarah Collins m. June 8, 1818 by Rev. John Littlejohn.
Anthony Weight [sic] [Wright] and Sarah Graham m. June 13, 1818 by Rev. John
    Littlejohn.

Vol. II, No. 26 – July 7, 1818
In Waterford on Tuesday, June 30th, 1818, by Rev. John Mines, Capt. Isaac VanDeventer to Mrs. Mary Braden, widow of the late Doct. Braden.

Vol. II, No. 32 – August 18, 1818
Died on 8th at Waterford, Mr. David Lacey.
On the 15th near Leesburg,Elizabeth Mead.

Vol. II, No. 34 – September 1, 1818
James Lane d. in Montgomery, Md. on August 20, 1818.

Vol. II, No. 36 – September 15, 1818
Robert Fulton and Louisa Wilkinson m. Thursday, September 3, 1818 by Rev. John Littlejohn.
Thomas W. Langton and Margaret Hains m. September 3, 1818 by Rev. John Littlejohn.
William Bateman and Catherine Spencer, all of this county, m. September 3, 1818 by Rev. John Littlejohn.

Vol. II, No. 37 – September 22, 1818
Thomas Rinaldo Johnson of Calvert Co., Md. and Sarah A. Mason of St. Marys Co., Md., m. on 8th inst. at Oakland, by Rev. Brady.

Vol. II, No. 39 – October 13, 1818
Walker Muse and Nancy Moffet, of this county, m. Thursday, September 10, 1818 by Rev. William Gilmore.
Peter Carper, of Frederick City, and Massy Fowler, of this city, m. September 24, 1818 by Rev. William Gilmore.
Mr. Marks [sic] and Hannah Daniel m. September 24, 1818 by Rev. William Gilmore.
Capt. Benjamin Mitchell and Martha Lane m. Sunday, October 4, 1818 by Rev. William Gilmore.
Dr. Thomas F. Tebbs of Prince William Co. and Margaret Binns of Leesburg m. Tuesday, October 6, 1818 by Rev. John Dunn.
Jacob Wildbahn [sic] and Anna Reed m. Thursday, October 8, 1818 by Wm. Gilmore.

Vol. II, No. 42 – November 3, 1818
In this county on the __ day of October, Mrs. Mary M'Gathah, in the 106 year of her age. Native of Ireland, resident of this country 57 years and Loudoun 40 years. Mother of 8 sons. Buried at Methodist burying ground in this town.
Nathanial Norton, age 50 years, d. October 21, 1818.
Married on 20th ult. by Gilmore, Mr. Christian Stoneburner to Miss Elizabeth M'Geath, both of this county.

Vol. II, No. 43 – November 10, 1818
John A. Binns and Mary Rose, youngest daughter of Capt. John Rose, m. Thursday, November 5, 1818 by Rev. Mr. Griffith.
Doctor Jno. Drish and Catherine Washington m. Monday, October 20, 1818 in Haymarket by Rev. John Mines.

Vol. II, No. 45 – November 24, 1818
In Waterford – David Shawen and Miss Francis [*sic*] A. Fox, all of this county, m. November 17, 1818 by Wm. Gilmore.

Vol. II, No. 46 – December 1, 1818
Thompson Mason, of Loudoun Co., and Ann Thomas, daughter of Wm. Thomas, Esq. late of St. Mary's Co. Md., m. November 19th inst.
Wm. Cooper of Waterford and Ellen Dailey of Leesburg m. Thursday, November 26, 1818 by Rev. John Mines.

Vol. II, No. 47 – December 8, 1818
John A. Washington and Amelia Saunders, both of Loudoun Co., m. Thursday evening last by Rev. Mr. Griffith.

Vol. II, No. 51 – January 5, 1819
John Martin and Mary Hawk m. Thursday, December 31, 1818 by Griffith.
John Smarr and Susan McCarty m. Wednesday, December 17, 1818 by Wm. Gillmore.
James Swartz and Ketura Jenkins m. Thursday, December 22, 1818 by Wm. Gillmore.
John Jackson and Mrs. Mary Davis m. Sunday, December 29, 1818 by Wm. Gillmore.
John Turner and Mary Fowler m. Thursday, December 31, 1818 by Wm. Gillmore.

Vol. III, No. 1 – January 19, 1819
Alfred Weeks of Fauquier Co. and Glarissa [Clarissa] Dowdle of Loudoun m. Thursday the 17th by Rev. Wm. Gillmore.
James Caldwell and Frances Pattin, both of Fauquier, m. Thursday, December 24, 1818 by Rev. Mr. Brown in Warrenton.
Thomas Childs, Esq., U.S. Army, and Ann Eliza Coryton, niece of Gen. Lynn of Alex., m. Thursday, January 5, 1819 by Rev. W. H. Wilmer at Alexandria, DC.

Vol. III, No. 2 – January 26, 1819
George Chichester, Esq. of Fairfax and Margaret Peyton, daughter of late Doctor Peyton of Stafford, m. Thursday, January 12, 1819.

Vol. III, No. 3 – February 2, 1819
David Carr and Susan Brown, both of this county, m. Sunday, January 24, 1819.

Vol. III, No. 4 – February 9, 1819
Hamilton Elgin of Loudoun Co. and Rebecca H. Thrift m. Tuesday, January 26, 1819 by Rev. Mr. Waters.
James Strother and Sarah Tillett, of this county, m. Thursday, February 4, 1819 by Wm. Gilmore.

Vol. III, No. 9 – March 16, 1819
Capt. Samuel Dawson of Loudoun Co. and Anne E. Mason, daughter of Thomson Mason, m. Tuesday, March 9, 1819 by Rev. O. Norris at Hollin Hall.

Vol. III, No. 13 – April 13, 1819
Samuel Hough Esqr and Jane Edwards, both of this county, m. Thursday, April 8, 1819.

Vol. III, No. 19 – May 25, 1819

Died on the __ day of April, Richard Allnutt, age 16, of Leesburg.

Vol. III, No. 23 – June 22, 1819

Hugh Smith and Elizabeth Jones, m. Thursday, June 17, 1819 by Rev. John Dunn.

David Boss and Eliza Hoskins, m. Thursday eve last by Rev. John Littlejohn (collector of Internal Revenue for 22 district of Va.)

Charles Binns Jr. and Martha Moffett, all of this county, m. June 17, 1819 by Rev. Wm. Gilmore.

Vol. III, No. 24 – June 29, 1819

Thomas Loveless and Catharine Davis, all of this county, m. Thursday, June 24, 1819 by Rev. Gilmore.

Capt. James Beavers and Sarah Smarr, all of this county, m. Thursday, June 24, 1819 by Wm. Gilmore.

Thomas Allwell, [*sic*] [Attwell] age 47, d. Thursday, June 24, 1819 near Middleburg.

Vol. III, No. 26 – July 13, 1819

At Woodstock, Shenandoah Co., B. L. Bogan (editor of *Woodstock Herald*) and Sarah Ott, daughter of Michael Ott, all of Shenandoah Co., m. Saturday, July 3, 1819 by Rev. Nicholas Smuchker.

At New Holland, S. C. Stanbaugh, Esq. (editor of *Free Press*) and Ann Wilder, of Lancaster, m. Sunday, June 23, 1819.

Vol. III, No. 27 – July 20, 1819

Lieut. William Seeders and Sarah Dreane m. Thursday, June 15, 1819 by Rev. John Littlejohn.

Sunday, July 18, 1819, Rev. John Littlejohn m. Mr. Asa Peck and Miss Ann Eliza Hough, all of this town.

At Ithica, N. Y., Augustin P. Searing and Delia Butler, daughter of Comfort Butler, m. July 18, 1819.

Vol. III, No. 29 – August 3, 1819

Hillory Hackinson and Eleanor Spates, both of Montgomery Co., Md., m. Tuesday, July 27, 1819 by Rev. John Littlejohn.

Samuel M. Boss and Elizabeth F. Fox, both of Leesburg, m. Thursday, July 29, 1819 by Rev. John Littlejohn.

Died on Saturday morning last, Mrs. Harriet Newton, consort of John Newton, printer.

Died yesterday evening, Mrs. Ann Eliza Peck, consort of Asa Peck.

Mrs. Martha Mines, consort of Rev. John Mines, d. Monday, August 2, 1819.

Vol. III, No. 31 – August 17, 1819

Died in Newtown, Va. on Saturday, 21st ult., Mr. John Sopher, teacher at the Newtown Academy.

Vol. III, No. 35 – September 14, 1819

Maryland Tuesday last by Rev. Griffith m. Mr. William Jacobs to Miss Catherine Shaw, Tuesday, September 3, 1819, all of this town.

Vol. III, No. 38 –October 5, 1819

Died in Leesburg jail on 29th ult., Mr. Samuel Gray of Waterford – died of a blow on the head by a Mr. Kid in the Leesburg jail. Both were inebriated at the race track.

Vol. III, No. 39 – October 12, 1819

John Robert Wallace, Esqr, late of U. S. Military Academy, Warrenton, Fauquier Co., and Elizabeth Macrae, of Dumfries, m. September 30, 1819 in Dumfries by Rev. Wm. Steel.

Vol. III, No. 41 – October 26, 1819

Mrs. Harriot Mateer, wife of James Mateer, d. at Hillsborough on Monday, October 18, 1819, and on October 23, 1819 Mrs. Mateer's infant child.

Vol. III, No. 42 – November 2, 1819

Died on the parade ground at Gum Spring Friday afternoon last, Mr. Thomas Myers, was seized with a violent discharge of blood from the stomach and expired almost immediately. We understand he had been long comsumptive. He has left a wife and two children.

Vol. III, No. 44 – November 16, 1819

Nathan Near and Eliza Potts m. Thursday, November 11, 1819 by Rev. Gilmore.

Vol. III, No. 45 – November 23, 1819

Joseph Caldwell Jr., editor of the *Virginia Reformer*, and Ann Mitchell, daughter of late Capt. John Mitchell of Shenandoah, near Front Royal, m. Sunday, November 14, 1819 by Rev. Reuben Finnell.

Vol. III, No. 46 – November 30, 1819

Giles Hammatt and Alice B. Barnett, all of this town, m. Thursday, November 24, 1819 by Rev. Griffith.

George W. Henry and Elizabeth Fox, both of Waterford, m. Sunday, November 14, 1819.

Vol. III, No. 47 – December 7, 1819

At Fredericksburg, Va., Rev. Abraham Spitler, Shenandoah Co., aged 72, and Mrs. Bathsheba Clark, Madison Co., aged 78y, m. November 28, 1819 by Rev. A. C. Booten.

Died 22nd ult. at Fountain Inn, Baltimore, Joseph Stover, Esqr., aged 65 of Strasburg, Shenandoah Co., Va.

Vol. III, No. 49 – December 21, 1819

Died suddenly on Friday last, Mr. Isaac Steers, long a respectable resident of Loudoun Co.

Vol. IV, No. 2 – January 25, 1820

Died on Saturday last, Mrs. Mary Fortney, of this town. Her remains interred Sunday in Methodist Burial Ground.

Died on same day, infant son of Mr. John H. Monroe, of this town.

Died on Sunday evening last, Mrs. Jane Halling, consort of Mr. William Halling, of Loudoun.

Vol. IV, No. 3 – February 1, 1820

Died at his farm near the Gum Springs on Sunday last (January 30, 1820), Capt. Joseph Lewis Sr. in the 81st year of his age.

Gen. Thomas Parker of Frederick Co. departed life on the 24th ult. of angina pectoris. Interred in Episcopal burying ground, Leesburg, on 26th with honors of war. [long obit]

Vol. IV, No. 4 – February 8, 1820

John Buskirk and Lucinda Grahame, both of Loudoun Co., m. February 1, 1820 by Rev. M. L. Johns at Fredericktown.

Vol. IV, No. 5 – February 15, 1820

Married on Tuesday evening last by Rev. A. Griffith, James Mills and Ann (Nancy) Page, both of this town.

Married at Baltimore on 3rd inst. by Right Rev. Dr. Kemp, John Marshall Jr., son of the Chief Justice U. S., and Elizabeth Maria, daughter of Dr. Ashton Alexander of Baltimore.

Vol. IV, No. 6 – February 22, 1820

Died at Union on Friday the 11th inst. in the 20th year of her age, Mrs. Emily Brown, consort of David Ellicott Brown.

Vol. IV, No. 8 – March 7, 1820

Died March 2, 1820, Mrs. Jane Hamilton, in the 97th year of age. Early Resident of Leesburg...resided for the last 60 or 70 years of her life. She has left posterity of the fourth generation.

Died March 2, 1820, Mrs. Ann Drane, in the 54th years consort of Mr. John Drane of this town.

Vol. IV, No. 9 – March 14, 1820

John Hamilton and Maria Janney, both of this county, m. Thursday, March 9, 1820 by Rev. John Mines.

Samuel Lawrence Gouverneur, Esq., N. Y. and Maria Hester Monroe, youngest daughter of President Monroe, m. by Rev. Hawley, city of Washington

Sprightly Mr. Cutsail, 78 years, and amiable Miss Fogle, 17 years, all of Frederick, Md., m. February 24, 1820 by Rev. Mr. Higgins.

Vol. IV, No. 10 – March 21, 1820

Rev. Mr. Mines married in this town on Thursday last Mr. William J. Weldon and Miss Ann Fouch, all of this county.

Died about 1 o'clock yesterday morning, Mrs. Sarah C. Chichester, in the 19th year of her age, consort of Mr. George M. Chichester, of this town. The funeral will take place this morning and proceed to the family burial ground at the farm of Samuel Clapham, Esqr.

Died in Alexandria, DC., on Saturday the 11th inst., General Thompson Mason, collector of the port of Alexandria.

Vol. IV, No. 12 – April 4, 1820

Married March 30 by Rev. Mines, John C. Clarke and Miss __ Tillett, all of this county.

Vol. IV, No. 14 – April 18, 1820

Married April 13 by Rev. Wm. Gilmore, Mr. Thomas Rallings and Miss Amelia Watts, both of this county.

Died near Haymarket on the 6th of April in the 19th year of her age, Mrs. Catharine H. Drish, consort of Dr. John Drish, after an illness of about 2 months.

Married at Philadelphia on Thursday evening, the 1st inst., by the Rt. Rev. Bishop White, Mr. Judah Bobson to the truly amiable and accomplished Miss Susan, only daughter of Zachariah Poulson, editor of the *American Daily Advertiser.*

Vol. IV, No 15 – April 25, 1820

Married in Wayne Co., NC on March 14th Mr. Bartholomew Crab, in the 68th year of his age, and Miss Susan Candy, age 16 years.

Died on Sunday the 16th inst., Mrs. Frances Ellzey, consort of Col. William Ellzey of this county.

At Lancaster, Pennsylvania on the 10th of April, in the 49th year of age, Col. William Hamilton, editor of *Lancaster Journal.*

Vol. IV, No. 20 – May 30, 1820

Died May 25, 1820, infant child of Enos Wildman of Leesburg.

Married on the 23rd ult. in the Isle of Wight Co.,Va. Mr. James Steele, age 76 years, and Miss Deborah Iron, age 71 years.

Vol. IV, No 22 – June 13, 1820

Married May 14 by Rev. Wm. Gillmore, Charles Lucas and Delilah King.

Married May 25 by Rev. Wm. Gillmore, Jacob Carnicle and Sarah Conwell, all of this county.

Married June 1 by Rev. Wm. Gillmore, James Roane and Mary Bartlett, all of Frederick Co.

Married June 1 by Rev. Williamson, William Beatty and Rebecca Todd, all of this county.

Married June 4 by Rev. Wm. Gilmore, Hiram W. Taylor and Rachel Ann Morgan, all of Fauquier Co.

Vol. IV, No. 23 – June 20, 1820

Died on Monday, June 12, 1820, in Georgetown, DC., John Hagerty, age 29 years.

Married June 8 by Rev. Dr. Wm. H. Wilmer in Alexandria, James English of Alexandria and Ann Maria Richards of West End Fairfax Co., Va.

Married May 15 by Rev. Mr. Waugh at Baltimore, Capt. George Gilpin of Alexandria and Mrs. Margaret Smull of Baltimore.

Vol. IV, No. 24 – June 27, 1820

Died on May 30, 1820 at Lexington, Va. J. N. Snyder, editor of *Lexington News-Letter.*

Married June 18 by Rev. Dr. Elbert, James Smith and Jane Atkins, eldest daughter of William Atkins of Harford Co., Md.

Vol. IV, No. 25 – July 4, 1820

Townsend Dade killed in a duel in King George Co., June 19th by Richard Stuart.

Vol. IV, No. 27 – July 18, 1820
Mrs. Ann E. Fishback, age 26 years, died July 10, 1820 at family residence in Loudoun Co.

Vol. IV, No. 28 – July 25, 1820
Miss Melinda Clark died at Mr. John Galleher's near Union on July 19, 1820
Miss Eliza Allen, 2nd daughter of Wm. Allen, died July 19, after an illness of 4 days.
Married July 17 by Thomas Burkby [sic] 'Minister of Gospel', Philip Nicholson and Eliza Rhyne, both of this county.
Married July 19 by same, Matthew Gates and Sarah Dorrell, both of Leesburg.
Married July 20th by Wm. Gilmore, James McDaniel and Nancy Carnicle, both of Leesburg.

Vol. IV, No. 29 – August 1, 1820
Married lately, in Boothbay, Robert Reed 4th, cousin to Robert Reed 5th, no relation to Robert Reed 6th, son of Robert Reed 1st, but no relation to Robert Reed 2nd, and Miss Alice Reed, daughter of Robert Reed 3rd.
Died September 4, 1820, James Hervey, age 3 years. Died September 17, 1820, William Harrison, age 7 years. Died September 18, 1820, Elzira, age 11 years. Died September 22, 1820, Huldy, age 9 years. All children of Mr. and Mrs. William George of Loudoun.
Died on 10 July, W. W. Bibb, Governor of Alabama, at his residence near Fort Jackson, at age 40 years.

Vol. IV, No. 30 – August 8, 1820
Married August 3rd by Thomas Birkby, William Dailey and Eleanor Martin, both of this county.
Died on Monday, July 31st ult. at Belmont after an illness of 14 days, Mrs. Eliza Lee, 41 years of age, wife of Ludwell Lee Esqr.
Died in Sadsbury township, Chester Co., Pa. on Friday, July 21st, Mrs. John Trevilla, aged 50 years.

Vol. IV, No. 31 – August 15, 1820
James Marsh, in 89th year of age, member of Society of Friends, died at residence in Loudoun Co. on June 30th.
Married August 6th by Thomas Birkby, Jonathan Dilly and Nancy Davies.
Died on the 8th inst., the Rev. James Muir, senior Pastor of First Presbyterian Church in Alexandria.

Vol. IV, No. 32 – August 22, 1820
Daniel McCarty Chichester, age 51, died August 7 at his residence in Fairfax Co.
Died 7th August at the home of Andrew Ramsay, Esqr., DC., the Hon. John Graham, late minister plenipotentiary at the court of the Brazils, Rio de Janeiro.
Died 8th August at Belle Air the residence of Jonathan Swift, Esqr., the Rev. James Muir, senior pastor of the First Presbyterian Church in Alexandria.

Vol. IV, No. 35 – September 12, 1820
Mrs. Maria Cook, consort of Wm. Cook, died at Col. Mercer's seat at Aldie on Monday, September 4.

Vol. IV, No. 36 – September 19, 1820

Cornelius Shawen, about 50 years old, died September 12 at his residence near Waterford. Member of community 16-17 years. [long obit]

Spencer William, infant son of Dr. John T. Wilson of Leesburg, died Sunday, September 17.

James Triplett, 21 year old son of James L. Triplett, Esq., died Tuesday, September 12, at his father's residence in Fairfax Co.

Vol. IV, No. 37 – September 26, 1820

Married September 21st by Thomas Birkby, Henry Orum and Mary Sandsberry, both of this county.

Vol. IV, No. 39 – October 10, 1820

Died at Hagerstown, Joseph Crane Saunders, 19 years old, youngest son of Major Cyrus Saunders of Washington Co. September 10.

Ferdinando Fairfax, Esq., lately of Washington, formerly of Virginia, d. September 25 at Mount Eagle near Alexandria.

Capt. Thomas Brook Beall, President of Farmers and Mechanics Bank of Georgetown, died Saturday, September 30. [long obit next issue]

Vol. IV, No. 40 – October 17, 1820

Col. Joseph Biays, 68 years old, died October 4 in Baltimore.

William Taylor, age 82 years, died September 11 at residence in Lunenburg Co., Virginia.

Vol. IV, No. 41 – October 24, 1820

William T. Swann, Esq., died Sunday, October 15, in Alexandria at age 35 years.

Robert C. Gray, of New Orleans, died 31st ult. of yellow fever, from town of Woodstock Va., printer by profession.

Charles Sower, age 32, editor of *Star of Federation*, Frederickstown, Md., died October 21.

Vol. IV, No. 42 – October 31, 1820

Susan Hague of Leesburg, died October 23, age 17 years.

Charles Neale of Leesburg, died October 23, age 17 years.

Wilson Cary Nicholas died October 10 at residence of Thos. J. Randolph, Albemarle Co., late governor of Virginia.

Married lately in Rochester, N.Y., Capt. Samuel Courier and Miss Sarah Clough, being his 6th wife.

Vol. IV, No. 43 – November 7, 1820

Mrs. Elizabeth Currie, died November 4 in this vicinity, buried in Presbyterian cemetery in town.

Vol. IV, No. 44 – November 14, 1820

Amelia Gullatt died November 13 at age 60 years, in Leesburg for 30 years.

Henry Franciso, 134 year old veteran of French and Revolutionary war, died on October 25 near Whitehall, N.Y.

Col. Daniel Boon died September 16 at Charrette Village, Missouri, at age 90 years.

Married November 13th by Thomas Birkby, Thomas Langley and Maria Burke, both of this county.

Vol. IV, No. 46 – November 28, 1820
Benjamin Saunders, age 80 years, died November 26 at residence in vicinity of Leesburg. Resident for almost half a century.
Married November 26th by Rev. Mr. Dunn, William Thompson of Fauquier and Mildred Ball of Leesburg.

Vol. IV, No. 47 – December 5, 1820
Ephraim Smith, infant son of Mr. Jacob Martin, of this town, died December 4.
Married in Lynn, on October 12th Thomas Swann to Mary Martin.

Vol. IV, No. 48 – December 12, 1820
Col. Wm. McGuire, U. S. Military Storekeeper at Harper's Ferry, died November 24.
Negro Frank, 114 year old native of Acra, on the Gold Coast of Africa, d. November 12 at Capt. Miller's in Woodstock, Va.
Elizabeth Lancaster, wife of Joseph Lancaster, founder of Lancasterian System of Education, died December 6 at Baltimore.
Benjamin Fenwick, son of Richard Fenwick in City of Washington, died December 8.
Married December 7th by Rev. Richard McAllister, Richard Key Watts Jr. of Montgomery Co., Md., and Helen G. Rose, daughter of Capt. John Rose of Leesburg.
Married on 6th inst. at Waterford Friend's Meeting House, William H. Miller of Alexandria and Amy Ann Phillips of Waterford, daughter of Thomas Phillips.
Married November 30th at Winchester by Rev. A. Beck, William Miller, merchant, and Harriett A. Baker, daughter of Henry W. Baker, merchant, all of Winchester.

Vol. IV, No. 49 – December 19, 1820
Charles Bennett, 40 year resident of Leesburg, died December 14 at age 80 years.
Married December 11 by Thomas Birkby, Terence Kerney and Miss E. McWard, both of this town.
Married December 14 by Thomas Birkby, Samuel Harper and Margaret Mulligan, both of Loudoun Co.

Vol. IV, No. 50 – December 26, 1820
Married December 21 by Rev. Mr. Dagg, William Right [*sic*] and Margaret Wilkinson, both of Loudoun Co.
Married at Edgewood, Hanover Co., December 4, 1820, by Rev. E. C. M'Guire, Rev. William Meade to Miss Thomasia Nelson, daughter of the late Thomas Nelson.

Vol. IV, No. 51 – January 2, 1821
Died December 25th in Washington, James Burrill Jr., 49 year old senator from Rhode Island.

Vol. IV, No. 52 – January 9, 1821
John Linn congressman from New Jersey died.

Vol. V, No. 1 – January 16, 1821
Married January 2 at Fredericktown, Md., James Wood, merchant of Leesburg, and Margaret Goin of Loudoun.

Married January 4 by Thomas Birkby, John R. Anderson and Abby Thomas, both of Loudoun.

Vol. V, No. 3 – January 30, 1821

Married January 25 by T. Birkby, James Norris and Sarah Magennis, both of this county.

Died at Baltimore, 18th inst., General Joseph Sterett, 48 years of age.

Died in Hartford Co., Md., on December 28th, 1820, John Molton.

Vol. V, No. 4 – February 6, 1821

Died on January 13, 1821, Benjamin Butler, at his son's home in Georgetown, Delaware, aged 106 years.

Died February 11, 1821, Mrs. Bethiab Crooce, aged 100 years, at South Bridgwater, Mass.

Vol. V, No. 5 – February 13, 1821

Charles Veal, age 47 years of Loudoun, died January 30. Resident of Loudoun since infancy.

Thomas Hawkins, age 74 year, Rev. Soldier of Frederick Co., Md., died January 25.

Married in Wilmington, Del. on the 1st of February 1821 by the Rev. Dr. Read, Mr. Jos. Cheesely to Miss Anne Phillips, alias Spring, both blind.

Vol. V, No. 6 – February 20, 1821

Lee Durham of Leesburg, only son of widowed mother, age 19 years, died February 19.

Married February 6 by Rev. Wm. Gilmore, Ammon Ewers and Nancy Tolbert, all of this county.

Married February 13 by Rev. Wm. Gilmore, Thomas Love and Leah White.

Vol. V, No. 7 – February 27, 1821

Married 15th inst. by Rev. Mr. McAllister, James Martin of Winchester and Sarah Murray of this village.

Died, Sarah Ann, infant daughter of Samuel Dailey, in the vicinity of this town.

Vol. V, No. 8 – March 6, 1821

Married Sunday, December 24 by Rev. Philip Matthews, John Beazley, age 72, and Susan Davenport, age 18, both of Pr. Edward Co. Va.

Vol. V, No. 9 – March 13, 1821

William Neale, "old inhabitant of this county," died yesterday.

Married March 6 by Rev. Thomas Littleton, Robert Chew and Dorcas Osburn of Loudoun.

Vol. V, No. 10 – March 20, 1821

Thomas H. Wey and Hannah Galleher, m. 1st inst. by Rev. James M. C. Hanson.

John N. T. G. E. Keene and Harriet Triplett, all of this county, m. February 8, 1821 by Rev. James M. C. Hanson.

Vol. V, No. 12 – April 3, 1821

Married Thursday, March 29 by Thomas Birkby, Eli Daniel and Elizabeth Waigley, both of this county.

Married Thursday, March 15 by Rev. Jonathan Helfenstein, Capt. C. Lewis of
Loudoun Co. and Ann M. Hoffman, daughter of John Hoffman, Esq. of
Frederick Co., Md.

Vol. V., No. 13 – April 10, 1821

Ezra Gilman of Waterford, about 40 years old, died April 3. Remains were
interred with masonic honours.
Married on 28th ult. at Llangollen, Mr. Frank Frances, timber merchant, 29 years
old, to Mrs. Roberts, widow, a lady of large property, aged 85. [London paper,
Jan 8].

Vol. V, No. 14 – April 17, 1821

Henry Koontz of Frederick Co., Md., age 94 years, died. [no date of death]
Married April 10 by Wm. Gilmore, Chas. Williams and Mary Steer, both of this
county.

Vol. V, No. 15 – April 24, 1821

Married Tuesday, on 10th inst., by Rev. John Mines, Samuel Murray and Mary
Ann Binns.
Married Thursday, April 12 by Rev. John Mines, John Carr and Jane Means, all
of this county.
Married Wednesday, April 18 by Thomas Birkby, Samuel Garner and Sarah
Orrison, both of this county.
Married Sunday, April 8 in Alexandria, DC., Isaac Cooper, 86 year old grocer,
and Miss Nancy ___ [*sic*], 19 year old housekeeper.

Vol. V, No. 16 – May 1, 1821

Mrs. Hannah Burton, age 37 years, consort of John Burton lately from Leeds,
England to this place, member of Methodist Church, died Sunday, April 21st.
Married Sunday, April 29 at Fredericktown, Md., John Surghnour and Elizabeth
Dailey, both of Leesburg.

Vol. V, No. 17 – May 8, 1821

Married on Tursday, March 29th at Herculaneum, Missouri, John W. Honey Esqr. to
Mary S. Austin, daughter of Mr. Horace Austin of Herculaneum.

Vol. V, No. 19 – May 22, 1821

Jonathan W. Dustin, age 28 years, formerly of N. H., died April 15 in Frederick
Co., Md. (for past 7 years.)
Married Monday, May 14, 1821 by Thomas Birkby, Oliver Garrett and Elizabeth
Cohee, both of this county.
Peter Miller killed 3 miles from this city on the place of Wm. Esher. [*Dem. Press*]

Vol. V, No. 21 – June 5, 1821

Joseph H. Windsor, formerly from Delaware but more recently from Leesburg,
died in Washington City on May 26.
Married Thursday, May 24, 1821 by Rev. Asa Shin at Baltimore, Jesse Lee and
Eliza Millemon, 2nd daughter of George M., all of Baltimore.

Vol. V, No. 24 – June 26, 1821

Rev. Hamilton Jefferson of Charlestown, Va., died Wednesday, June 13, in
Baltimore.

Vol. V, No. 27 – July 17, 1821

Patrick McIntyre, Esq., in 43rd year at Leesburg, late editor of the *Washingtonian*, died July 9, buried at Methodist Episcopal churchyard.

Married Thursday, July 5 by Rev. Mr. Wilmer, Lt. William B. Davidson, U.S. Army, and Elizabeth Chapman Hunter, daughter of Gen. John Chapman Hunter of Fairfax Co.

Vol. V, No. 29 – July 31, 1821

Edward Cooksey died July 24, George and Harrison Cooksey died of bilious fever July 25, all sons of Obadiah Cooksey near Waterford.

Alfred McVicker, in 23rd year, of near Winchester, died July 14, after being thrown from a horse on July 4th.

Vol. V, No. 30 – August 7, 1821

Mrs. Matilda D. Low died July 28, and consort of deceased William Low, age 23, died August 2, at Hamilton's Mill, Loudoun, died of bilious fever. Remains interred at Methodist buring ground in town.

Married Sunday, July 27 by T. Birkby, William Hawke and Jane Perfect, both of Leesburg.

Married Thursday, August 2 by T. Birkby, Jonathan Russell and Elizabeth Moldon, both of Leesburg.

Vol. V, No. 32 – August 21, 1821

Miss Margaret B. Peyton, in 18th year, daughter of Henry Peyton Jr. of Fauquier Co., died August 6 at her father's home.

Col. Joseph Swearingen of Shepherdstown, Jefferson Co., Va., died August 9 in 68th year. Buried at family burial ground.

Robert Thomas of Fairfax, died July 2 at age 107 years, born in Westmoreland Co., moved to Fairfax in early boyhood, remembered when site of Alexandria was a howling wilderness inhabited by wild deer and wolf.

Vol. V, No. 34 – September 4, 1821

Died on August 21 at Waterford, of bilious fever. George McCormick, age 22 years. Left Baltimore when young.

Died at Baltimore on August 26, Charles Wirgman. Masonic Grand Master.

Vol. V, No. 35 – September 11, 1821

Mrs. Jane Wright of near Waterford, died August 16 in her 63rd year.

William Wright Jr. of near Waterford, died August 26 in his 22nd year.

William Wright Sr. of near Waterford, died August 31 at age 57 years. Husband and father to the above.

Mrs. Elizabeth Janney, consort of David Janney of Waterford, died August 31 in 31st year.

Mrs. Lydia Wilkinson, consort of Thomas Wilkinson of Waterford, died September 2.

Samuel Murray of Leesburg, died after a short illness September 10 in his 79th year. Respectable citizen of this town for nearly half a century.

Vol. V, No. 36 – September 18, 1821

Mrs. Elizabeth Livingston, consort of John Livingston of Waterford, died August 31 at age 31 years.

Mr. John H. Talbott of Brownsville, Pa, died at Waterford of billious fever August 10th at age 26 years.

Mrs. Mary Neal of Waterford, died August 12th at age 32 years.
Mrs. McGarvick, consort of Patrick McGarvick, died August 13th.

Vol. V, No. 38 – October 2, 1821
Died Thursday, September 20th, Dr. James M. Scott in Leesburg, son of James
Scott of Winchester.

Vol. V, No. 39 – October 9, 1821
Died September 16th at Waterford, David Janney, of prevailing fever, age 40
years. Husband of Mrs. Janney who recently died leaving 6 children.
Died Saturday, September 29th at her father's, Mr. George Rhodes, near
Leesburg, Mrs. Milly Shepherd, consort of Charles Shepherd, age 21 years,
leaving 2 children, youngest born day before she died.
Died Saturday, September 29th near Noland's Ferry, Loudoun Co., Mrs. Elizabeth
Beatty, relict of the late David Beatty, age 71 years.
Married 25 ult. by Rev. John L. Dagg, Mr. Charles Gullatt of this town to Miss
Rebecca B. Lewis.
Married at Aldie on the 27th by Rev. John Dunn, Lewis Berkley, Esqr. of
Evergreen to Frances C. Noland, daughter of William Noland.

Vol. V, No. 40 – October 16, 1821
Died at Philadelphia on Saturday, October 6th Commodore Alexander Murray Sr.,
officer of the Navy of the U. S.
Died at Washington, D. C. on October 9th, Mrs. Elizabeth Lowry, age 82 years.
Died at Lancaster, Pa. on October 1st, Mr. George Price, late editor of the *Free
Press*, age 29 years.

Vol. V, No. 41 – October 23, 1821
Died on Saturday, October 13th, at his home 8 miles from Leesburg, Mr. Isaac
Nickols, age 79 years.
Died at Ossian Hall, Fairfax Co., on Sunday, October 14th, Capt. Thomas Gregg,
formerly of Loudoun.
Died at his residence in Round Hill, Fairfax Co., Major George Tripplett, in his
55th year.

Vol. V, No. 42 – October 30, 1821
Died at his residence in Loudoun Co. near Middleburg on October 16th, Mr.
Francis Hereford, age 54 years. Member of M. E. church.
Died on Wednesday, October 10th, Mr. John Eckis of Taney Town, Maryland, age
82 years.

Vol. V, No. 43 – November 6, 1821
Died at Aldie, Loudoun Co., Thursday, October 25th, Clementina B. Richards,
age 17 years, youngest daughter of Rev. Geo. Richards, formerly of
Portsmouth, N. H. Buried Leesburg Methodist Episcopal Church.
Died at Waterford, Loudoun Co., October 17th, Mrs. Phebe Cole, age 22 years,
consort of Mr. Lewis Cole.

Vol. V, No. 45 – November 20, 1821
Married on Tuesday, November 13th by Rev. John Mines, Mr. Thomas Russell of
this town and Miss Ellenor Tillett, daughter of Capt. Samuel Tillett of this
county.

Vol. V, No. 46 – November 27, 1821
Married Thursday, November 22nd by Rev. Jno. G. Walt, Dr. __ Wilson and Miss
Charlotte Rose, youngest daughter of Capt. John Rose of this town.

Vol. V, No. 47 – December 4, 1821
Died on Tuesday, November 27th, Mr. Wm. Sheid in 35th year, of this county.
Died at Park Gate, Prince William Co., Richard B. Alexander of Kentucky.
Married on Thursday, November 29th by Rev. William Gilmore, Mr. William D.
Daniel and Miss Sarah Garrett, both of this county.

Vol. V, No. 48 – December 11, 1821
Died on Tuesday, December 4th, Mr. John Donohoe, age 63 years, a native of
Loudoun. Member of Methodist church.

Vol. V, No. 49 – December 18, 1821
Married Thursday, December 13th near Waterford by Rev. John Mines, Cyphas
Hank and Miss Phebe Mock, all of Loudoun Co.

Vol. V, No. 50 – December 25, 1821
Married Thursday, December 13th by Rev. John Mines, Mr. Hiram McVeigh and
Miss Jane Elgin, of this county
Married Tuesday, December 18th by Rev. Wm. Gilmore, Mr. Charles D.
Vermillion and Jane Tillett, all of this county.
Married Thursday, December 20th by Rev. Thomas Birkby, Mr. William Lightfoot
and Miss Catharine Whitmore, all of this county.
Married Thursday, December 20th by Rev. Wm. Gilmore, Mr. John Wornel and
Miss Rachael Wildman, also of this county.
Married Thursday, December 13th by Thomas Birkby, Mr. Joseph Hough and
Miss Rachel Russell, both of this county.

Vol. V, No. 51 – January 1, 1822
Married Thursday, December 27th by Thomas Birkby, Mr. David Conner and Mrs.
Ann Newton, both of this county.
Married Thursday, December 27th by Thomas Birkby, Mr. William Saunders and
Miss Mahala Tillett, all of this county.
Married Thursday, December 27th by Thomas Birkby, Mr. Stephen Roberts and
Miss Malinda Roach, all of this county.

Vol. V, No. 52 – January 8, 1822
Died at his home in this vicinity, Wednesday, January 2nd, Mr. Henry Dyer, age
38 years.
Married on Thursday, January 1st by Rev. William Gilmore, Mr. David Simpson of
Harrison Co. and Miss Elizabeth Gregg of Loudoun Co.

Vol. VI, No. 1 – January 15, 1822
Died on January 8th at his residence in Waterford, Capt. John McGeath, in 67th
year of his age, soldier of the revolution and present at the capture of Lord
Cornwallis in 1781.
Married in Fauquier Co., Thursday, December 27 by Rev. Williamson, Mr.
Thomas P. Knox of Warrenton and Miss Catherine Routt.

Married in Middleburg on Thursday, January 3rd by Rev. Williamson, Mr. Burr W. Harrison of this town and Miss Sarah H. Powell, daughter of Major Burr Powell of Middleburg.

Married on December 19th by Rev. Gold, Mr. James Holderly of Guyandatte, Va. and Mrs. Ariana Love of Mason Co., formerly of Fairfax, Va.

Married on Tuesday, January 8th by Thomas Birkby, Mr. Henry Claggett and Miss Eveline Carr, daughter of William Carr, the former of Montgomery, the latter of Loudoun.

Vol. VI, No. 2 – January 22, 1822

Married at Frederick Town, Maryland on Wednesday, December 26th by Rev. Helfinstein, Mr. Daniel Hiram and Miss Maria Potts, both of Loudoun.

Vol. VI, No. 8 – March 5, 1822

Died in Baltimore on Sunday, February 23rd, Mr. Thomas N. Binns, age 49 years, formerly of Leesburg.

Married Tuesday, February 27th by Thomas Birkby, Mr. John Simpson and Miss Matilda Swartz, all of this county.

Vol. VI, No. 10 – March 19, 1822

Died on Tuesday, March 12th, Mrs. Sarah Price, age 50 years, relict of the late Capt. Benjamin Price.

Died in Leesburg on Sunday, March 17th, Miss Ann Potter, age 15 years, youngest daughter of Ebenezer Potter.

Vol. VI, No. 14 – April 16, 1822

Died April 10th, Mr. Silas Wherry of Loudoun, age 45 years, after short illness.

Vol. VI, No. 15 – April 23, 1822

Married Thursday, April 18th by Thomas Birkby, Mr. Marks Watkins and Miss Mary Marks, daughter of Thomas Marks, all of this county.

Died February 22nd, Mrs. Frances D. Williams, age 41 years, consort of Notley C. Williams, of cancer of the breast.

Vol. VI, No. 16 – April 30, 1822

Married Tuesday, April 23rd by Thomas Birkby, Mr. Joseph Cavan and Miss Nancy Templer, both of this county.

Married April 14th in Fredericktown, Md. by Rev. Schaeffer, Mr. Joseph Umbrage and Miss Elizabeth Russell, both of this county.

Vol. VI, No. 18 – May 14, 1822

Died May 5th, Mrs. Cecilia Stribling, age 27 years, consort of Capt. Francis Stribling.

Vol. VI, No. 19 – May 21, 1822

Married on Thursday, May 16th by Thomas Birkby, Mr. Lewis Grigsby and Miss Malinda Torbet, all of this county.

Married Thursday, May 16th by Rev. John G. Watt, Dr. William S. Eaches and Miss Ann R. Bennett, daughter of Charles Bennett, all of this county.

Vol. VI, No. 20 – May 28, 1822

Married Thursday, May 23, by Thomas Birkby, Mr. William Hammontree and Miss Ann Torrison, both of Loudoun.

Vol. VI, No. 21 – June 4, 1822

Died near Leesburg, May 28th, Mrs. Eleanor Handey, age 33 years, consort of
Mr. William H. Handey, buried at North Fork with infant son. Besides mother
of Mrs. Handey, left husband and 5 small children.

Died near Charlestown, Va. on Thursday, May 9th at his home, Mr. William
Grayson Orr, 39th year of his age.

Vol. VI, No. 22 – June 11, 1822

Died in Leesburg, Friday, June 7, Mrs. Letitia Goff, age 38 years. Member of
Methodist Church.

Vol. VI, No. 23 – June 18, 1822

Married on Tuesday, June 11, by Thomas Birkby, Mr. Jesse Miller and Miss
Rebecca Davis, all of Loudoun.

Vol. VI, No. 24 – June 25, 1822

Married on Thursday, June 20, by Rev. John Dunn, Mr. Wilson C. Seldon Jr. and
Miss Louisa Alexander, both of this county.

Married Sunday, June 23, by Thomas Birkby, Mr. Samuel Baldwin and Miss
Elizabeth Stoneburner, both of Loudoun.

Died Monday, June 17th, Mr. George E. Cordell, age 81 years, of Leesburg.
Interred at M. E. Church.

Vol. VI, No. 25 – July 2, 1822

Married at Shepherds Town, Va. on June 5th, Mr. Edward Bell, editor of the
Virginia Monitor, and Miss Catharine Eaty.

Married on Thursday, June 27, by Thomas Birkby, Mr. Daniel Dulaney and Miss
Eleanor Conner, both of Leesburg.

Vol. VI, No. 28 – July 23, 1822

Died in vicinity of Waterford on Monday, July 15th, Mr. Joseph Lovett, a young
man.

Died in Leesburg, Thursday, July 18th, Mrs. Sarah Ryan, age 47 years.

Vol. VI, No. 29 – July 30, 1822

Married on Thursday, July 25, by Rev. Wm. Gilmore, Mr. Robert Barrett and Miss
Martha Moffett, both of Loudoun.

Died Thursday, July 25th, Mrs. Elizabeth Lucas, age 36 years. Remains interred
Valley Meeting House.

Vol. VI, No. 30 – August 6, 1822

Married on Thursday, August 2 by Rev. Wm. Gilmore, Mr. Gainer Pierce of the
western country and Miss Sinah McGeath of this county.

Died on 8th ult. at Mount Pleasant, Prince William Co., Mrs. Willie E. Newman,
relict of the late Thos. Newman Esqr, in the 58th year of her age. She raised a
family of 10 children.

Vol. VI, No. 32 – August 20, 1822

Died at Middleburg Tuesday, August 6th, Mr. James Church. Wife and children
predeceased, leaves 2 small children. Native of Scotland. Last 20 months
was principal of the female academy in Winchester.

Died at Winchester, August 2nd, James Scott, age 54 of Leesburg.

Died Friday, August 17th, Benjamin Franklin Edwards, infant son of Samuel M. Edwards Esqr of this town.

Vol. VI, No. 33 – August 27, 1822

Died in Leesburg, Tuesday, August 20th, Mrs. Bethany Rice, age 72 years. Member Baptist Church. Interred New Valley burying ground.

Died on August 9th at her residence in St. Mary's Co., Md., Miss Jane Monroe, 60 years old one time resident of Leesburg.

Died Monday, August 19th at Shepherdstown, Jefferson Co., Va., Thomas Van Swearingen, member of congress for that district.

Died on 11th inst., at house of George Lower in Washington Co. Md., Mr. Cyrus R. Saunders, 26 years old, printer, son of Cyrus R. Saunders Sr. of Williamsport.

Vol. VI, No. 34 – September 3, 1822

Married at Fredericktown on Thursday, August 29th by Rev. Jonathan Helfenstein, Mr. Robert Barret Jr. and Miss Mary C. Killen, both of Loudoun.

Married Thursday, August 20th by Rev. Wm. Gilmore, Mr. Henry Lafaver and Miss Mary Fouch.

Vol. VI, No. 35 – September 10, 1822

Married in Richmond Va. on August 8th, Mr. James Semple of Essex Co. and Miss Mary P. Garlick of King William.

Married at Prospect Hill on Thursday, August 29th by Rev. Pressman, James Foster and Miss Elizabeth, eldest daughter of Capt. Henry Fairfax, all of Prince William Co. Va.

Married near Fredericktown, Md. on Monday September 2nd by Rev. Thompson, Mr. Lott Clues and Miss Edith Brown, daughter of Mr. Isaac Brown.

Married near Fredericktown, Md. on Monday September 2nd by Rev. Thompson, Thomas Jefferson Bennett and Miss Susan Brown, daughter of Mr. Isaac Brown, all of Loudoun Co. Va.

Died Monday, September 2 at Harper's Ferry Va., Lt. Col. Jacinth [sic] Laval, military store keeper at that place.

Died on 15th ult. near Russellville, Logan Co., Rev. Valentine Cook, Methdoist preacher.

Vol. VI, No. 36 – September 17, 1822

Died Tuesday, September 10th in this vicinity in his 39th year, Mr. Charles Thrift, formerly deputy sheriff of this county.

Died Tuesday, September 10 near Noland's Ferry, Mr. David Beatty, a native of this county.

Died on Thursday, September 12th at Aldie, Mr. James Simpson of that place.

Died on 3rd, William Davison, postmaster at Winchester.

Died at his residence near Shepherdstown, on 7th inst., Capt. Abraham Shepherd, 68 years old.

Vol. VI, No. 37 – September 24, 1822

Married on Thursday, September 19th by Rev. Wm. Gilmore, Mr. James Frazier, age 80 years, and Miss Ann Dawson, age 50 years, both of this county.

Died at Dumfries, Va. on 12th inst., Timothy Brundige, Esqr., merchant and postmaster of that place.

Died on 14th inst. at his residence in Barnesville, Md., Leonard Hays, Sr., 63 years old.

Died at Washington City on 17th inst., Rev. Samuel Davis, 28 year old Methodist minister.

Died on Wednesday night last, editor's [B. W. Sower] infant daughter Maria, aged 11 months 11 days.

Vol. VI, No. 38 – October 1, 1822

Died in Waterford on September 23, Richard Janny, age 14 years, eldest son of Mr. Mahlon Janny.

Died on Wednesday, September 25th at his residence near Leesburg, Mr. James McSorley, age about 30 years, resident of Leesburg 3 years, a native of north Ireland.

Died in this town, 24th ult., Joseph Beard Esqr, mayor of the corporation, 49 years old. Mason procession to family burial gound in Maryland about 8 miles from Leesburg. [Communicated]

Vol. VI, No. 39 – October 8, 1822

Died at residence of his mother in Fairfax Co. on October 3rd Simon Summers (of John), age 21 years.

Vol. VI, No. 40 – October 15, 1822

Married Thursday, September 26th by Rev. James Reid, Mr. Thompson Byrd of Prince William Co. and Miss Levinah Rose of Loudoun Co.

Married at Bellevoir on Tuesday, October 8th by Rev. Dr. Wilmer, Mr. Dan'l Haines of Jefferson Co. and Miss Frances Henderson of Fairfax Co. Va.

Died in this vicinity on Wednesday, October 7th, Mrs. Rebecca Elgin, age 56 years, consort of Major Gustavus Elgin, after illness of about 15 or 20 minutes.

Died at Waterford on Thursday, October 8th, Marab, wife of Mr. John E. Palmer, age 40 years, member of Society of Friends.

Died Friday, October 9th, William Thomas Thompson, 9 month old son of Thompson Mason of Loudoun.

Died in Leesburg on Saturday, October 10, Mr. David Bowen, age 22 years, a native of Lancaster, Pa. for the year last part a resident of Leesburg.

Vol. VI, No. 41 – October 22, 1822

Died in Waterford Monday, October 7th, Mr. Bushrod William Mason Fox, son of the late Mr. William Fox, in the 16th year of his age. [long obit]

Died at residence near Brookville, Md., Thomas Moore, for several years past principal engineer for Virginia board of public works.

Died in this town on Monday last, 14th inst., John Thomas Rose, 13 months, only child of Richard K. Watts Jr., of Montgomery Co., Md.

Vol. VI, No. 42 – October 29, 1822

Died on Sunday, October 6th in German Settlement, Loudoun Co., Mrs. Mary M. Shover, age 78 years, relict of the late Capt. Adam Shover, after 15 minute illness.

Vol. VI, No. 43 – November 5, 1822

Died on Wednesday, October 30th in German Settlement, Loudoun Co., Mrs. Elizabeth George, relict of the late John George, in her 87th year.

Vol. VI, No. 45 – November 19, 1822

Married on Thursday, November 7th by Rev. John L. Dagg, Mr. William Rogers and Miss Elizabeth, daughter of Mr. James Hixon, all of this county.

Married on Thursday, November 7th by Thomas Birkby, Mr. Thomas Green and Miss Elizabeth Dailey, daughter of Aaron Dailey, all of this county.

Married on Thursday, November 14th by Rev. William Gilmore, Mr. Alfred Taylor and Miss Mary Race, both of this county.

Died in this vicinity on November 8th, Mr. William Hall, age 60 years, arrived in Leesburg from Ireland 40 years ago.

Vol. VI, No. 46 – November 26, 1822

Married on Tuesday, November 12, at Georgetown, DC. by Rev. Balch, Mr. Harry Upperman Sr., age 80 years, and Miss Margaret Gibbs, aged 65 years, all of that place.

Married Tuesday, November 21, by Thomas Birkby, Mr. Joseph Shorb and Miss Mary E. Tillett, both of Loudoun.

Married Tuesday, November 21 by Thomas Birkby, Patrick J. Hawe, Esq., late co-editor & propietor of the *Washingtonian*, and Miss Catharine, daughter of Mr. Jacob Fadely, all of this town.

Vol. VI, No. 47 – December 3, 1822

Married on Thursday, November 28, by Thomas Birkby, Mr. Samuel D. Waltman and Miss Catharine L. Drish, both of this town.

Married on Thursday, November 28, by Rev. Christopher Frye, Mr. __ [Corbin] Buckmaster and Miss Catharine Davis, all of this town.

Died on Wednesday, November 27th, Ann Rebecca, infant daughter of Mr. Isaac Wright of this town.

Vol. VI, No. 48 – December 10, 1822

Married in Fredericktown, Md. on November 24 by Rev. Schaeffer, Mr. William Carter and Miss Frances Nolan, both of Loudoun Co.

Married on Thursday, November 21st by Rev. Allen, Mr. George Dale, merchant of Leesburg, and Miss Eliza, daughter of Col. George Minor of Fairfax Co.

Vol. VI, No. 49 – December 17, 1822

Married on Tuesday, December 10th by Rev. Dr. Chapman, John Monday and Margaret Philips, both of Loudoun.

Died on Tuesday, December 10th John Mathias Sr., county surveyor of Loudoun, aged 62 years, a native of Great Britain.

Died on __ in Washington Co. Md., Mr. Cyrus Sanders.

Vol. VI, No. 50 – December 24, 1822

Married in Baltimore on Sunday, December 15th, by Rev. Daniel Hitt, Rev. Andrew Hemphill of Va. and Mrs. Ruth A. Green of the former place

Married on Thursday, December 19th by Thomas Birkby, Mr. Evan Wilkinson and Miss Sarah Currie, both of this county.

Married on Thursday, December 19th by Thomas Birkby, Mr. Asa Peck and Miss Patience W. Saunders, both of this county.

Died on Thursday, December 12th in German Settlement, Loudoun Co., Mr. Benjamin Heater, age 20 years.

Vol. VI, No. 51 – December 31, 1822

Married on Thursday, December 19th by Rev. William Gilmore, Deskin D. Monroe of Loudoun and Miss Mary E. McCarty of Fairfax.

Married on Sunday, December 22 by Rev. William Gilmore, Dr. Erasmus G. Tillett of Loudoun and Miss Sarah Coffer of Fairfax.

Died on Thursday, December 26, at his late residence in this vicinity, Mr. Charles Bennett.

Vol. VI, No. 52 – January 7, 1823

Died at her residence near Lanesville on Friday, December 27th, Mrs. Rebecca Sheid, consort of Mr. George Sheid, 45 years.

Vol. VII, No. 1 – January 14, 1823

Married in Washington on Monday, December 30th by Rev. O. B. Brown, Mr. Ferdinand Fairfax Stuck of Loudoun Co. and Miss Jane, eldest daughter of Mr. Isaac Cooper of Washington.

Died on January 3rd John Mitchell in the 9th year, only son of Matthew Mitchel of this town.

Vol. VII, No. 2 – January 21, 1823

Married on Thursday, January 16th by Rev. William Gilmore, Mr. George Fox and Miss Maria Roach, both of this county.

Married on Thursday, January 16th Mr. Gratis Adams and Miss Matilda Heskett, both of Loudoun.

Died __ at age 9, Hannah Heaton, eldest daughter of Dr. Jonathan Heaton.

Vol. VII, No. 5 – February 11, 1823

Married on Thursday, February 6th by Rev. Thomas Birkby, Mr. Peyton B. Smith and Miss Anne Campbell, both of this county.

Vol. VII, No. 6 – February 18, 1823

Married on February 6th at Fredericktown, Md., Mr. John Collins and Miss Miranda Henry, both of this county.

Died at Woodgrove in Loudoun on February 1st Mr. William King, age 63 years.

Died on Tuesday, February 4th Mrs. Jane Carr, consort of Mr. John Carr of this county.

Died on Saturday, February 8th Mr. Samuel Frank of Loudoun.

Died on Sunday, February 9th William Wooddy Sr., postmaster in this town.

Vol. VII, No. 7 – February 25, 1823

Married on Thursday, February 13th by Rev. William Gilmore, Levi McCaffrey and Miss Tamson Bailes, both of this county.

Died at his residence in this county, Eli Heaton Handey, age 23 years.

Died on Wednesday, February 19th at his residence near Leesburg, Mr. Henry Saunders, aged 68 years.

Vol. VII, No. 9 – March 11, 1823

Died at her residence Mountsville, Loudoun Co., on Thursday, Mrs. __ Mount, consort of Mr. Ezekiel Mount.

Vol. VII, No. 10 – March 18, 1823

Died in Leesburg on Monday, March 10th, James Hansbrough, infant son of Samuel Carr, Esq.

Vol. VII, No. 11 – March 25, 1823

Married on February 27th by Rev. William Gilmore, Mr. William Swarts and Miss Arminda Johnson, both of this county.

Married on Tuesday, March 18th by Rev. William Gilmore, Dr. Isaac Eaton and Miss Malenda Craig, the former of Mount Gilead, both of this county.

Died at Catoctin Mills on Tuesday, March 18th, Mrs. Elizabeth Copeland, consort of Mr. John Copeland, age 30 years.

Died on March 14th Mrs. Amelia Smith, age 30 years, consort of Ralph Smith of this town.

Died on Sunday, March 23, Mrs. Sophia Hilliard, consort of Mr. Joseph Hilliard of this town, her age 33 years.

Vol. VII, No. 12 – April 1, 1823

Married Wednesday, March 26 by Thomas Birkby, Mr. Lee Thompson and Miss Emily Gregg, both of Loudoun.

Married Sunday, March 30 by T. Birkby, Mr. Solomon Harlin of Frederick Co. Md. and Miss Christeener Winpigler.

Vol. VII, No. 13 - April 8, 1823

Died Saturday, March 29th at Hawling's Ferry, Mr. Henry Huff, age 55 years.

Vol. VII, No. 16 – April 29, 1823

Died Friday, April 18th, John Turner, 17 year old orphan.

Died Saturday, April 19th at age 57 years, Mr. Samuel Laycock, resident of Leesburg.

Died Wednesday, April 23rd at age 50 years, William Hawling, resident of Leesburg.

Vol. VII, No. 17 – May 6, 1823

Married Tuesday, April 29th by Rev. William, Enos Trayhorn and Miss Sarah Alder, both of this county.

Vol. VII, No. 18 – May 13, 1823

Married at Friends Meeting House in Waterford on April 23rd, Robert H. Miller, merchant of Alexandria, and Anna, daughter of Elisha Janney of Hillsborough.

Died on Tuesday, April 29th, Mrs. Margaret Bayly, consort of John Bayly, Esq. of this county.

Vol. VII, No. 19 – May 20, 1823

Married on May 18th by Rev. Peyton of Washington, Mr. John Fitzhugh of Prince William and Miss Frances Sharpe of Fauquier Co.

Vol. VII, No. 20 – May 27, 1823

Died on May 19th at age 23 years, Mrs. Eliza Harrison, wife of Russell Harrison, at residence in Loudoun.

Died in Leesburg on Thursday, May 22nd, Mr. Thomas Edwards, age 64 years.

Vol. VII, No. 21 – June 3, 1823

Married on Thursday, May 29th by Rev. Thomas Birkby, Mr. Jacob Shutt, merchant of Shepherdstown, and Miss Caroline T. Laslie of this county.

Married on Sunday, June 1st by Rev. Thomas Birkby, Mr. William Norris and Mrs. Milly Ann Harwood.

Died at sea on board the brig Resolution on his passage from St. Thomas to Alexandria on May 10th, in the 58th year of his age, John Janney, merchant of Alexandria, of Society of Friends.

Vol. VII, No. 22 – June 10, 1823

Married on Thursday, May 29th by Rev. Wm. Gilmore, Mr. Samuel Trayhorn and Miss Susan Brown, both of Loudoun.

Married on Thursday, May 29th by Rev. Wm. Gilmore, Mr. Wesley Carr and Miss Edna Gulick, both of this county.

Vol. VII, No. 23 – June 17, 1823

Married Thursday, June 12th by Rev. Wm. Gilmore, Mr. Ludwell Gulick and Miss Elizabeth Tillett, both of this county.

Married Thursday, June 12th by Rev. Thomas Birkby, Mr. William W. Lawrence and Miss Philippa Jones, both of Leesburg.

Vol. VII, No. 24 – June 24, 1823

Married on Tuesday, June 17th in Frederick Co. Va. by Rev. Walls, Capt. Francis Stribling of the county and Miss Rebecca Litler, at home of Capt. Charles W. Litler.

Married on Tuesday, June 17th in Frederick Co. Va. by Rev. Walls, Thomas Stribling of Hopewell and Miss Rachael Ann Litler, at home of Capt. Charles W. Litler.

Married on Wednesday, June 18th by Rev. Thomas Birkby, Mr. John Burton of this town and Mrs. Sophia Arkless of Fauquier, both born in England.

Vol. VII, No. 26 – July 8, 1823

Married Thursday, July 3rd by Thomas Birkby, Edmund F. Carter and Mrs. Sarah Smith, both of this county.

Died Saturday, June 28th at his residence in Loudoun Co., David Fulton, aged 66 years.

Died July 2, Dr. Charles B. Ball, age 30 years.

Vol. VII, No. 27 – July 15, 1823

Died on July 2nd at Contemplation, home of Gen. John C. Hunter of Fairfax Co., Mrs. Sarah Triplett, age 80 years.

Died in Aldie on Saturday, July 12th Frederick Edwards, 10 months old, youngest son of Daniel P. Conrad.

Vol. VII, No. 30 – August 5, 1823

Married at Mellona in Fauquier on Tuesday, July 29th by Rev. R. Latham, Capt. William H. Handey of Loudoun and Mrs. Eve Graham of Fauquier.

Married Thursday, July 31 by Rev. Thomas Birkby, Mr. David Beale, age 69 years, and Miss Hannah Saunders, age 46 years, both of this county.

Vol. VII, No. 31 – August 12, 1823

Died on August 2nd at age 70 years, Samuel Hough Sr. of Waterford.

Vol. VII, No. 33 – August 26, 1823

Died in this vicinity on August 15, Miss Mary Nelson, age 22 years.

Died August, James Henry Flinn, infant son of Samuel Flinn.

Died August 21st at age 25 years, Mrs. Mildred Flinn, wife of Samuel Flinn.
Died at his residence a few miles from this town on Saturday, August 23,
Stephen C. Rozsel.

Vol. VII, No. 34 – September 2, 1823
Died in this vicinity on Thursday, August 28th at age 47 years, Mr. Major Hunt.
Died on Sunday, August 31st in 71st year, Presley Saunders Sr. of Loudoun.

Vol. VII, No. 35 – September 9, 1823
Married on Thursday, September 4th by Rev. Thomas Birkby, Mr. John Ramsay
and Miss Elizabeth Dorrel, both of this county.
Married on Thursday, September 4th by Rev. William Gilmore, Mr. Eli Everett and
Miss Ann Davis, both of this county.
Died in Leesburg Wednesday, September 3rd Mrs. __ McCarty.
Died on Sunday, September 7 at age 61 years, Mr. Mark Wood of Loudoun.

Vol. VII, No. 36 - September 16, 1823
Married on Tuesday, September 9th by Rev. Thomas Birkby, Mr. Abner Whitaker
and Miss Hannah Dillon, both of this county.
Married on Thursday, September 11th by Rev. Thomas Birkby, Mr. Mahlon
Warner and Miss Lucinder Curry, of this county.
Died in this town on Tuesday, September 9th at age 39 years, Mrs. Mary Head.
Died in This town on Thursday, September 11th at age 59 years, Mrs. Louisa
Hough, consort of Bernard Hough.

Vol. VII, No. 37 – September 23, 1823
Died in Bedford, Pa, on Sunday, August 31st Capt. William M. Littlejohn of
Leesburg.
Died in Frederick Co., Va. on Saturday, September 6th Francis Stribling Sr.
Died in this town on Friday, September 19th at age 21 years, John Jacobs.
Died on Friday, September 19th at age 26 years, James Mansfield.

Vol. VII, No. 38 – September 30, 1823
Died at Hillsborough on Saturday, September 20th at age 53 years, Thomas
Hough.
Died on Tuesday, September 23 at age 25 years, Mr. Samuel Donohoe.

Vol. VII, No. 39 – October 7, 1823
Died at her residence in Loudoun, Monday, September 29th at age 88 years, Mrs.
Mary Fouche.
Died at his residence in Loudoun near Noland's Ferry on October 2nd at age 54
years, Casper Ekart.

Vol. VII, No. 40 – October 14, 1823
Married on Thursday, October 9th by Rev. Thomas Birkby, Samuel Carter and
Miss Ranche [Rachel??] Johnson, both of the county.
Married on Thursday, October 9th by Rev. Thomas Birkby, Mr. George Norwood
and Miss Mary D. Kaighn of this county.
Died at Waterford on Thursday, October 9th Asa Moore of Society of Friends.

Vol. VII, No. 41 – October 21, 1823
Married on Tuesday, September 30th by Rev. John G. Watt, Mr. James Brady
and Miss Honour Houser, both of this county.

Married on Thursday, October 9th by Rev. John G. Watt, Mr. Mordecai Elgin and
    Miss Sarah Allen, all of this county.
Died at residence of his father in Jefferson Co., Va. on Wednesday, September
    24th, Isaac Lafferty.
Died in this vicinity on Wednesday, October 15th at age 28 years, Jonathan Hall.

Vol. VII, No. 42 – October 28, 1823
Married on Thursday, October 16th by Rev. Thomas Birkby, John Morris and Miss
    Elizabeth Dorrell, both of Leesburg.
Married on Thursday, October 16th by Rev. Thomas Birkby, Asa Jackson and
    Miss Susan M. Rhodes, both of this county.
Died on Friday, October 10th in Montgomery Co., Md., Thomas Green, and on
    Saturday, October 11th his wife Mrs. Green.

Vol. VII, No. 43 – November 4, 1823
Married on Tuesday, October 28th by Rev. Wm. Williamson, Captain Hamilton
    Rogers and Miss Mary Hawling of this county.
Died at Carlisle, Pa. on Tuesday, October 21st, Mrs. Mary Duncan Lee, wife of
    Richard H. Lee of Leesburg.
Died Friday, October 24th at age 21 years, Mrs. Rebecca Fulton, consort of David
    Fulton.
Died Thursday, October 30th Jane Sidney Lee Saunders, 6 years old daughter of
    Major James Saunders.

Vol. VII, No. 45 – November 18, 1823
Married Thursday, November 6th by Rev. Thomas Birkby, Mr. Thomas O'Neale
    and Miss Mary Iden, both of Loudoun.
Married Thursday, November 6th by Rev. Thomas Birkby, Mr. Alexander P.
    Brackenridge and Miss Elizabeth Newton, both of Loudoun.
Married Thursday, November 13th by Rev. Thomas Birkby, Mr. Wesley
    Donaldson and Mrs. Nancy Saunders, both of Loudoun.

Vol. VII, No. 46 – November 25, 1823
Married Thursday, November 6th by Rev. Wm. Gilmore, Mr. Christopher
    Stoneburner and Miss Eliza Wildman, both of Loudoun.
Married Thursday, November 20th by Rev. Wm. Gilmore, Mr. Moses Hicks and
    Miss Elizabeth Davis, both of Loudoun.

Vol. VII, No. 47 – December 2, 1823
Married Thursday, November 27th by Rev. Wm. Gilmore, Mr. Alexander Lee and
    Miss Alice Jones, both of Loudoun.
Married Thursday, November 27th by Rev. Wm. Gilmore, Mr. John C. Hanley and
    Miss Uree Eaton, both of Loudoun.

Vol. VII, No. 48 – December 9, 1823
Married by Rev. Robert Burch, Mr. Richard Vallendingham and Miss Mary Goran,
    both of Fairfax [no date given].
Married Sunday, November 30th by Rev. Robert Burch, Mr. Thomas Darne and
    Miss Catharine Lewis, both of Loudoun.
Married on Tuesday, December 2nd by Rev. Thomas Birkby, Mr. Leven W.
    Shepherd and Miss Catharine Eversol.
Died on Saturday, December 6th at age 30 years, Mrs. Sarah Hammett, consort
    of Edward Hammett.

Vol. VII, No. 49 – December 16, 1823
Married Thursday, December 11th by Rev. Wm. Gilmore, Mr. Washington
Hummer and Mrs. Martina B. Sheid, all of this county.
Married Thursday, December 11th by Rev. Thomas Birkby, Mr. Wm. Lloyd and
Miss Elizabeth Rogue, both of the county.

Vol. VII, No. 50 – December 23, 1823
Married on Thursday, December 18th by Rev. Thomas Birkby, Mr. Charles Crook
and Miss Deborah Marks, both of this county.

Vol. VII, No. 52 – January 6, 1824
Married on Thursday, December 25 by Rev. Wm. Gilmore, Mr. Thomas Jones
and Miss Hannah Orrison, both of this county.

Vol. VIII, No. 2 – January 20, 1824
Married Thursday last by Rev. Wm. Gilmore, Elijah Holmes and Miss Elizabeth
Rogers, both of Loudoun.

Vol. VIII, No. 3 – January 27, 1824
Married Tuesday eve the 13th inst. by Rev. George M. Frye, Mr. Abraham Carrell
of Winchester and Miss Nancy, daughter of Lewis Lider of this county.
Married Wednesday eve last by Rev. Thomas Birkby, Mr. Wm. Schooley and
Miss Abigail Myers, all of this county.
Married on Thursday last, (22nd Jan) by Rev. Thomas Birkby, Mr. Edwin A.
Stover and Miss Ann Bogue, all of town.
Married Thursday eve by candle light on the Potomac River, by Rev. Robert
Burch, Mr. Francis Dulin and Miss Margaret Hoskinson, all of this county.
Died on the 17th inst. at his residence in Baltimore Co. Md., Oliver Matthews in
the 103rd year of his age.

Vol. VIII, No. 4 – February 3, 1824
Married Tuesday eve last (Jan 27) by Rev. Mr. Johnson, Townsend McVeigh,
Esq. of this county and Miss Karen Thrift of Fairfax.
Married Thursday last (Jan 29) by Rev. Thos. Birkby, Conrad Long and Nancy
Crooks, both of this county.

Vol. VIII, No. 5 – February 10, 1824
Married on 29th ult. (Jan 29) by Rev. Robert Burch, Dr. Benedict M. Lane and
Susan Cockerill, both of Fairfax Co.
Married 5th inst. (Feb 5) by Rev. Robert Burch, Samuel B. T. Caldwell of
Leesburg and Mary Hough of Waterford.
Married 5th inst. (Feb. 5) by Rev. Thos. Birkby, John Stowe and Catharine Cost,
both of this county.
Married 5th inst. (Feb. 5) by Rev. Thos. Birkby, John Beatty and Catharine
Whitmore, all of this county.

Vol. VIII, No. 6 – February 17, 1824
Died at Birmingham, England on the 11th of December last, Mr. Henry Foxall of
Georgetown, who was a pious christian and well known as the proprietor of
the Georgetown foundry in the District of Columbia.

Vol. VIII, No. 7 – February 24, 1824

Married in Ryegate, Vt., Col. Jacob Blanchard and Miss Thomas Jefferson Cameron, daughter of Judge Cameron and grand-daughter of Gen. Stark. The excentricities of some of the sons-in-law of the veteran Stark were scarcely less remarkable than his own. The whole family were admirers of Jefferson. Previous to the birth of the lady, whose marriage is above announced, the father predicted that the infant would be a son, and insisted at all events whether male or female, it should be named Thomas Jefferson.

Married on the 4th inst. (Feb 4) by Rev. Mr. Green, Hiram Opie Bell of Frederick Co. and Frances Elizabeth Roach of this city.

Married on the 12th inst. (Feb. 12) by the Rev. John M. Sockman [sic], Daniel Householder and Priscilla S. Gregg, both of this county.

Married on Thursday last (Feb. 14) by Rev. Wm. Gilmore, William Trenary of Frederick Co. and Susannah Lafaber of Loudoun.

Vol. VIII, No. 8 – March 2, 1824

Married Thursday the 12th ult. (Feb 12) by Rev. Thos. Birkby, John Irey and Massy Warner, both of this county.

Vol. VIII, No. 9 – March 9, 1824

Married Tuesday eve (Mar 2) by Wm. Gilmore, Joseph P. Megeath and Elizabeth Cochran, both of this county.

Married in Md. on Thursday last (Mar 4) by Rev. Mr. Lee, Samuel Pinor of Baltimore, age 70 years, and Hannah Selby of Snow Hill, age 80 years.

Married Thursday eve (Mar 4) by Rev. Robert Burch, Thomas Jackson and Jane Hancock of Loudoun Co.

Died in this state on the 15th ult., Wm. Fleming, Esq., Presiding Judge of the Court of Appeals of Virginia.

Died on the 15th ult., Laurance Augustine Washington at his residence in Wheeling, age 50 years.

Died on the 1st inst. after protracted illness in Washington, The Hon. Wm. Lee Ball, aged about 45 years, Representative in Congress from Virginia.

Vol. VIII, No. 11 – March 23, 1824

Married Thursday last (Mar 18) in Md. by Rev. Thos. Birkby, Wm. P. Fox, Esq. and Catharine E. Sullivan, both of this county.

Married Thursday last (Mar 18) by Rev. Thos. Birkby, Walter Evans of Fairfax Co. and Mary F. Nichols, daughter of Thos. of Loudoun.

Vol. VIII, No. 12 – March 30, 1824

Married in Frederick Co. on 16th inst. (Mar 16) by Rev. Dr. Chapman, John Heiskell, late ed. of *Winchester Gazette*, and Sarah White, daughter of John White, Esq.

Married at Waterford on Thursday last (Mar 25) by Rev. Birkby, Jacob G. Paxson and Matilda I. Potts of Loudoun Co.

Died on 22nd inst., John W. Wager of Harper's Ferry.

Died on 23rd, Wm. P. Craighill, Esq., Paymaster of Harper's Ferry.

Vol. VIII, No. 13 – April 6, 1824

Discovery of body of Col. Charles Elgin in Potomac where he was lost on March 9.

Vol. VIII, No. 14 – April 13, 1824
Married on Thursday last (Apr 8) by Birkby, John L. Parsons and Jane Wilson both of this county.

Vol. VIII, No. 15 – April 20, 1824
Married Tuesday eve last (Apr 13) by Rev. Mr. Burch, Dr. Jonathan N. Bradfield and Miss Sarah, daughter of Abiel Jenners, Esq., all of this county.

Vol. VIII, No. 16 – April 27, 1824
Married on 15th inst. (Apr 15) by Birkby, Hillary Jarvis and Sally Neale, both of this county.

Married Thursday last by Birkby, William Howell and Elizabeth Flowers, all of Loudoun.

Vol. VIII, No. 17 – May 4, 1824
Married 11th ult. (Apr 11) by Rev. R. Burch, John Taylor and Eve Buckey, both of Fairfax.

Married 22nd ult. (Apr 22), James Sinclair and Emily Sanders, both of Loudoun.

Married 22nd ult. (Apr 22) in Georgetown by Rev. Balch, John M. Dorrell and Julia M. Daily, both of Leesburg.

Vol. VIII, No. 20 – May 25, 1824
Married Thursday last (May 20) by Birkby, Charles Hogan and Margaret Martin, both of this county

Died on Tuesday last (May 18) at home in vicinity of Leesburg, William Darne, in 43rd year, buried at Methodist burial ground same day.

Vol. VIII, No. 21 – June 1, 1824
Died at Baltimore 24th ult. (May 24) at 49 years, Gen. William H. Winder.

Vol. VIII, No. 22 – June 8, 1824
Married 26th ult. (May 26) at Friends Meeting House at Waterford, Dr. George Harris, late of Baltimore, and Sarah Ann Littler of Waterford.

Vol. VIII, No. 23 – June 15, 1824
Married Tuesday last (June 8) by Birkby, Richard C. Barton and Delilah Burditt, all of this county.

Vol. VIII, No. 24 – June 22, 1824
Died Saturday night last (June 19), Miss Emily Wherry, aged about 18 years.

Vol. VIII, No. 25 – June 29, 1824
Died Tuesday eve, June 22, Julia Ann Moss, killed by lightning at her father's house near Upperville.

Married in this town 24 ult. by Birkby, Claudius T. Devall and Harriot E. Langley.

Vol. VIII, No. 26 – July 6, 1824
Married on Sunday last in Fredericktown Md., Samuel Sterrett and Lydia Kitzmiller, both of this town.

Married in Bath M. E., Decan Samuel Dunlap, aged 85 years, to Hulda Ham, aged 70 years.

Vol. VIII, No. 28 – July 20, 1824

Died on Wednesday last after a few hours illness at his late residence, Exedra, Loudoun County, Dr. James Heaton, in the 65th year of his age, highly respected and much regretted. Born Sussex County, New Jersey, Jan. 12, 1759, came to Loudoun County in 1786.

Vol. VIII, No. 29 – July 27, 1824

On Thursday last Dr. Claggett was called upon to visit a lad by the name of Fox who from the carelessness or curiosity incident to youth, while wainting at Weldon's Mills, had his right hand caught and shockingly mangled by some of the machinery attached to the carding establishment. Upon examination it was found necessary to amputate the hand which operation was immediately performed. The boy is a resident of this county and about 11 years of age.

Vol. VIII, No. 30 – August 3, 1824

Married Thursday last (July 29) by Rev. Wm. Gillmore, Joseph Leak and Elizabeth Myers, both of this county.

Vol. VIII, No. 31 – August 10, 1824

Died in Leesburg on the 31st ult., Nancy Margaret, infant daughter of James Mateer.

Vol. VIII, No. 32 – August 17, 1824

Married on 9th inst. (Aug 9) by Birkby, Reuben Reily and Jane McCarty, both of Loudoun.

Vol. VIII, No. 33 – August 24, 1824

Died 14th inst. at Dalecarlin, Fauquier Co., Va., Mrs. Margaret C, wife of Dr. Thomas Triplett.

Vol. VIII, No. 34 – August 31, 1824

Married Thursday last (Aug 26) by Gilmore, Charles Carter and Malinda Craven, both of Loudoun.
Died in Franklin, Mo on night of 6th ult., Joseph Jones Monroe, bro. of Pres. Monroe.
Died in Jefferson Co., 12th inst., Capt. Smith Slaughter, in 61st year.

Vol. VIII, No. 35 – September 7, 1824

Died in Pa. on the 16th of August at 95 years, Charles Thompson, sole secretary of Congress during Rev.

Vol. VIII, No. 36 – September 17, 1824

Died 7th inst. Jonathan Sheppard of this county, aged 29 years, son, husband and father, left widow and infant child and venerable father 72 years.
Died Sunday morn last, Ann Ball, youngest daughter of L. P. W. Balch, Esq. of this town, aged 16 months.

Vol. VIII, No. 37 – September 21, 1824

Married Thursday last (Sept 16), Joseph Hilliard of Leesburg and Ann Hough of Waterford.

Vol. VIII, No. 38 – September 28, 1824
Married Thursday last (Sept. 23) by Gilmore, Alfred Dulin and Sarah E. Reese, both of this county.

Vol. VIII, No. 39 – October 5, 1824
Died in the German Settlement in Loudoun Co. on the 17th ult. Mr. Charles Crim, aged about 83 years.

Died in the German Settlement in Loudoun Co. on the 28th ult. (Sept 28), Mr. Daniel Shoemaker, aged about 48 years.

Died in Waterford on the 29th ult. (Sept 29) Jas. D. French.

Died on Thursday last, September 30, Sam'l N. Smallwood, Esq., mayor of the City of Washington, in the 54th year of his age.

Died on Sunday evening last (Oct 3), Alexander Cooper Jr. of this town.

Abiel Jenners departed this life on the first day (Sunday) evening, about six o'clock, on the 26th ult. in the 52nd year of his age. He was born at Concord, in the State of Massachusetts, and emigrated when a young man to the city of Washington, at which place he married Deborah Young, a native thereof, and removed with his family to this county in 1802, where he has resided ever since. [continues about his characteristics]

Vol. VIII, No. 40 – October 12, 1824
Died at U. S. Cantonment at Belle Fontan, Missouri, on Tuesday 7 ult. (Sept 7), Mrs. Elizabeth Littlejohn late consort of Dr. Samuel Littlejohn, of the United States Army.

Vol. VIII, No. 41 – October 19, 1824
Died in the 19th ult. assending the Missouri, Dr. Samuel Littlejohn, husband of Elizabeth Littlejohn who died Sept 7. Dr. Littleton [Littlejohn] was formerly of this town but more recently of Sacketts Harbour, N. Y.

Died on the 9th inst. (Oct 9) near Waterford, Stephen Scott, an aged member of the Society of Friends.

Died on the 11th inst. (Oct 11) Randolph Rhodes in the 22nd year of his age, son of George Rhodes in the vicinity of this town.

Died on Saturday morning last (Oct 16) Mrs. Ann McCabe of this town.

Vol. VIII, No. 42 – October 26, 1824
Married on the 20th inst. on the Maryland bank of the Potomac by the Rev. William Green, Mr. Baylis Castleman and Miss Nancy Lynch, both of Loudoun Co.

Died in the neighborhood of Waterford on the 15th inst., Hannah Schooley, wife of William Schooley, of Society of Friends.

Vol. VIII, No. 43 – November 2, 1824
Married on Tuesday last (Oct 26) by Rev. John G. Watt, Levi Cooksey and Elizabeth Wood, both of this county.

Married on Tuesday last (Oct 26) by Rev. John G. Watt, Jer [*sic*] Moore and Jane Wright, all of Loudoun Co.

Died on Tues. morning last, after an illness of 11 days, Mr. Lewis Lyder, an old resident of this county, and for sometime a respectable member of the Methodist Church.

Vol. VIII, No. 44 – November 9, 1824

Married 4th inst. (Nov 4) by Gilmore, Strother Bell of Frederick Co. and Jane Ann Potts of Loudoun.

Died Tuesday morn last (Nov 2) Dr. John T. Wilson, in the 36th year of age, left widow and small child.

Died 15th September, Mrs. Margaret Ann, consort of Wm. Lander, 2nd daughter of Charles & Susan Drish of Leesburg.

Vol. VIII, No. 45 – November 16, 1824

Married Tuesday eve last (Nov 9) by Gilmore, Jesse Orrison and Mary Gheen, all of this county.

Married Thursday last (Nov 11) by Gilmore, Matthew Orrison and Elizabeth Ann Garner, both of Loudoun.

Married Thursday last (Nov 11) by Birkby, Henry Adams and Priscilla McKimmie, all of this county.

Died in vicinity of this town, Mrs. Mary Mason, relict of late Gen. Stephen Thompson Mason.

Vol. VIII, No. 46 – November 23, 1824

Married Thursday eve 18th inst. by Rev. Tuston, Archibald Carr and Emily, daughter of Geo. Gulick, all of Loudoun Co.

Died in Waterford Sunday morn the 7th inst., Mrs. Elizabeth Thomas, wife of Isaac P. Thomas, left 4 small children.

Vol. VIII, No. 47 – November 30, 1824

Married on Sunday eve 21st inst. by Birkby, Benjamin Brown and Ann Schooley, both of this county.

Married Thursday eve 25th inst. by Rev. John G. Watt, Rev. George M. Frye of Winchester and Mrs. Mary Daves of Loudoun Co.

Married 5th ult. (Oct 5) by Rev. Robt. Burch, Dr. Joseph B. Fox and Amanda O. Leslie, all of Loudoun Co.

Married 29th inst. by Rev. Robt. Burch, Balis Castleman and Nancy Lynch, both of Loudoun Co.

Vol. VIII, No. 48 – December 7, 1824

Married Tuesday eve last (Nov 30) in Hillsborough by the Rev. Tuston, Dr. Geo. W. Taylor and Ann Eliza White, daughter of late Maj. White, all of this county.

Vol. VIII, No. 49 – December 14, 1824

Married Thursday last (Dec 9) by Gilmore, James P. Lovett and Huldah Gulick, all of this county.

Married Thursday last (Dec 9) by R. Tuston, Norval Chamblin and Sarah Vandeventer, daughter of late Dr. Vandeventer, all of Loudoun Co.

Vol. VIII, No. 50 – December 21, 1824

Died in this town on the 7th inst. after illness of 15 days, Mrs. Mary P. Buck, wife of Mr. Samuel Buck, aged 36 years, left husband and seven children.

Vol. VIII, No. 51 – December 28, 1824

Married Thursday the 16th inst. by Gilmore, Wesley S. McPherson and Anna Thrift, all of Loudoun Co.

Married Sunday the 19th inst. by Gilmore, Joseph Randall Jr. and Lucinda Collins, both of Fauquier.

Married Thursday last (Dec 23) by Birkby, Ezra Bolen and Nelly Conwell, both of this county.

Vol. VIII, No. 52 – January 4, 1825

Married 23rd ult. in Middleburg by Rev. Davis, Mr. Kerfoot and Catharine Sowers.

Married 23rd ult. in Middleburg by Rev. George Roszel, John Murry and Catharine Rector.

Married 23rd ult. in Middleburg by Rev. George Roszel, Philip Tutt and Catharine Ashby.

Vol. IX, No. 1 – January 11, 1825

Married Thursday, 23rd ult. (Dec 23) by Rev. Dunn, Capt. George M. Chichester of Loudoun Co. and Mary, eldest daughter of Washington Bowie.

Married Tuesday last (Jan 4) by Birkby, Matthew Sypherd and Eliza Brown, both of this county.

Married Thursday last (Jan 6) by Birkby, Henry Stoneburner and Sarah Ann Frye, both of Loudoun.

Died 2nd inst., Mrs. Helen Curtis, aged inhabitant of this town.

Vol. IX, No. 2 – January 18, 1825

Married on 6th instant by Rev. Bascom, Wm. C. Conine and Mary Ann Wilcox, both of Baltimore.

Married Monday 10th inst. by Birkby, Francis Millar and Anne Jones, both of this county.

Died Monday 10th inst., Jacob Myers, aged 77, many years resident of Loudoun.

Vol. IX, No. 3 – January 25, 1825

Married Sunday the 16th inst. by Gilmore, James H. Whaley of Fairfax and Mary A. Hutchison of Loudoun.

Vol. IX, No. 4 – February 1, 1825

Married Thursday last (Jan 27) by Birkby, Joseph Hogue and Elizabeth Butler, both of city.

Vol. IX, No. 5 – February 8, 1825

Married in Alexandria on Thursday the 27th ult. by Rev. Burch, Charles W. D. Binns, Esq. of town and Marianne T. S., daughter of Walter S. Alexander, Esq. of Alexandria.

Married Tuesday eve last by the Rev. Post, Septimus Tustin and Elizabeth Maria, daughter of Stephen B. Balch of Georgetown, DC.

Died at Winchester on the 27th ult., Hon. Hugh Holmes, Judge of Gen'l Court.

Died Thursday eve last, Louisa Drain, daughter of John Drain.

Vol. IX, No. 7 – February 22, 1825

Married Thursday eve last by Birkby, Norval Osburn and Elizabeth Potts, both of this county.

Married on Sunday eve by Birkby, James Thomas and Ann Murry of town.

Died in this town Wednesday eve last, Thomas Clifford in the 23rd year of his age.

Died on Friday last, Adam Goff, a soldier of the Revolutionary War and for many years a resident of Leesburg.

Vol. IX, No. 8 – March 1, 1825
Married Thursday eve last, Mason P. Chamblin and Duanna, daughter of Capt. Isaac Vandeventer, both of this county.

Died Friday morn last, George Henry, infant son of Giles Hammat of town

Vol. IX, No. 9 – March 8, 1825
Married by Rev. John Dunn on Thursday the 17th ult., John Holmes, Esq. and Lydia Vansickle, all of this county.

Vol. IX, No. 10 – March 15, 1825
Married Thursday the 3rd inst., by Birkby, William L. Simpson and Hannah Moffett, both of this county.

Married on Thursday last by Birkby, Edward Hammett and Elizabeth Donohoe, both of Loudoun.

Vol. IX, No. 11 – March 22, 1825
Married Thursday eve last by Birkby, John Dailey and Elizabeth McDaniel, all of this county.

Married on Thursday last by Rev. Tuston, Andrew Copeland and Jane Copeland, all of Loudoun.

Married on Thurs. last by Rev. Robt. Burch, Samuel Tebbs and Hannah, daughter of Chas. Binns of town.

Vol. IX, No. 12 – March 29, 1825
Married Thursday last by Gilmore, Walter Williams and Ann E. Harwood, both of Fairfax.

Married eve of Thursday last by Gilmore, Briton Saunders and Ann Eckart, of Loudoun.

Vol. IX, No. 14 – April 12, 1825
Married Thursday eve the 31st ult. by Gilmore, Alexander Beard and Susan Tillett, both of this county.

Vol. IX, No. 15 – April 19, 1825
Married Tuesday last by Birkby, John Hanley and Hannah Craven, both of this county.

Married Thursday last by Rev. Tuston, Alexander Lawrence, of Frederick Co., and Emily McCormick, daughter of John McCormick, Esq. of town.

Vol. IX, No. 16 – April 26, 1825
Married on the 19th inst. in Millwood, Frederick Co., by Rev. Meade, Edmund Tyler, Esq., of Loudoun Co., and Alice Jane, daughter of late Rev. George Richards of Portsmouth, New Hampshire.

Died in this town on Tuesday eve last, Martin Cordell, aged about 50 years.

Died also in town Sunday last, Mary Jane Dowling, about 16.

Vol. IX, No. 17 – May 3, 1825
Long obituary of M. J. Dowling, only daughter of Mrs. Catherine Dowling.

Vol. IX, No. 18 – May 10, 1825
Married on Thursday last by Rev. John Dunn, James McIlhany, Esq. and Margaret, eldest daughter of Richard H. Henderson, all of town.

Vol. IX, No. 19 – May 17, 1825

Married Thursday 5th inst. by Rev. Sockman, Jacob Everhart and Sarah, daughter of Peter Stuck, all of this county.

Died, Mrs. Emily Sinclair, aged 17, consort of Mr. James Sinclair of this town, fell from carriage and left infant child. [no date given].

Vol. IX, No 21- May 31, 1825

Married Tuesday eve the 10th inst. at Llangollen, Loudoun Co., Cuthbert Powell Jr., Atty at Law of Romney, Va., to Miss Mary E., 2nd daughter of Cuthbert Powell, Esq. of Loudoun.

Married Thursday eve last by Gilmore, Daniel Brown and Ann Watkins, all of this county.

Died in this town on Wednesday last, Miss Harriot Harrison.

Died Thursday morn last, Henry Darnes aged 4, son of late William Darnes.

Vol. IX, No. 23 – June 14, 1825

Married at Baltimore Tuesday eve by Rev. Bishop Soule, Rev. Joseph Frye formerly of Winchester, and Cornelia M., daughter of Richard Lawrence of that city.

Married Tuesday, 31 May, by Rev. Evans, James S. Carter of Culpeper and Jemima Leith of Loudoun.

Married Thursday last by Rev. Thomas Birkby, Nicholas Kline and Elizabeth Smarr, all of this county.

Vol. IX, No. 24 – June 21, 1825

Married Charlestown, Jefferson Co., Tuesday eve last by Rev. Alexander Jones, Thos. A. Moore, Esq., atty at law, to Jane Cramer, 3rd daughter of Dr. Samuel J. Cramer, all of this place.

Died on Saturday, June 11th Rev. John Summerfield, in 27th year of age and 8th year of ministry.

Vol. IX, No. 25 – June 28, 1825

Died in Leesburg on Sunday the 19th inst., Joseph Dailey, in the 17th year of his age.

Died on Tuesday last in Leesburg, Cuthbert P. Surghnor, aged about 8 months, infant of James Surghnor of Leesburg.

Vol. IX, No. 26 – July 5, 1825

Died on the 22nd ult., Sylvester Whitefield, youngest son of L. P. W. Balch, Esq. of this town.

Died on the 24th ult. in Richmond, Dr. John Adams, mayor of that city.

Died at his residence in Richmond on Tuesday 21st ult., William Munford, 52, many years clerk of the House of Delegates of Virginia.

Vol. IX, No. 28 – July 19, 1825

Married at Alexandria on Tuesday, July 12 by Rev. Elias Harrison, Mr. Alfred Mitchel of Waterford and Miss Mary Biers of Alexandria.

Vol. IX, No. 29 – July 26, 1825

Died on Wednesday, July 20th, Amanda, infant daughter of John A. Binns of Leesburg.

Married Tuesday, July 19th, by Rev. Thomas Birkby, Mr. Christian Nuswanger [*sic*] and Miss Mary Russell, all of Loudoun.

Died at Union in Loudoun Co. on July 16th Cornelius Vandeventer, 35 years, leaves widow & son.

Died, at Manchester, Mass., Henry Ward, of US Navy, aged 34, native of Salem. [More about circustances of his death].

Died at Bath, Maine, Capt. Levi Patterson, aged 55.

Died on Wednesday, the 20th inst. Amanda the infant dau. of John A. Binns Esqr. of this town.

Died in Prince William Co., on Friday, 15th instant, Mrs. Catharine Drewery, age 103 years. She was a native of Virginia.

Vol. IX, No. 30 – August 2, 1825

Married at Roxton, Jefferson Co., on 21st July by Rev. Jones, Charles G. Eskridge, Esq. of this place and Miss Isabella, daughter of John Kennedy, Esq. of Charlestown.

Vol. IX, No. 31 – August 9, 1825

Married on Thursday, 28 July, by Rev. Thomas Birkby, Mahlon T. Norris and Miss Rachel Davis, all of this county.

Married on Sunday, 31st July by Rev. Thomas Birkby, Mr. Ishem Hill to Miss Eleanor Vermillion.

Died in Leesburg on Thursday, August 4th, Mr. Andrew Young (a hatter) age 22 or 23.

Vol. IX, No. 32 – August 16, 1825

Died in Upperville on August 1st Mrs. Christiania Miley, age 88 years. Member Methodist Church for 50 years.

Died in Middleburg, Loudoun Co., August 5th Mr. Samuel Noland, age 40 years.

Died in Leesburg, Friday, August 12th Mr. Presley Foley, age 42 years. Interred by Masonic Brethern.

Vol. IX, No. 34 – August 30, 1825

Died on Sunday, August 14th Armistead Mason Mitchell, 7 years old, eldest son of Col. Benjamin Mitchell.

Married in Washington, DC on the 25th inst. by Rev. Mr. McCormick, John Walter Crouse, to Miss Mary Margaret Smith, both of this town.

Vol. IX, No. 35 – September 6, 1825

Married Thursday, August 4th, by Rev. Robert Burch, Mr. Richard F. Peyton of Loudoun and Miss Vurlinda Yates of Pohick.

Died in Leesburg on Monday, August 15, Mr. Mungo Dykes, age 64 years.

Died in Leesburg on Wednesday, August 31st, Eliza Maria Caldwell, 9½ month old daughter of S. B. T. Caldwell.

Vol. IX, No. 37 – September 20, 1825

Married on Thursday, September 8th by Rev. William Gilmore, Mr. John B. Hunter of Loudoun and Miss Sibyl Deneale of Fairfax.

Married on September 11th by Rev. Tuston, Mr. Marca Tarlton and Miss Amelia Vermillion of this county.

Died in Leesburg, Monday, August 29th, Mrs. Elizabeth Woodly , age 32 years.

Died Saturday, September 3rd, Mrs. Elizabeth Dailey, consort of Mr. John Dailey of this vicinity.

Died near Leesburg Monday, September 12th, Mr. John Wildman, 81 years old, a native of Bucks Co. Pa, resident of Leesburg 50 years.

Vol. IX, No. 38 – September 27, 1825

Died on August 15th in Lewisburg, Greenbrier Co. Va., Alexander Langley (a hatter) formerly of Leesburg.

Died on 20th ult. in Delaware Co., Pa., Gideon Gilpin.

Vol. IX, No. 39 - October 4, 1825

Died on 9th ult. at Bloomingdale, New Jersey, Mr. Wm. Summerfield, father of the late John Savage, age 54.

Died in Alexandria on Thursday night, Dr. Elisha C. Dick, in 72nd year. He was one of the physicians who attended George Washington.

Vol. IX, No. 40 – October 11, 1825

Died September 23rd at his home near Hillsborough, Mr. James White, age 41 years. Member of Methodist Episcopal Church.

Died October 3rd near Leesburg, Reuben Schooley Sr., Quaker.

Died October 3rd Samuel Nichols, Quaker.

Vol. IX, No. 42 – October 25, 1825

Died Sunday, October 16th 7 year old Frances Ellen, eldest daughter of James and Eleanor Newton.

Married Thursday, October 13th by Rev. Tuston, Mr. Thomas Pooley and Miss Mary Ann Maguire, both of Georgetown, DC.

Vol. IX, No. 43 – November 1, 1825

Married Thursday, October 27th by Rev. Thomas Birkby, Mr. Johnston Erwin and Miss Penelope Thompson, both of this county.

Died in Leesburg on Wednesday, October 20th 31 year old Miss Mary Dykes.

Died in Union on Friday, October 22nd Dr. Wm. H. Dorsey, a native of Calvert Co. Md., some years living in Loudoun.

Died in Washington Co. Md. on September 17th Rev. Daniel Hitt, age 58 years.

Vol. IX, No. 44 – November 8, 1825

Died in Leesburg, Wednesday, November 3rd, John Moore, 4 month old son of Mr. William H. Jacobs.

Vol. IX, No. 45 – November 15, 1825

Married at Vine Mont near Charlestown Va. on Thursday, November 3rd by Rev Tuston, Mann R. Page, Esq. and Miss Helena Margaret Beale, both of Jefferson Co.

Vol. IX, No. 46 – November 22, 1825

Married on Thursday, November 10th by Rev. John Dunn, Joseph Lewis, Esq. and Miss Elizabeth O. Grayson, eldest daughter of Benjamin Grayson, Esq., all of Loudoun.

Died on Wednesday, November 16th, Henry Clagett, infant son of John Surghnor of this town.

Vol. IX, No. 48 – December 6, 1825

Married in Amissville on Thursday, November 17th by Rev. R. Bashaw, Mr. Benjamin P. Ferguson of Loudoun and Miss Edna Amiss, daughter of P. Amiss, Esq. of Culpeper Co., Va.

Vol. IX, No. 50 – December 20, 1825

Married in Leesburg, 24 November, Griffin Taylor of Frederick Co. and Miss
    Susan Chilton of Leesburg. [Winchester paper]
Married on Thursday, December 1st, by Rev. Wm. Gilmore, Mr. Jno. Van Sickler
    and Miss Mahalie Fred, all of this county.
Married on Thursday, December 1st, by Rev. George Reed, Mr. John Mount of
    Waterford and Miss Eliza Thomas, daughter of Daniel W. Thomas of
    Winchester.
Married in Fairfax on Tuesday, December 6 by Rev. J. G. Watt, I. Comstock and
    Miss Cynthia, 3rd daughter of Sebastian McPherson, all of Fairfax.
Married on Thursday, December 8th by Rev. Thos. Birkby, William Cruit [sic] and
    Miss Hannah Moon, all of Waterford.
Married on Thursday, December 8th by Rev. Thos. Birkby, Noah Hixon and
    Cecilia Hough, all of Loudoun.
Married Tuesday, December 13th by Rev. Thos. Birkby, Thos. Wiley and Miss
    Pleasant McFarling, all of this county.
Married Thursday, December 15th by Rev. Thos. Birkby, Thomas Loveloss [sic]
    and Miss Elizabeth Curry, all of this county.
Married Thursday evening, December 15th by Rev. Thos. Birkby, Lawson Littleton
    and Miss Cecilia Nickolls, all of this county.

Vol. IX, No. 51 – December 27, 1825

Married in Washington City on Thursday, December 15th by Rev. O. B. Brown,
    Thomas J. Noland and Miss Sarah C. Myers, both of Middleburg, Loudoun
    Co.
Married on Thursday, December 15th by Rev. Dr. Wilmer, Dr. Hugh H. McGuire of
    Winchester, Va. and Miss Ann Eliza, daughter of William Moss, Esq. of
    Fairfax Va.

Vol. IX, No. 52 – January 3, 1826

Married on Thursday, December 29th by Rev. Thomas Birkby, Mr. Wm.
    Sidebottom and Miss Elizabeth Y. Crider, both of Loudoun Co.
Married on Thursday, December 29th by Rev. Thomas Birkby, Mr. Joshua
    Ratcliffe of New Market, Md. to Miss Nancy Taylor of Waterford.

Vol. X, No. 1 – January 10, 1826

Married at Rose Mont, Fauquier Co., on Tuesday, December 6th by Rev. Stephen
    G. Roszel, Jno. M. Chunn, Esq. and Miss Ann Mariah, eldest daughter of
    Washington Cocke, Esq.
Married at Rose Mont, Fauquier Co., on Tuesday, January 3rd by Rev. French S.
    Evans, Marshall Ashby, Esq. and Miss Lucinda, 2nd daughter of Washington
    Cocke, Esq.
Died at Llangollan, the residence of Cuthbert Powell Sr., Esq. on Thursday
    evening last (Jan 5th) in the 25th year of his age, Cuthbert Powell Jr., Esq. of
    Romney, Hampshire Co. Va.

Vol. X, No. 2 – January 17, 1826

Married December 15th by Rev. William Gilmore, Mr. George Sagar and Miss
    Delia Carter, both of this county.
Married on Thursday, December 29th by Rev. French S. Evans, Peter Gregg,
    Esq. and Miss Emily L. Craine, all of this county.
Married January 3rd by Rev. William Gilmore, Mr. Wm. Fletcher and Miss Harriot
    Lake, both of Fauquier Co.

Married Thursday, January 5th by Rev. William Gilmore, Mr. Ludwell Lake and
  Miss Agnes Martin, both of Fauquier.
Married Thursday, January 12th by Rev. Thomas Birkby, Mr. Jonathan Painter
  and Miss Delilah, daughter of Mr. Lambert Myers, all of this county.
Married Thursday, January 12th by Rev. Thomas Birkby, Mr. Jacob Towner and
  Miss Sarah Laws, all of this town.
Died Thursday, January 12, Mr. John Shaw Sr. of Leesburg. Interred Methodist
  burying ground.

Vol. X, No. 3 – January 24, 1826

Married on Thursday, January 19th by the Rev. Tuston, Mr. Henry McCartor and
  Miss Martha Curry, all of this county.
Married on Thursday, January 19th by Rev. Thomas Birkby, Mr. Tho. Mashall and
  Miss Elizabeth, daughter of Capt. Skillman, all of Loudoun.

Vol. X, No. 4 – January 31, 1826

Married January 10th at Locust Hill, Leesburg, Professor Bonnycastle of the U. of
  Va. and Ann Mason, eldest daughter of Chas. Tutt, Esq.
Married in Fairfax on Tuesday the 17th of January by Rev. John Johnson, Mr.
  Edmund P. Richards and Miss Matilda Leigh, all of Fairfax.
Married on Tuesday, the 17th of January, by Rev. John Johnson, Mr. Edward
  Johnson and Miss Mary Leigh, all of Fairfax Co.
Married on Thursday, January 12 by Rev. John G. Watt, Mr. George Harmen and
  Miss Elizabeth Peake, all of Fairfax Co.
Married on January 12 by the Rev. Burch, Mr. Amos Janney of Loudoun and
  Miss Mary Ann Rowles, daughter of Maj. George Rowles of Bolivar near
  Harper's Ferry.
Married on Tuesday, January 24th by Rev. Thomas Birkby, Mr. Benjamin Dawes
  and Miss Margaret Dykes, both of this town.
Married on Tuesday, January 24th by Rev. Baker, Mr. Conrod R. Dowell and Miss
  Malinda, daughter of Morris Osburn, Esq., both of this county.
Married on Thursday, January 26th by Rev. Thos. Birkby, Mr. Richard Hill and
  Miss Delilah Jones, all of the county.
Married on Thursday, January 26th by Rev. Thos. Birkby, John Janney, Esq. of
  this town and Miss Alcinda S. Marmaduke of Hillsborough.

Vol. X, No. 5 – February 7, 1826

Died at St. Johns on Friday, 23rd of Dec, Mr. McNall of Fairfax. Choked, accidental
  death at Inn.

Vol. X, No. 7 – February 21, 1826

Married 16 June 1825 by Rev. Robert Burch, Mr. William Tucker and Miss Ellen
  Underwood.
Married 19 June 1825 by Rev. Robert Burch, Mr. Turner Dawson and Miss
  Lucinda Tole.
Married 26th July 1825 by Rev. Robert Burch, Mr. Alfred Poulton and Miss Lydia
  Lyder.
Married July 31st 1825 by Rev. Robert Burch, Mr. John Lewis and Miss Sarah
  Green.
Married August 4, 1825 by Rev. Robert Burch, Mr. Richard Peyton and Miss
  Verlinda I. Yeates.
Married November 1, 1825 by Rev. Robert Burch, Mr. Nelson Shepherd and
  Miss Caroline Glasscock.

Married November 1, 1825 by Rev. Robert Burch, Mr. Andrew Hesser and Miss Mary Bitzer.

Married December 1, 1825 by Rev. Robert Burch, Mr. George Hammontree and Miss Margaret Miller.

Married December 6, 1825 by Rev. Robert Burch, Mr. Amos Gulick and Miss Sarah M. Beale.

Married 10th January, 1826 by Rev. Robert Burch, Mr. Thomas Nichols and Miss Barbara Akers.

Married 9th February 1826 by Rev. Robert Burch, Mr. David Fulton and Miss Phebe Gibson, both of Loudoun.

Married 9th February 1826 by Rev. Robert Burch, Mr. Thomas Francis and Miss Helena Gulick, both of this county.

Married 9th February 1826 by Rev. Thomas Birkby, Mr. Amos Neptune and Miss Hetty Jeffries, both of Loudoun.

Married 16th February 1826 by Rev. Thomas Birkby, Mr. Giles Brown and Miss Harriot Briscoe, all of Loudoun.

Vol. X, No. 8 – February 28, 1826

Married February 14th by the Rev. Wm. Gilmore, Enoch Garrett and Miss Hannah Battson, both of this county.

Died at Waterford, February 16th James Moore, an old and respectable member of Society of Friends.

Vol. X, No. 10 – March 14, 1826

Married 20 January by Rev. James Reid, Mr. William Cayton and Miss A. Buckley, all of Fairfax Co.

Married 28 January by Rev. James Reid, Mr. James Buckley and Miss Julia Ann Gold, all of Fairfax Co.

Vol. X, No. 11 – March 21, 1826

Married Thursday, March 9th by Rev. William Gilmore, Mr. Amos Whitacre and Miss Nancy Tavener, all of this county.

Died at Snickersville on March 11th Mr. Robert Chew of Loudoun.

Vol. X, No. 12 – March 28, 1826

Married Thursday, 23 March, by Rev. William Gilmore, Mr. John Werts and Miss Mary Mock, all of this county.

Died March 14th Mrs. Isabella Eskridge, consort of Charles G. Eskridge, Esq. of this town and only daughter of John Kennedy, Esq. of Jefferson.

Vol. X, No. 13 – April 4, 1826

Married on Thursday, March 30th by Rev. Septimus Tuston, Mr. Jonathan McArtor and Miss Minerva Beans, all of the county.

Vol. X, No. 14 – April 11, 1826

Married on Tuesday, April 4, by Rev. Wm. Gilmore, Mr. Thomas Priest Jr. and Miss Phebe Ann Urton, both of Fauquier.

Vol. X, No. 15 0 April 18, 1826

Married on Thursday, April 13, by Rev. Tuston, Mr. Samuel Suffron and Miss Mary Ann Carr, daughter of Mr. Thomas Carr, all of this county.

Married on Thursday, April 13, by Rev. William Gilmore, Mr. Samuel Underwood of this county and Miss Jane Grigsby of Fauquier Co.

Vol. X, No. 16 – April 25, 1826

Married on the 19th March by Rev. Thomas Birkby, Mr. Joshua Reiley to Miss Nancy McDaniel, both of this town.

Married on April 2nd by Rev. Thomas Birkby, Mr. James McKim to Mrs. Margaret Campbell, both of this county.

Married on the 4th of April by Rev. Thomas Birkby, Captain John J. Mathias and Miss Caroline F. Osburn, daughter of Col. Nicholas Osburn, both of this town.

Married on Thursday, April 20, by Rev. William Gilmore, Mr. Enos Gore and Miss Sarah Davis, both of Loudoun.

Married on Tuesday, April 18, by Rev. William Gilmore, Mr. James Gilmore of this town and Miss Eleanor Steer of Loudoun.

Vol. X, No. 17 - May 2, 1826

Married in Baltimore on the 20th April by Rev. John Davis, Mr. William Hauk, late of Leesburg, and Miss Caroline M. Hattan of Baltimore.

Died on the 18th April in Georgetown, DC, Stacy Hanes, 61 years old, of Loudoun.

Vol. X, No. 18 – May 9, 1826

Married on Tuesday, May 2nd, by Rev. Septimus Tuston, Mr. John Shaw and Miss Cynthia Corwin, all of this town.

Died at Boydstown, Va. on April 17th Rev. Elam J. Morrison, age 25, graduate of N.C.U. in 1821, leaves widowed mother.

Died in this town on Wednesday, May 3, Mr. John Hilliard, age 82 years, a soldier of the revolution.

Died on Wednesday, May 3, Miss Mary Potter.

Vol. X, No. 21 – May 30, 1826

Died on Wednesday, May 24th Captain Martin Kitzmiller of this town.

Vol. X, No. 22 – June 6, 1826

Married on Saturday, 27th May, at Georgetown, DC, by Rev. Septimus Tuston, Major General Alexander Macomb of U. S. Army and Mrs. Harriet B. Wilson, daughter of Rev. Dr. Balch, Pastor of Presbyterian Church in that place.

Vol. X, No. 23 – June 13, 1826

Married June 8th by Rev. Burch, Frederick Morris, age 24, and Mrs. Susannah Pool, aged 45, all of Middleburg.

Vol. X, No. 25 – June 27, 1826

Married in Baltimore on Tuesday, June 20, by Rev. Henshaw, Mr. Hezekiah Niles, editor of *Niles Weekly Register*, and Miss Sally Ann, daughter of the late John Warner, Esq.

Vol. X, No. 31 – August 8, 1826

Died near Hillsborough on June 15th Archibald Morrison, 78 years old, of Loudoun.

Died July 18th at Red Sulphur Springs, Monroe Co., Va., Thomas R. Mott, Esq., cashier of the Leesburg Branch of the Valley Bank.

Died in this town Wednesday, August 2nd Charles William Chilton, aged 20.

Vol. X, No. 32 – August 15, 1826

Married on August 3 by Rev. William Gilmore, Mr. William M. Herrick and Miss Rowena Holmes, both of Mount Gilead, Loudoun Co.

Died in Fairfax Co., Monday, 7th August, at 62 years, Mr. George Sweeny, a native of Ireland.

Died in this town on Tuesday, August 8, Miss Ann C. Lee.

Died on Sunday, August 13, John, infant son of John H. Monroe of this town.

Vol. X, No. 33 – August 22, 1826

Married on Tuesday, August 15 by Rev. Thomas Birkby, Mr. George Marlow and Miss Mary W. Smith, all of this county.

Married Tuesday, August 15 by Rev. Thomas Birkby, Mrs. Jonas P. Schooley and Miss Sarah Ann Smith, all of the county.

Vol. X, No. 34 – August 29, 1826

Married on Thursday, August 24, by Rev. Tuston, Mr. Mahlon McCarty and Mrs. Eliza Thomas, all of this county.

Died Sunday, August 27, Mrs. Emily Lawrence, consort of Alexander Lawrence of Leesburg and daughter of John McCormick, Esq.

Vol. X, No. 35 – September 5, 1826

Married August 17th by Rev. William Gilmore, Mr. Richard Persons and Miss Maria Beard, all of this county.

Married August 24th by William Gilmore, Mr. John Webster and Miss Elizabeth T. Timms, both of this county.

Died on August 22nd at Salem, Fauquier Co., Dr. Samuel Summers.

Vol. X, No. 36 – September 12, 1826

Died on Sunday, September 3rd, Mrs. Catharine Lane, late consort of Col. Joseph Lane, at age 84 years.

Died on Sunday, September 3rd, Margaret, infant daughter of Edward Hammett.

Died on September 4th, Samuel Clapham, Esq. of Loudoun, of pulmonary complaint under which he had long laborered.

Died on Friday, September 8th in vicinity, Thomas Spiller, age 35 years.

Vol. X, No. 37 – September 19, 1826

Married at Centre Farm on September 7th by Rev. Robt. Burch, Mr. Cageby [sic] [Catesby] Jones and Miss Susan Nicewarner, both of Loudoun.

Died September 9th Mr. John L. Stovin, age 28 years.

Vol. X, No. 38 – September 26, 1826

Died in Leesburg, Monday, September 18, Mrs. Mary Monroe, 26 year old consort of Mr. John H. Monroe. [long obit]

Married on Thursday, September 21 by Rev. Joseph Baker, Mr. Robert Keyes of Jefferson and Miss Sarah Caroline Williams of Hillsborough, Loudoun Co.

Died vicinity of Leesburg on September 8th Capt. Josiah Moffett, age 89 years, a soldier of the revolution present at Yorktown surrender.

Died on Wednesday, September 20, Sarah, and her husband died on Thursday, September 21, Enoch Schooley, Quakers of Waterford.

Died at Winchester, on 13th ult., Thomas Marshall Esq. of that town.

Vol. X, No. 39 – October 3, 1826

Died in Winchester 13 September, Thomas Marshall.

Died September 22nd, Miss Elizabeth Given Hains, age 17 years, a cousin of
Elizabeth Mount, eldest daughter of Joseph Hains.
Died 29 September, James Allen Jr., age 18 years.

Vol. X, No. 40 – October 10, 1826
Died Monday, 2nd October, Mrs. Susan L. Williams, consort of Notly C. Williams,
Esq., age 45 years, after an illness of 6 days.
Died in Prince William Co. on September 14th Mrs. Alice Taylor, relict of William
R. Taylor deceased.
Died at Winchester Va. on September 22, Mrs. Powell, consort of Hon. Alfred H.
Powell, rep. to congress from Winchester.
Died in Leesburg on Friday, October 5, Samson Blincoe, Esq., attorney at law.

Vol. X, No. 41 – October 17, 1826
Died at Staunton, Va. on the 6th October, General John Brown.
Died on Wednesday in Leesburg, Mr. Henry S. Cooke.

Vol. X, No. 42 – October 24, 1826
Died at Aldie on Thursday, October 12th Mrs. Alice Jane Tyler, consort of
Edmund Tyler, Esq., age 29 years, married 18 months before death.

Vol. X, No. 43 – October 31, 1826
Died in Loudoun Co., October 12th Mrs. Mary Ritchie, age 89 years.
Died Sunday, 29th October, at his brother's residence, Mr. John Shepherd, printer
late of Winchester.

Vol. X, No. 44 – November 7, 1826
Died at Springfield, Loudoun Co., at the residence of Mr. John H. Halley, on
Tuesday, October 17th Thomas Jefferson Halley, merchant at Brentsville Va.,
age 24 years.
Died in Leesburg on Thursday, November 2nd Margaret Hough, age 13 years,
only daughter of Mr. John Hough.
Died at Belmont, home of Ludwell Lee, Esq., Richard Henry, only son of Richard
H. Lee.
Died Saturday, 28th October, at Caton, Mrs. Louisa E. F. Selden, age 21 years,
consort of Wilson C. Seldon of Loudoun.

Vol. X, No. 45 – November 14, 1826
Died 3 November, John Hutchison Sr. of Loudoun Co., age 71 years.
Married on Thursday, November 9, by Rev. William Gilmore, Mr. Benjamin
Hough and Miss Elizabeth Orrison, both of Loudoun.
Died at residence of John Bayly in the county on 31 October, Mrs. Mary Bayly,
relict of Pierce Bayly, age 74 years.

Vol. X, No. 47 – November 28, 1826
Married Thursday, November 23, by Rev. Thomas Birkby, Mr. David Shawen and
Miss Elizabeth Fox, both of this county.

Vol. X, No. 48 – December 5, 1826
Married lately by Rev. Thomas Birkby, Mr. Jonathan Potterfield and Miss
Deborah Thompson, both of this county.

Married on Tuesday, Nov. 28, at Fairfax Court House by Rev. Septimus Tuston, Mr. Thos. W. Coleman of Loudoun and Miss Ann M. Ratcliffe of the former place.

Vol. X, No. 50 – December 19, 1826
Died at Milton on 2nd inst., Andrew Monroe, last surviving brother of the late Presdietn fo U. S. The deceased was a soldier in the Revolutionary War.

Vol. X, No. 51 – December 26, 1826
Died in Baltimore on Friday, December 8th Emily Ann, only daughter of William Wooddy, age 3 years. (Communicated)

Vol. X, No. 52 – January 2, 1827
Died in Baltimore on Sunday, December 24th second son of Wm. Wooddy, William Wallace A. Wooddy, age 6 years.

Vol. XI, No. 1 – January 9, 1827
Married 27 Dec by Rev. Septimus Tuston, Mr. James Lawder and Miss Mary Gibbons, all of this county.
Married by Rev. Septimus Tuston on January 4th Mr. Henry German and Miss Ruth Vanskiver, all of this county.
Died on Thursday, January 4th, Sarah Frances Vandeventer, age 3 years, daughter of Capt. Isaac Vandeventer.

Vol. XI, No. 2 – January 16, 1827
Married recently by Rev. Septimus Tuston, Mr. Joseph Lacock and Miss Emily White, all of this county.
Married Thursday, January 11th by Rev. Septimus Tuston, Mr. John B. Patterson, printer of Winchester, recently of this town, and Miss Mahala S. Norton of this county.

Vol. XI, No. 3 – January 23, 1827
Died on Thursday night of a paralytic stroke experienced two days previous, Mrs. Mary Boss, age 72 years. The deceased had been a respectable resident of this town for many years and member of Methodist Episcopal Church for half a century.
Died lately in Exeter, New Hampshire, Miss Anna Rogers, aged 78, a descendant of the Rev. John Rogers, of London, who was burnt at Smithfield in 1555.

Vol. XI, No. 6 – February 13, 1827
Married on Thursday, February 8th by Rev. Thomas Birkby, Mr. Giles Tillett and Miss Reubanion Skeckels, both of this county.

Vol. XI, No. 7 – February 20, 1827
Married in Dover, Loudoun Co., on 6 February, by Rev. Johnson of Fairfax, Mr. Hamilton Rogers and Miss Ann, daughter of James Hixon, all of this county.
Married on Thursday, February 8, by Rev. William Gilmore, Mr. William Ewers and Miss Ruth White, both of this county.
Married on Thursday, February 15th by Rev. Thomas Birkby, Mr. Elijah Paxson and Miss Elizabeth Norwood, both of this county.
Married on Thursday, February 15th by Rev. Thomas Birkby, Mr. James Tillett and Miss Uree Humphrey, all of this county.

Vol. XI, No. 8 – February 27, 1827

Married on December 28, Mr. John P. Gilbert, formerly of Leesburg, and Miss Sarah L., eldest daughter of the late Judge Dawson near Pinckneyville, Mississippi.

Vol. XI, No. 10 – March 13, 1827

Married on Tuesday, March 6 by Rev. William Gilmore, Mr. John R. Morgan of Fauquier and Miss Lucidney Debell of Frederick Co.

Vol. XI, No. 11 – March 20, 1827

Married on February 22 by Rev. Septimus Tuston, Mr. Henry Powers and Miss Mary Quaile, both of Georgetown, DC.

Married on Thursday, March 13 by Rev. Septimus Tuston, Mr. John Fulton and Miss Jane E. Taylor, both of this county.

Vol. XI, No. 13 – April 3, 1827

Married on March 21 by Rev. L. Fullerton, Mr. Humphrey Fullerton of Franklin Co. Pa. and Miss Eleanor Davidson of Washington Co., Md.

Vol. XI, No. 17 – May 1, 1827

Married lately by Rev. Francis Moore, Mr. John McKenney and Mrs. Mary Jackson, both of Harper's Ferry, her 5th marriage (now but 28), 3rd by Moore.

Died Saturday, April 14th, Rev. John Dunn, Pastor of the Episcopal Church, age 58 years.

Vol. XI, No. 18 – May 8, 1827

Married April 31st by Rev. Septimus Tuston, Capt. George W. Henry and Miss Duanna Hamilton, all of this county.

Vol. XI, No. 19 – May 15, 1827

Died April 28 at his residence near Waterford, Mr. John Bowman, age 50 years.

Vol. XI, No. 20 – May 22, 1827

Died at Martinsburg, Sunday, May 6th Mr. John Alburtis, age 49 years, late editor of the *Shepherdstown Journal*, formerly editor of *Martinsburg Gazette*.

Vol. XI, No. 21 – May 29, 1827

Married May 8th by Rev. Martin, Mr. Daniel G. Smith of this town and Miss Eleanor Buckey of Frederick Co., Md.

Married May 17th by Rev. Septimus Tuston, Doctor Wilson D. Drish and Miss Martha Adams, all of this county.

Died a few days ago at his residence in Middletown valley, Md., Mr. Adam Routzong, long a respectable inhabitant of this county, age 91 years, and had lived with his wife Catharine 65 years. She survives him and is now in the 93rd year of her age. Their offspring was 130 in number, viz 12 children (of whom 8 are still living), 63 grandchildren, and 55 great grandchildren.

Died on the 4th inst. in Fredericktown, Md. at the advanced age of 96 years, Mr. Michael McCann, a Revolutionary pensioner, who, after living comfortably had saved upwards of $100, which he has bequeathed to an old friend.

Vol. XI, No. 22 – June 5, 1827

Married May 27th by Rev. William Gilmore, Mr. George Cridler of Md. and Miss Margaret Monroe of this town.

Married May 29th by Rev. William Gilmore, Mr. Eli McVeigh of Loudoun and Miss Jane Hutchinson of Fairfax.

Vol. XI, No. 23 – June 12, 1827

Married at Waterford in a meeting of the Society of Friends on May 30, Henry S. Taylor and Hannah J. Brown, daughter of William Brown, all of this county.

Married on Thursday, June 7th by Rev. Septimus Tuston, Mr. James P. Lovett and Miss Lucinda Doudel, all of this county.

Vol. XI, No. 25 – June 26, 1827

Married Thursday, June 21 by Rev. Septimus Tuston, Mr. James Sinclair and Miss Leonah Vandeventer, all of this county.

Married Thursday, June 21 by Rev. Septimus Tuston, Mr. Jesse Hatch and Miss Jane Hawling, all of this county.

Vol. XI, No. 26 – July 3, 1827

Married on Tuesday, June 26 by Rev. Septimus Tuston, Mr. Elias Pool and Miss Margaret Tillett, both of this county.

Died in Georgetown, DC. on June 27th Mrs. Elizabeth Balch, consort of Rev. Dr. Balch, mother of Mrs. Tuston of this place. Mrs. Balch was the eldest daughter of late Col. George Beale of Georgetown, and had been united to her venerable partner more than half a century. Member of Presbyterian Church.

Vol. XI, No. 27 – July 10, 1827

Died in Georgetown, in the 62nd year of her age, on the 27th June, Mrs. Eliza Balch, consort of Rev. Stephen B. Balch, D.D., pastor of the Presbyterian church in that place.

Vol. XI, No. 28 – July 21, 1827

Married Thursday, July 12, Rev. William Gilmore, Mr. Nathaniel Allison and Miss Catharine Cordell, all of this town.

Died Sunday, July 8th at the seat of Col. Wm. D. Merrick, Elizabeth Ann, age 16 months, daughter of Thomson Mason of Loudoun Co.

Vol. XI, No. 29 – July 28, 1827

Married on Tuesday, July 17th by Rev. Dr. McCan, P. C. MacCabe, Esq. of Jefferson and Miss Maria C. Lee, only daughter of the late George Lee, Esq. of Farmwell, Loudoun Co.

Married on Thursday, July 19th by Rev. Dr. McCan, Dr. George Lee and Miss Sarah M. Henderson, daughter of Richard H. Henderson Esqr., all of this town.

Vol. XI, No. 31 – August 11, 1827

On Tuesday evening last, Stephen B. Balch, aged four years, son of James C. Wilson of Georgetown, fell from the piazza of his grandfather, the Rev. Dr. Balch, and fractured his head in such a manner as to cause his death in six hours.

Died at New York, on the 22nd ult. after a short and painful illness, William Chambers, M.D., so celebrated for his cure of intemperance.

Vol. XI, No. 33 – August 25, 1827

Married Tuesday, 21 August, by Rev. William Gilmore, Dr. Erasmus G. Tillett and Miss Emily Furguson, both of this county.

Died, at P. Hurt's Tavern, eight miles north of Nashville, Major Robert Bailey, of Bucksville, Kentucky, formerly a resident of this city, and well known in this district and in Virginia.

Vol. XI, No. 38 – September 29, 1827

Married on Thursday, September 20th by Rev. Jackson, Richard Henry Lee and Miss Anna Eden Jordan, both of Leesburg.

Vol. XI, No. 41 – October 20, 1827

At his residence in Baltimore on Friday of last week, the venerable Col. John Eager Howard, a distinguished soldier of the Revolution.

Vol. XI, No. 42 – October 27, 1827

Married on Thursday, October 18th by Rev. Thomas Birkby, Mr. Elijah Hatcher and Miss Jane Craig, both of this county.

Married on Thursday, October 25th by Rev. Thomas Birkby, Mr. Curtis Grubb and Miss Harriett Hough, both of this county.

Vol. XI, No. 43 – November 3, 1827

Married Tuesday, October 31 by Rev. Thomas Birkby, Capt. John More of Florida (late of this town) and Miss Matilda L. Beard, of this county.

Married Thursday, November 1st by Rev. Thomas Birkby, Mr. Lawson Herell and Miss Nancy Moreland, both of this county.

Vol. XI, No. 45 – November 17, 1827

Married Thursday, November 8th by Rev. William Gilmore, Mr. Lewis Francis and Miss Alvira Amanda Norton, both of Loudoun.

Vol. XI, No. 46 – November 24, 1827

Married Tuesday, 20 November by Rev. Joseph Baker, Mr. Taliaferro M. M'Ilhany and Miss Ann, daughter of Hugh Rogers, all of this county.

Died Thursday, November 15th, Capt. Benjamin Hagerman, on road near Aldie. On Saturday, the brethren from Union and Middleburg Lodges, joined by the transient brethren of Aldie, paid the last tribute of respect to his memory.

Died November 14th at his residence, Major Robert Braden, age 63 years, of Waterford.

Died November 15th at residence in vicinity of this town, Mr. Aaron Daily, for many years a resident of Loudoun.

Vol. XI, No. 48 – December 8, 1827

Died in Leesburg, Friday, November 30, John Drish, age 74 years.

Died Tuesday, December 3, James McNellege, age 71 years.

Died Wednesday, December 4, Mrs. Ann Dykes.

Vol. XI, No. 49 – December 15, 1827

On the receipt in Leesburg of the melancholy intelligence of the death of Mr. Julius Hamilton, of this county, who died in Baltimore, where he had gone for the purpose of completing his medical education, the company of "Leesburg Independent Blues" assembled at the Eagle Tavern.

Vol. XI, No. 50 – December 22, 1827

Died at Harper's Ferry, November 29, John McKenney, age 26 years, married just 8 months. He was 5th husband of Mrs. Mary Jackson, who is yet under the age of 29 years.

Died in Baltimore, Sunday, December 2nd, Rev. Dr. George Roberts, of the Methodist Church.

Vol. XII, No. 1 – January 12, 1828

Married January 3 by Rev. William Gilmore, Mr. John Swann and Miss Elizabeth Timms, both of this county.

Vol. XII, No. 3 – January 26, 1828

Married at Washington City, January 3 by Rev. R. Post, Mr. Roberdeau Annin and Miss Helen C. M'Cormick, both recently of this town.

Died in Washington DC., January 11, Mr. William W. Lawrence, formerly of Leesburg, aged 24 years.

Vol. XII, No. 4 – February 2, 1828

On Wednesday last, in the vicinity of this town, Nelly Cross, a coloured woman, in the 114th year of her age. She had descendants of the 5th generation.

Vol. XII, No. 5 – February 9, 1828

Died in city of Baltimore, January 29, Rev. Ambrose Marechal, Catholic Archbishop of Baltimore.

Vol. XII, No. 6 – February 16, 1828

Married January 29 by Rev. Thomas Birkby, Major Frederick Carper of Fairfax and Miss Martha Mead of this county.

Married January 31 by Rev. William Gilmore, Mr. Joshua Nichols and Miss Naomi White, both of Loudoun.

Married on February 7th by Rev. Thomas Birkby, Mr. Thomas Roberts and Miss Alice Mock, both of this county.

Married on February 7th by Rev. Thomas Birkby, Mr. Jesse Tribby and Miss Elizabeth Virts, both of this county.

Married Thursday, January 31 by Rev. Thomas Birkby, Mr. Jesse S. Wilson and Miss Elizabeth F. Richards, both of this town.

Married Thursday, January 31 by Thomas Birkby, Mr. Charles Lewis Garner and Miss Elizabeth Moffett, both of this county.

Vol. XII, No. 7 – February 23, 1828

Married Tuesday, February 19th, Mr. John F. Barrett of Maryland and Miss Caroline M. E. Wade, daughter of John Wade of this county.

Died at Russellville, Ky, on March 16th at 71 years of age, Mrs. Monica Littlejohn, consort of Rev. John Littlejohn (M. E.) both formerly of Leesburg. The deceased was formerly a resident of Leesburg; and had been, at the time of her death, fifty-three years a member of the Methodist Episcopal church.

Vol. XII, No. 8 – March 1, 1828

Married Tuesday, February 25 by Rev. Thomas Birkby, Mr. Thomas Moss and Miss Sarah A. Binns, daughter of Simon A. Binns, both of this county.

Married Thursday, February 28 by Rev. Thomas Birkby, Mr. Thomas Moffitt and Miss Eliza Landis, both of this county.

Vol. XII, No. 10 – March 15, 1828

Died at Ellicott's Mills, Md., on February 24, a Quaker formerly of Bristol, Pa, Joseph Atkinson, age 65 years. Member of Society of Friends, a native of Bristol, Pa., and for last 36 years resident in Ellicott's Mills, Md.

Died at Leesburg Friday last week, Mr. Robert H. Mathias, age 29 years, member of Leesburg Independent Blues.

Vol. XII, No. 11 – March 22, 1828

Married March 19th by Rev. Thomas Birkby, Mr. Lewis Sullivan and Miss Lydia A. Janney, both of this county.

Vol. XII, No. 12 – March 29, 1828

Married Thursday, March 20, by Rev. William Gilmore, Mr. James McClain of Loudoun and Miss Honoria Ann Barry of Alexandria.

Vol. XII, No. 13 – April 5, 1828

Died in Leesburg, April 1st at residence of Chas. Binns, Dr. Thomas F. Tebbs, age 34 years, had recently moved to Washington City.

Vol. XII, No. 14 – April 12, 1828

Died at his residence in Washington City on March 28, Dr. William Thornton, many years superintendent of the patent office in the Department of State.

Died at Leesburg on Thursday, April 10, Mr. Alexander Couper, age 80 years.

Vol. XII, No. 15 – April 19, 1828

Married on Tuesday, April 8, by Rev. William Gilmore, Mr. Sydnor Williams and Miss Mary S. Brown, both of this county.

Vol. XII, No. 16 – April 26, 1828

Married on Thursday, April 17th by Rev. Joseph Baker, Mr. Bushrod Anderson and Miss Ann, daughter of James Wornal, both of this county.

Vol. XII, No. 17 – May 3, 1828

Married on 24 April, Mr. John W. Wood and Miss Ann Edwards, both of this town.

Vol. XII, No. 20 – May 24, 1828

Died May 13, Mrs. Eve Handey, age 55 years, consort of William H. Handey of Fauquier Co. Va., at Mellona, her late residence.

Died on Wednesday, May 21st, in this vicinity, Mr. Charles Thornton, age 40 years.

In Norristown, Pa. on the 7th inst., Mrs. Catharine Sower, consort of David Sower, Sr., in the 66th year of her age.

Vol. XII, No. 21 – May 31, 1828

Married on Sunday, 25th May, by Rev. William Gilmore, Mr. William Wright and Miss Parmelia [*sic*] Brown, all of this county.

Married Wednesday, May 28th by Rev. Septimus Tuston, Mr. Noble S. Braden and Miss Elizabeth Williams, both of Waterford.

Vol. XII, No. 22 – June 7, 1828

Married on Tuesday, May 13 at Emmitsburg by the Rev. David Bossler, Mr. Daniel Potterfield of Loudoun and Miss Mary Danner of Emmitsburg.

Married Sunday, May 25, by Elder James Reid, Mr. John Cook and Miss Matilda Harrison, both of Fairfax Co.

Married Sunday, May 25, by Elder James Reid, Mr. Jeremiah Cockrill and Miss Winny Tillett, both of Fairfax.

Married Thursday, May 27, by Rev. Charles B. Tippett, Mr. Stacy Taylor and Miss Mary Hollingsworth, all of Loudoun.

Vol. XII, No. 23 – June 14, 1828

Married in this town on Tuesday, June 10 by Rev. Thomas Birkby, Mr. John Robbin of Maryland, age 73 years, and Miss Nancy Bell of Loudoun, age 26 years.

Vol. XII, No. 26 – July 5, 1828

In City of Washington, on 25th ult., Richard W. Meade, Esq., long a respectible merchant of Cadiz.

Vol. XII, No. 30 – August 2, 1828

Married July 17 by Rev. Charles B. Tippett, Mr. John Flowers and Mrs. Catharine Monroe, both of this town.

Married Monday, July 29th by Rev. Charles B. Tippett, Mr. Amor Hunt and Miss Ellen Willson.

Died on Sunday, July 27, Thomas Fouch, age 73 years, of vicinity.

Vol. XII, No. 32 – August 16, 1828

Married on Tuesday, August 12, by Rev. Chas. B. Tippett, Mr. Patrick McGee to Miss Margaret Dailey.

Vol. XII, No. 33 – August 23, 1828

Died August 1st, Mrs. Pleasant Osburn, consort of Mr. Richard Osburn of this county.

Vol. XII, No. 35 – September 6, 1828

Married on Thursday, August 28, by Rev. Charles B. Tippett, Mr. James Moreland and Miss Nancy Jones, both of Loudoun.

Married on Thursday, August 28 by Rev. Charles B. Tippett, Mr. David Boren and Miss Caroline McCarter, both of Loudoun.

Married on Thursday, August 28 by Rev. Charles B. Tippett, Mr. Archibald M. Lyles of Maryland and Miss Harriet T. Fitcher of this town.

Died in Leesburg on Saturday, August 30th, Mr. Benjamin Dawes, innkeeper age 41 years.

Vol. XII, No. 37 – September 20, 1828

Married at N.Y. on September 3rd, Capt. Henry Saunders, late of this town, and Miss __ North, daughter of Gen. North of the city of New York.

Married on Thursday, September 11 by Rev. William Gilmore, Mr. William M. Harle and Miss Eliza Veale, both of this county.

Married on Thursday, September 11 by Rev. William Gilmore, Mr. James Hill and Miss Elizabeth Woodford, both of Loudoun.

Vol. XII, No. 38 – September 27, 1828

Married on Thursday, September 18 by Rev. William Gilmore, Mr. Edward D. Potts and Miss Eliza Ann Thompson, all of this county.

Died Saturday, September 20th at his residence, Jesse Hoge, age 44 years, of this county.

Vol. XII, No. 39 – October 4, 1828
Died at Benedict, Maryland, September 2nd Mr. John Bogue, age 30 years, formerly of Leesburg.

Vol. XII, No. 42 – October 25, 1828
Died on 4th inst., at Camp No. 10, at the head of the Rapids of the Maumee River, Ohio, after an illness of ten days, Asa Moore, Esq., late U.S. Ass't civil engineer, in 31st year of his age, a man of sicence and the son of an eminent engineer of Virginia [*National Intelligencer*]

Vol. XII, No. 46 – November 22, 1828
Married Thursday, November 20th by Rev. Jackson, Mr. John B. Ball and Miss Sarah Ann Fouch, all of Loudoun.
Died in Washington City on November 12, Mr. Alexander Henderson, age 21 years, at home of kinsman, Dr. Henderson.

Vol. XII, No. 48 – December 6, 1828
Married on November 27 by Rev. Charles B. Tippett, Mr. Edward Francis and Miss Ann E. B. Hamilton, all of Leesburg.
Died in Georgetown, DC., November 24th 3 weeks after her marriage to Rev. Dr. Stephen B. Balch, Mrs. Elizabeth Balch.

Vol. XII, No. 49 – December 13, 1828
Married at Belle Field by Rev. William Williamson on Thursday, November 27, Abner Gibson, Esq. and Mrs. S. E. Powell, both of Middleburg.
Died Friday, November 28th in Leesburg, Mary A. Orr, eldest daughter of the late Dr. John D. Orr.

Vol. XII, No. 51 – December 27, 1828
Married Tuesday, December 2nd by Rev. William Armstrong, Capt. Benjamin Shreve of Loudoun county and Miss Mary Elizabeth, daughter of Mr. Daniel Trundle of Montgomery Co., Maryland.
Married on December 18th by Rev. William Gilmore, Mr. Poynts O. Galleher and Miss Mary F. Baldwin, both of Loudoun.
Married Tuesday, December 23 by Rev. William Gilmore, Mr. Jonah W. Orrison and Miss Nancy Neile, all of this county.

Vol. XII, No. 52 – January 3, 1829
Married Tuesday, December 23 by Rev. Dr. Green, Mr. Alexander Turner of Loudoun to Miss Jane Parker of Fauquier Co.
Married Tuesday, December 23 by Rev. Chas. B. Tippett, Mr. William Torryson and Miss Mary W. Birkby, all of Leesburg.
Died Sunday, December 28 at his residence in the vicinity of this town, Capt. Aaron Saunders, age 72 years.

Vol. XIII, No. 2 – January 17, 1829
Died December 15th 1828, Margaret Weadon, wife of John Weadon of Union, aged 35 years.
Died Sunday, January 11, Mrs. Margaret Sinclair, relict of the late George Sinclair of this county, age 58 years.

Vol. XIII, No. 3 – January 24, 1829

Married December 25th by Rev. Thos. Birkby, Mr. Alfred Shields and Miss
Catharine Mathias, both of Loudoun
Married December 30 by Rev. Thomas Buck Jr., Mr. Isaac R. Cloud and Miss
Amelia Ann, daughter of Samuel Buck, all of Shenandoah
Married on January 1st by Rev. Thomas Birkby, Mr. Robert S. Reed of Fairfax
and Miss Catharine Cockrell of this county.
Married on January 8th by Rev. Thomas Birkby, Mr. Samuel Thompson and Miss
Sarah Tribby, both of Loudoun.
Married on January 8th by Rev. Thomas Birkby, Mr. John D. Wilson and Miss
Mary Wells, both of Montgomery Co., Maryland.
Married on January 8th by Elder Jas. Reid, Mr. Foley Thompson and Miss Mary
Davis, both of Fairfax Co.
Married on January 8th by Elder Jas. Reid, Mr. Presley W. Sears and Miss Harriet
A. Caton, both of Fairfax.
Married on January 13 by Rev. Mr. Brown, Caldwell Carr, Esq. of Upperville,
Fauquier Co., and Miss Cornelia, 2nd daughter of Enoch Reynolds, Esq. of
Washington.
Married January 13 by Rev. Thos. Birkby, Mr. Edward Thompson and Miss
Rebecca Sullivan, both of Loudoun.
Married January 15 by Rev. Thos. Birkby, Mr. John A. McCormick and Miss Ann
E. Fadely, both of this town.
Married January 20 by Rev. Thos. Birkby, Mr. William W. Hammontree and Miss
Dorcas Manly, both of this town.
Died on the 15th of January at his residence in Georgetown in the 66th year of his
age, Lt. Col. Isaac Roberdeau, of the Topographical Bureau in the
department of war, over which he has presided from its creation, with zeal
and fidelity.

Vol. XIII, No. 4 – January 31, 1829

Married Thursday, January 22nd, by Rev. Wm. Williamson, Capt. Lloyd Noland of
Fauquier and Miss Elizabeth Smith of Middleburg.

Vol. XIII, No. 5 – February 7, 1829

Married January 22 at Valley View, Fauquier Co by Rev. George Lemmon, Judge
R. H. Field of Culpeper Co. and Miss Alice Logan Gibson, daughter of Wm.
Gibson of Fauquier.

Vol. XIII, No. 6 – February 14, 1829

Married on Thursday, February 5 by Rev. Thomas Birkby, Mr. John Myers and
Miss Mary Perry, both of this county.
Married on Tuesday, February 10 by Rev. Chas. B. Tippett, Mr. Josias Adams
and Miss Mary Hill, both of Leesburg.
Married on Thursday, February 12 by Rev. Thomas Birkby, Mr. Martin Kyser and
Miss Barbara Razor, both of Loudoun.

Vol. XIII, No. 7 – February 21, 1829

Married Thursday, February 12 by Rev. Chas. B. Tippett, Mr. James Humphreys
of Lower Marlboro, Calvert Co. Maryland, and Miss Rebecca McClosky of this
town.
Married on Monday, February 16th by Rev. Thos. Birkby, Mr. Benjamin F. Taylor
and Miss Nancy Taylor, both of this county.

Married on Tuesday, February 17th by Rev. Thos. Birkby, Mr. Thomas Hatcher
and Miss Nancy L. Gregg, both of Loudoun.

Married on Tuesday, February 17th by Rev. Thos. Birkby, Henley H. Gregg and
Miss Amey Hogue, all of Loudoun.

Died in Leesburg on February 20th Mrs. Elizabeth Wooddy, 55 year old relict of
late William Wooddy, for many years postmaster of this town.

Vol. XIII, No. 8 – February 28, 1829

Died on Tuesday, February 24, at his residence in Leesburg, Robert R. Hough,
age 42 years.

Vol. XIII, No. 9 – March 7, 1829

Married Thursday, February 26th by Rev. Thomas Birkby, Mr. Samuel Jenkins
and Miss Louisa Hough, both of Loudoun.

Married Tuesday, March 3rd, by Rev. Thomas Birkby, Charles B. Hamilton and
Miss Sarah C. Luckett, both of Loudoun.

Vol. XIII, No. 10 – March 14, 1829

Married Thursday, March 5th by Rev. Wm. Gilmore, Mr. Patrick McGarvack and
Mrs. Sarah Garner, both of Loudoun.

Died at her residence on March 6th Mrs. Mary Rhodes, age 54 years.

Vol. XIII, No. 11 – March 21, 1829

Married on March 12th by Rev. Thomas Birkby, Mr. Elmond Hogue and Miss
Sarah Orrison, both of Loudoun.

Married on March 12th by Rev. Thomas Birkby, Mr. Isaiah B. Beans and Miss
Elizabeth Moss, both of Loudoun.

Married on Tuesday, March 17th by Rev. Thomas Birkby, Rev. Thomas Green of
Frederick Co. Md. and Miss Jane Shelton of Montgomery Co.

Married on Thursday, March 19th by Rev. Thomas Birkby, Mr. Landon C. Carter
and Miss Mahala Batson, both of Loudoun.

Died in Leesburg, Sarah Ann Annin, infant daughter of the late Robert R. Hough,
in her 3rd year.

Vol. XIII, No. 12 – March 28, 1829

Married on March 12th by Rev. Wm. Gilmore, Mr. Joshua T. Hope and Miss
Massa Gore, both of Loudoun.

Married on Thursday, March 26th by Rev. Thos. Birkby, Mr. John W. Littleton and
Miss Elizabeth A. Tavenner, both of Loudoun.

Died on Saturday, March 21 at his residence in Fairfax, Mr. Cyrus Saunders, age
36 years.

Died in Leesburg, Wednesday, March 25th, Mr. John Drean, age 72 years,
member of Methodist Episcopal Church.

Vol. XIII, No. 14 – April 11, 1829

Married on Sunday, March 8th by Rev. James Reed, Mr. George Sheid of
Loudoun and Miss Serena G. Dulin of Fairfax.

Married on Tuesday, March 10th by Rev. James Reed, Mr. James Rouse of
Loudoun and Miss Sarah E. Sheid of Fairfax.

Died in Leesburg on Monday, April 6th, Mr. Andrew Monroe, a 64 year old
auctioneer.

Vol. XIII, No. 15 – April 18, 1829
Married on Thursday, April 2nd by Rev. O. R. Brown, Mr. William Slater of
Loudoun Co. and Miss Margaret Cooper, daughter of Mr. J. Cooper of
Washington City.
Married on Tuesday, April 14 by Rev. Dr. Green, Mr. Edward Washington of
Kentucky and Miss Ann Elizabeth Ellzey of Loudoun.

Vol. XIII, No. 16 – April 25, 1829
Married at New Lisbon, Ohio on March 12th by Rev. A. G. Richardson, Mr. James
Harvey Shields, formerly of Leesburg, and Miss Sarah Arter of New Lisbon,
Ohio.
Married on Thursday, April 16th by Rev. Wm. Gilmore, Mr. Carter Moss and Miss
Susan Beveridge, all of this county.

Vol. XIII, No. 18 – May 9, 1829
Married in Leesburg on Tuesday, May 5th by Rev. Thos. Jackson, Col. Asa
Rogers of Loudoun and Miss Ellen L. Orr, daughter of the late Dr. John D. Orr
of Frederick Co., Va.
Married in Leesburg on Tuesday, May 5th by Rev. Thos. Birkby, Mr. John
Connard and Miss Elenor Gregg, both of Loudoun.
Died in Leesburg on Tuesday, Mary 5th Miss Ann M. Drean.

Vol. XIII, No. 20 – May 23, 1829
Married on Thursday, May 14th by Rev. Thomas Birkby, Mr. Lewis Steele and
Miss Matilda Workman, both of Loudoun.
Married on Thursday, May 21st by Rev. Thomas Birkby, Mr. Nathan Gregg and
Miss Susan R. Gregg, all of this county.
Married on Thursday, May 21st by Rev. Thomas Birkby, Mr. Thomas E. Hatcher
and Miss Elizabeth P. Gregg, all of Loudoun.

Vol. XIII, No. 21 – May 30, 1829
Married April 29th at Brandon in Prince George Co., Va. by Right Rev. Bishop
Moore, Alfred H. Powell of Winchester, Va. and Miss Elizabeth Harrison.
Died in Leesburg May 18th, Mrs. Elizabeth Towner, age 81 years, a member of
Methodist Episcopal Church.
Died on May 23rd, John Wilson Reiley, son of Joshua Reiley of this town, in the
12th year of his age.

Vol. XIII, No. 22 – June 6, 1829
Married on Tuesday, June 2 by Rev. Chas. B. Tippett, Mr. Aaron Russell and
Miss Tamsen Underwood, all of Loudoun.
Died in Waterford on April 16th, Mrs. Mary E. Dulaney, consort of Capt. Zachariah
Dulaney.

Vol. XIII, No. 24 – June 20, 1829
Married Thursday, June 11th by Rev. William Gilmore, Mr. Maaziah Thomas and
Miss Elizabeth Furr, all of Loudoun.

Vol. XIII, No. 25 – June 27, 1829
Died Saturday, June 20th, Lewis M. Smith, Postmaster at Aldie.
Died Sunday, June 21st, Capt. Thos. Moralle, 53 years old, of Leesburg.

Vol. XIII, No. 27 – July 11, 1829

Married on Thursday, July 9th by Rev. Thomas Birkby, Mr. William Hammatt of Parkersburg, formerly of Leesburg, and Miss Sophia Watters of Leesburg.

Married at St. Louis, Mo., on 2nd ult., Dr. S. W. Roszel, son of Dr. George Roszel, sometime since presiding elder of this district, to Miss Sophronia, eldest daughter of the late Daniel Bosley, dec'd, formerly of Baltimore.

Vol. XIII, No. 30 – August 1, 1829

Married at Washington City on July 23rd by Rev. Wm. Ryland, the Rev. French S. Evans and Miss Georgiann Clinton, 3rd daughter of Major William O'Neale of that city.

Vol. XIII, No. 31 – August 8, 1829

Married on Thursday, July 30, by Rev. William Gilmore, Mr. Adam Barr and Miss Mary Beatty, all of this county.

Died in Leesburg on July 30, Mrs. Mary Hanna, age 86 years, member of Presbyterian church.

Vol. XIII, No. 32 – August 15, 1829

Died on August 7th in vicinity of Leesburg, Malcolm V. Downs, age 19 years, and Hamilton M. Downs, age 18 years, sons of James Downs.

Vol. XIII, No. 34 – August 29, 1829

Married at Martinsburg, Va. on August 13 by Rev. Medtar, Mr. Archibald Fadely, printer, formerly of Leesburg, and Miss Rosanna Young, daughter of Adam Young, all of Martinsburg.

Died on August 7th in Clarksburg where he lived for 2 years, Hamilton Bennett, age 20 years, native of Loudoun.

Died August 19th at Morven his residence near Leesburg, John Swann, age 28 years, eldest son of Thomas Swann of Washington.

Died at his residence in vicinity of Leesburg, Sunday, August 23, Mr. David Martin.

Vol. XIII, No. 36 – September 12, 1829

Died at his residence at Ellicott's Two Mills, Maryland, Edward Stabler Hough, age 44 years, brother of the late Robert R. Hough of this town.

Vol. XIII, No. 37 – September 19, 1829

Married in Leesburg on Tuesday, September 15, Mr. __ Mathias and Miss Martha Oswald, all of Leesburg.

Vol. XIII, No. 39 – October 3, 1829

Died in Leesburg on Sunday, September 27, Mrs. Darcus Brady, age 65 years.

Died of Leesburg on Tuesday, September 29, Mrs. Martha Oswald, age 58 years, resident of this town.

Vol. XIII, No. 44 – November 7, 1829

Married on Tuesday, November 3rd by Rev. Chas. B. Tippett, Mr. George Rhodes and Miss Catharine Dyer, all of this county.

Vol. XIII, No. 45 – November 14, 1829

Married at Glebeland on the 6th of October by Rev. W. Thornton, Dr. Alpheus W. Gibson of Culpeper and Miss Harriet A., 2nd daughter of John Aldridge of Loudoun.

Died at residence of his father, Stephen Wilson, in this county, on Friday, November 6th, Dr. Isaac Wilson, age 32 years.

Vol. XIII, No. 46 – November 21, 1829

Died on Monday, November 16, Ellen, age 6 years, youngest daughter of George K. and Jane Fox of Leesburg.

Died on Thursday, November 19, Mr. David Wooddy of Leesburg, age 37 years.

Vol. XIII, No. 48 – December 5, 1829

Married on November 26th, Mr. John P. Smart of this vicinity and Miss Emily Hilliard of this town.

Died in this town on November 27th, Mr. Robert W. Dykes, age 28 years.

Vol. XIII, No. 50 – December 19, 1829

Married on Thursday, December 17 by Rev. William Gilmore, Mr. William Jackson and Miss Margaret Stoneburner, both of Loudoun.

Died on the 6th of December at his residence near Centreville, Fairfax Co., Coleman Brown, age 85 years, a Baptist.

Vol. XIII, No. 51 – December 26, 1829

Married on Thursday, December 17th by Rev. Job Guest, John P. H. Short and Miss Elizabeth J., only daughter of the late Thomas Atwell.

Married on Tuesday, December 22 by Rev. Chas. B. Tippett, Mr. Richard Howser and Miss Mary Ann Hague, all of this county.

Vol. XIII, No. 52 – January 2, 1830

Married Thursday, December 10th by Rev. Dr. Williamson, Robert Y. Conrod of Winchester Va. and Miss Elizabeth W., daughter of Burr Powell, Esq. of Middleburg.

Vol. XIV, No. 1 – January 9, 1830

Married at Mount Gilead, Loudoun Co., on Sunday, January 3 by Rev. William Gilmore, Mr. James R. Chenoweth of Harper's Ferry and Miss Eliza Davis of Pennsylvania.

Vol. XIV, No. 2 – January 16, 1830

Married September 3rd by John Davis, Mr. Bartlett Clements and Mrs. Belinda Jane Pendleton.

Married September 3rd by John Davis, Mr. John W. Allen and Miss Mary Clements, daughter of Bartlett Clements.

Married December 10, 1829 by Rev. William Duncan, Mr. David Allen and Joyce T. Clements, 2nd daughter of Bartlett Clements.

Married December 31, 1829 by Rev. William Duncan, Mrs. Samuel Ballard and Nancy B. Clements, 3rd and last daughter of Bartlett Clements.

Married at Prospect Hill, Frederick Co. Va., on December 31st by Rev. Dr. Hill, Rev. E. C. Hutchinson of Leesburg and Miss Lucy B., daughter of the late Capt. Archibald Randolph.

Married Thursday, January 7 by Rev. Chas. B. Tippett, Mr. Harrison Kent and Miss Melinda Henry, both of this county

Married Tuesday, January 12 by Rev. Thos. Birkby, Mr. William C. Luckett and Miss Matilda Jacobs, both of this county.

Vol. XIV, No. 3 – January 23, 1830

Married on December 15th by Rev. Guest, Mr. John Francis of Loudoun and Miss Alpheina Maddaux of Fauquier.

Married on Thursday, January 14 by Rev. Thomas Birkby, Mr. James E. Stonestreet and Miss Amelia Tillett, both of this county.

Married on Thursday, January 14 by Rev. Gilmore, Mr. George McMullen and Miss Edith Craven, both of Loudoun.

Married on Thursday, January 14 by Rev. Gilmore, Mr. John Tavenner and Miss Uree Drake, all of this county.

Vol. XIV, No. 4 – January 30, 1830

Married on Thursday, January 21st by Rev. Jackson, William H. Gray, attorney-in-law of this place, and Miss Frances, daughter of Col. Wm. Ellzey of this county.

Died in Leesburg on Saturday, January 23, Mrs. Jane G. Fox, consort of George K. Fox.

Died at Middleburg on Tuesday, January 19, Jane Ann Eliza, age 10 months, only daughter of Hiram McVeigh.

Vol. XIV, No. 6 – February 13, 1830

Married on Thursday, February 11th by Rev. Thomas Birkby, Mr. William Dodd and Mrs. Mary Hunt, both of this county.

Vol. XIV, No. 7 – February 20, 1830

Married on Tuesday, February 16th by Rev. Thomas Birkby, Mr. William L. Craven of Albermarle and Miss Eleanor Craven of this county.

Vol. XIV, No. 8 – February 27, 1830

Married on February 16th by Rev. Jackson, Benjamin Smith, merchant of Middleburg, and Miss Sarah Blincoe of this town.

Died near Waterford February 11st inst., Mrs. Judith Divine, consort of Jacob Divine, age 69 years.

Vol. XIV, No. 9 – March 6, 1830

Married on Tuesday, March 2nd by Rev. William Gilmore, Mr. Thomas Richards and Miss Margaret Orrison, both of this county.

Vol. XIV, No. 11 – March 20, 1830

Died in Leesburg, Tuesday, March 16th, Mr. William Hawling, age 25 years.

Died in vicinity of Leesburg, Wednesday, March 17th, Mrs. __ Newton, consort of Mr. Jos. T. Newton.

Vol. XIV, No. 14 – April 10, 1830

Married on Thursday, March 18 by Rev. Thomas Birkby, Mr. William Greenlease and Miss Lydia N. Brown, both of this county.

Married on Thursday, March 25 by Rev. Thomas Birkby, Mr. Lewis Ruse and Miss Jemima Stone, both of this county.

Married on the same day by the same [Birkby], Mr. Edward Tillett to Miss Susan Ball, both of this county.

60   *Northern Virginia Genealogy*

Married on Tuesday, March 30th by William Gilmore, Mr. William Wilkinson and Miss Abigail Carter, both of this county.
Married Thursday, April 1st by Rev. Thomas Birkby, Mr. Philip Setzer and Miss Emily Beach, both of this county.
Married Thursday, April 1st by Rev. Thomas Birkby, Mr. Josiah Conwell and Miss Mary Ann Porter, both of this county.
Married Tuesday, April 6th by Rev. Geo. M. Frye, Mr. E. I. Hancock and Miss E. F. Potts, both of this county.
Married Wednesday, April 7th by Rev. Thomas Birkby, Mr. James Templer and Miss Balsora Gregg, both of this county.
Married on Thursday, April 8th by Rev. Thomas Birkby, Mr. Samuel Piggott and Miss Sarah Verts, both of this county.

Vol. XIV, No. 15 – April 17, 1830
Died in Leesburg on Sunday, 11 April, Mr. Thomas Russell, age 50 years.
Died in Leesburg on Sunday, 11 April, Mr. Peter Ish, after a protracted illness.

Vol. XIV, No. 16 – April 24, 1830
Married on Thursday, April 15th by Rev. Saml. Clark, Mr. John Inser and Miss Mary Jane Wooddy, all of Leesburg.
Died at Audley, in Frederick Co., Va., on the 9th inst., Mrs. Betty Carter, relict of the late Charles Carter, Esq. & niece of the late Gen. George Washington, in the 65th year of her age, after a long and painful illness.

Vol. XIV, No. 18 – May 8, 1830
Married on Wednesday, April 21st by Rev. Thomas Birkby, Mr. William Bolon and Miss Mary Ann Whitacre, both of Loudoun.
Married in Middleburg on Thursday, April 29 by Rev. Wm. Williamson, Edwin A. Keeble, Esq., attorney in law of Murfreesborough, Tennessee, and Miss Susan R., daughter of Dr. Richard Cochran.
Married on Thursday, April 29 by Rev. William Gilmore, Mr. Arthur Rogers and Miss Hannah Nichols, both of this county.
Married on Thursday, May 6th by Rev. Thomas Birkby, Mr. Burr Smith Walker and Miss Mary Ann Swartz, both of this county.

Vol. XIV, No. 19 – May 15, 1830
Married in Dumfries, Prince William Co. on Thursday, May 6th by Rev. Thomas C. Thornton, Edmund Tyler, Esq. of Aldie and Miss Mary K, daughter of late James Smith, Esq. of Richmond.
Died in Loudoun on May 4th, Francis Stribling, formerly of Loudoun but recently of Frederick Co.

Vol. XIV, No. 21 – May 29, 1830
Married on May 20th by Rev. William Gilmore, Mr. Robert Power to Miss Arminda Gheen, both of Loudoun.
Died in Parkersburg, Wood Co., Va. on May 4th, Mrs. Winifred Hammett, consort of Samuel Hammett, formerly of this town.
From the *National Intelligencer*, Cambridge, Md., May 22' 1830. Died, William H. Fitzhugh, Esq. of Fairfax Co., Va., who had just arrived here on a visit (to his matrimonial connections). He died yesterday morning at 8 o'clock, at the residence of the Hon. Charles Goldsborough, his father-in-law.

Vol. XIV, No. 23 – June 12, 1830

Married on Tuesday, May 25th by Rev. John Davis of Alexandria, Capt. James H. McVeigh, merchant, and Miss Scynthia A., daughter of Rev. Job Guest, both of Middleburg, Va.

Married Thursday, May 27th by Rev. Mr. Kalbfus, Mr. Matthew Elgin of Loudoun and Miss Ann Broadwater of Fairfax Co., Va.

Died on the 24th April, near Bainbridge, Ohio, Mr. William Taylor, in the 86th year of his age; leaving 14 children, 124 grandchildren and 75 great grandchildren. He was a native of Monmouth County, New Jersey.

Vol. XIV, No. 26 – July 3, 1830

Married on June 24th by Rev. William Gilmore, Mr. Andrew Beveridge and Miss Rebecca H. L. Race, both of Loudoun.

Vol. XIV, No. 27 – July 10, 1830

Died in Hillsborough on July 4th Mr. Solomon Parsons, a native of Massachusetts, aged upwards of 50 years.

Vol. XIV, No. 28 – July 17, 1830

Died on Sunday, July 11 at residence of his brother in vicinity of Leesburg, Thompson Fouche, age 39 years.

Vol. XIV, No. 30 – July 31, 1830

Married on Saturday, July 24th by Rev. Mr. Baker, Mr. Craven Ashford and Miss Ann E. Evans, both of Fairfax Co.

Died July 23rd at her residence near Middleburg, Mrs. Sarah Roszel, aged about 87 years, and for the last half century a worthy member of the M. E. Church.

Vol. XIV, No. 31 – August 7, 1830

Married in Loudoun on June 29th by Rev. E. C. Hutchinson, Mr. Jonathan Potterfield and Miss Sarah Sackman, daughter of Rev. Mr. Sackman of the Lutheran Church.

Died Sunday, July 25th after a painful lingering illness, Rebecca T. Brown, daughter of John Brown of this county.

Vol. XIV, No. 32 – August 14, 1830

Died at the residence of Robert Y. Brent on August 9th near the city of Washington, George Graham, Esq., Commissioner of the General Land Office.

Vol. XIV, No. 34 – August 28, 1830

Married on Thursday, August 26th by Rev. Mr. Hutchinson, Mr. William Spense of Middleburg and Miss Elizabeth Kirk of this place.

Vol. XIV, No. 35 – September 4, 1830

Departed this life, on the 6th of August, 1830, in Morgan County, Ohio, Mrs. Louisa Fulton, consort of Mr. Robert Fulton, Jr., formerly of this county. (Communicated).

Vol. XIV, No. 36 – September 11, 1830

Married on Tuesday, September 7th by Rev. William Gilmore, Mr. Phenias Osburn and Miss Margaret Osburn, daughter of Mr. Morris Osburn, all of Loudoun.

Vol. XIV, No. 38 – September 25, 1830
Died on Sunday last, Mr. James F. Newton, late of this vicinity, after a severe and protracted illness.

Vol. XIV, No. 39 – October 2, 1830
Married Thursday, August 26 by Rev. Thomas Birkby, Mr. Henson Combs and Miss Maria Towperman, both of this county.

Married Thursday, August 26, by Rev. Thomas Birkby, Mr. Henry Young and Miss Rebecca Combs, all of this county.

Married September 2nd by Rev. Thomas Birkby, Mr. George Simpson and Miss Helen Fichter, all of this county.

Married September 2nd by Rev. Thomas Birkby, Mr. Jacob Sockman and Miss Sarah Winegardner, all of this county.

Married September 9 by Thomas Birkby, Mr. Jeremiah Miller and Miss Mary Thompson, all of this county.

Married Tuesday, September 21 by Thomas Birkby, Mr. Townsend McBee and Miss Sarah Blaker, all of this county.

Married Tuesday, September 21 by Rev. Joseph Baker, Mr. Thomas Rogers and Miss Elmina S., daughter of Charles Chamblin, all of this county.

Married Thursday, September 23 by Rev. Thomas Birkby, Mr. Henry G. Samsell and Miss Ann Nixon, all of this county.

Married Thursday, September 23 by Rev. Thomas Birkby, Mr. William Brown and Miss Mary Mercer, all of this county.

Married Thursday, September 23 by Rev. Samuel Clarke, Mr. John H. Bennett and Miss Mary Isabella White, all of this county.

Vol. XIV, No. 40 – October 9, 1830
Married in Baltimore on Sunday, October 3 by Rev. Mr. Pausel, Mr. Thomas H. Long of Baltimore and Miss Mary Jane Hawk of Leesburg.

Vol. XIV, No. 41 – October 16, 1830
Died on October 6 near Leesburg, Mrs. Mary Apsey, in the 71st year of her age, consort of William Apsey, Sen.

Died on Saturday, October 9th in this vicinity, Mr. James Carr, aged about 50 years.

Vol. XIV, No. 42 – October 23, 1830
Married Thursday, October 21 by Rev. William Gilmore, Mr. Michael Morallee and Miss Emily Patience Osburn, both of Leesburg.

Vol. XIV, No. 43 – October 30, 1830
Married Thursday, October 28 by Rev. Thomas Birkby, Mr. John Brown and Miss Emily Boling, both of this county.

Married Thursday, October 28 by Rev. Thomas Birkby, Mr. Thomas Schley Rinker and Miss Ann Feichter, all of Loudoun.

Vol. XIV, No. 44 – November 6, 1830
Married Thursday, October 28 by Rev. William Gilmore, Mr. Benjamin Davis and Miss Sarah White, both of Loudoun.

Married Thursday, October 28 by Rev. William Gilmore, Mr. James McGeath and Miss Margaret Drake, both of Loudoun.

Married Thursday, October 28 in Alexandria by Rev. John P. McGuire, Chas. L. Powell Esq. of Loudoun and Miss Selina, eldest daughter of John Lloyd Esq. of the former place.

Married Thursday, October 28 in Middleburg, Lt. Thomas Hammersly, of U.S. Navy, and Mrs. Emily A. Noland.

Vol. XIV, No. 45 – November 13, 1830

Married Thursday, November 4th at the residence of John Jolliffe Esq. in Frederick Co. by Rev. Septimus Tuston, Robert Worthington of Charlestown, Jefferson Co. and Miss Catharine Helm, daughter of late Col. Meredith Helm Esq. of Frederick.

Died in Winchester on October 4th, Mrs. Mary Rust, age 97 years. Deceased had been a member of the Presbyterian church for upwards of 50 years.

Vol. XIV, No. 46 – November 20, 1830

Married on Monday, November 8 by Rev. Thomas Birkby, Mr. Jacob Yachy and Miss Harriet Neale, both of Loudoun.

Married Tuesday, November 9 by Rev. Thomas Birkby, Philip Griffith and Miss Agatha Gant, both of Loudoun.

Married Thursday, November 11 by Rev. Thomas Birkby, Mr. Gustavus Elgin and Miss Elizabeth Cross, both of Loudoun.

Married Thursday, November 18 by Rev. Thomas Birkby, Mr. Isaac Fry and Miss Isaphene Cartor, both of Loudoun.

Married Thursday, November 18 by Rev. William Wickes, Mr. Dolphin Nichols and Miss Anna Tracey, both of Loudoun.

Vol. XIV, No. 47 – November 27, 1830

Married on Tuesday, November 23 by Rev. William Gilmore, Mr. James Rogers and Miss Martha Hawling, both of Loudoun.

Married Thursday, November 25 by Rev. William Gilmore, Mr. Issachar Brown, age 70 years, and Miss Margaret Griffith, age 45 years, both of Loudoun.

Died in Winchester, Va. of small pox, on Thursday the 18th inst., Mr. Beverly Simpson, shoemaker, aged 24. He was married but three weeks previously. The deceased was a native of Alexandria.

Vol. XIV, No. 48 – December 4, 1830

Married at Easton Talbot Co. Md., Tuesday, November 9, Rev. Stephen B. Balch of Georgetown, DC., and Mrs. Jane Parrott of Easton, formerly of Georgetown.

Married Thursday, December 2 by Rev. William Wickes, Mr. Washington Boteler of Maryland and Miss Mary Ellen, daughter of Presley Cordell Esq. of Leesburg.

Vol. XIV, No. 49 – December 11, 1830

Married on Tuesday, November 30 by Rev. Samuel Clarke, Mr. George Sinclair and Miss Ruthyann Belt, both of Loudoun.

Vol. XIV, No. 50 – December 18, 1830

Married on December 9th by Rev. William Monroe, Mr. Asa B. Cordell of Leesburg and Miss Lucinda Littleton Dixon of Charlestown, Jefferson Co. Va.

Died at Leesburg, December 10, Daniel Tilton Esq. The gentleman came to Leesburg some seven or eight months ago, and employed himself as an instructor of youth. He has left among his papers a commission signed by

President Adams in 1798, appointing him a Judge of the Federal Court in the Mississippi Territory; and at one period, he held a commission of Captain in the Army of the United States. About 1810 to 1816, he resided in Philadelphia, in circumstances of easy affluence. These facts are mentioned in the hope that they may meet the eye of some of his children, whose place of residence is unknown to the writer. Capt. Tilton was probably about 60 years of age. [The editors of the public journal of extensive circulation, in the states of North Carolina and Illinois (where it is believed the deceased has children residing) are repectfully requested to insert this obituary notice.]

Vol. XIV, No. 51 – December 25, 1830
Married at Romney on December 7th by William H. Foote, Joseph W. Bronaugh, attorney at law of Upperville, Loudoun Co., Va. and Miss Nancy S., daughter of William Naylor.

Married on December 7th by Rev. Jacobs, Mr. Ezekiel Daugherty of Frederick and Miss Sarah, daughter of John Copsey of Hampshire Co.

Died on December 16th after a protracted illness, Mrs. Julia Clagett, consort of Dr. Henry Clagett of this town.

Died Friday, December 17th Mr. Samuel Carr, aged about 50 years, for a long time a respectable merchant of this place.

Died in Bloomfield, Loudoun Co., Va. on December 17th Mr. Charles Rivers, age 65 years.

Vol. XIV, No. 52 – January 1, 1831
Married on Thursday, December 23 by Rev. Charles Kalbfus, Mr. Erastus Todd of New York and Miss Ann Leigh of Fairfax Co., Va.

Married Friday, December 24 by Rev. Samuel Clarke, Mr. William H. Galleher and Miss Frances B. Eidson, both of Loudoun.

Married Thursday, December 30 by Rev. William Gilmore, Mr. Joel Brown and Miss Mahala Barr, both of Loudoun.

Vol. XV, No. 2 – January 15, 1831
Married on Thursday, January 6th by Rev. William Gilmore, Mr. William C. Palmer of Loudoun and Miss Lucinda Hutchison of Fairfax Co., Va.

Died Monday, January 10th, Mrs. Mary McCabe, aged about 37 years, consort of Dr. John H. McCabe of Leesburg.

Vol. XV, No. 4 – January 29, 1831
Died at his residence in Alexandria, DC. on January 18, Edward Stabler, in the 62nd year of his age, a minister of Society of Friends.

Vol. XV, No. 5 – February 5, 1831
Married Thursday, January 13 by Rev. John McElhenny at White Sulphur Springs, Lt. Levin M. Powell, of the U.S. Navy, son of Alfred H. Powell, Esq. of Winchester, and Miss Virginia Augustin, daughter of James Caldwell of the former place.

Married in Washington City on Thursday, January 27th by Rev. S. G. Roszel, Mr. Thomas Francis of Loudoun and Miss Sarah Ann, daughter of the late William Mount of Prince William Co.

Married Tuesday, February 1 by Rev. Littlejohn, Mr. John Vandeventer and Miss Harriot A. Darne, both of Loudoun.

Died at Greenville, Tennessee on January 23rd Lewis F. Douglas, formerly of Leesburg, in the 24th year of his age.

Vol. XV, No. 6 – February 12, 1831

Married Sunday, January 23 by Rev. Thomas Birkby, Mr. Washington Dennis and Miss Frances M. Stoneburner, both of Loudoun.

Married Saturday, January 29 by Rev. Thomas Birkby, Mr. Malcolm Jameison of Centreville and Miss Julia Margaret Thompson of Loudoun.

Married Thursday, February 10 by Rev. Thomas Birkby, Mr. Jonathan Myers and Miss Malinda Reed, both of this county.

Vol. XV, No. 7 – February 19, 1831

Married Thursday, February 15 by Rev. Samuel Clarke, Capt. John H. Monroe of this town and Miss Catharine E. Solomon, recently of Baltimore.

Jonesborough (Ten.) Jan 29. Died in Greenville, Ten. on the 23rd inst. Lewis Fordyce Douglas, Esq. in the 25th year of his age. About the 1st of September last, Mr. Douglas left Loudoun County, Va. his native place, to explore some of the western country, with the view of making an eligible location. From Loudoun, he went immediately to the White Sulphur Springs, where he was attacked by bilious fever. Upon a partial recovery of health he proceeded to Fayette County, Ky. With his relatives in the neighborhood of Lexington, he spent some weeks. ... From Kentucky he arrived at Greenville, six or seven weeks since. Upon his arrival, he was in tolerable health, such as enabled him to enjoy the society of his relatives, to visit whom, was his object in the journey hither. ... Mr. Douglas was educated at the University of Virginia, and subsequently qualified himself for the profession of his coice, at the law school of Judge Tucker. (Communicated)

Died Sunday, February 13, Joseph B. Rodney, son of the late Caesar A. Rodney of Delaware, at the residence of Capt. Terrett in Fairfax Co., Va. where he was on a visit. His death was occasioned by an accident.

Died at Winchester on February 15 after a short illness, John Easten Cooke, aged about 5 years, son of John R. Cooke, Esq.

Vol. XV, No. 8 – February 26, 1831

Married on Thursday, February 17 by Rev. Thomas Birkby, Mr. Harrison Russel and Miss Jemima Neale, both of this county.

Married on Tuesday, February 22 by Rev. Thomas Birkby, Mr. Gilford Gregg and Miss Semina Gregg, both of this county.

Died at his residence in Leesburg on Thursday, February 17, Mr. Richard N. Love.

Vol. XV, No. 9 – March 5, 1831

Married on Tuesday, March 1 by William Gilmore, Mr. Arthur Orrison of Loudoun and Miss Ann Louisa Hutchison of Fairfax.

Vol. XV, No. 11 – March 19, 1831

Married on Tuesday, March 15 by Rev. Butler, Edward E. Cooke and Miss Margaret L. Harrison, all of Loudoun.

Died at the residence of his mother in the county on March 8th Dr. Albert Heaton, age 29 years.

Died at her residence in Haliford [*sic*] Co. Va. on February 15, Mrs. Dorothea Winston, widow of the late Judge Edmond Winston and before that widow of Henry Clay.

Died at his residence in Winchester, Va. on March 9th Judge Robert White, age 72 years.

Vol. XV, No. 12 – March 26, 1831

Married on March 17 by Rev. William Gilmore, Mr. Bailey Barton and Miss Sarah Warnall, both of this county.

Married March 22 by Rev. William Gilmore, Mr. Theodore N. Davisson and Miss Sarah Rogers, both of this county.

Vol. XV, No. 13 – April 2, 1831

Married on Thursday, March 24, by Rev. Thomas Birkby, Mr. James Saunders Jr. and Miss Roena Eleanor Bale, both of Loudoun.

Married on Thursday, March 24 at Goose Creek Meeting, Asa M. Bond of Waterford and Sarah Alice, daughter of Bernard Taylor of this county.

Died in Leesburg, Tuesday, March 29, Josephine Bethany, only daughter of Augustine G. Monroe, aged 18 months 3 days.

Vol. XV, No. 14 – April 9, 1831

Married on Thursday, March 24 by Rev. M. Frye, Mr. Zedekiah Kedwell [sic] and Miss Mary Ropp, both of Loudoun.

Married on March 21 by Rev. Thomas Birkby, Mr. Solomon F. Hogue and Miss Juliana Janney, both of Loudoun.

Married on March 21 by Rev. Thomas Birkby, Mr. Nathan Cochran and Miss Mary McGavack, both of Loudoun.

Married Tuesday, April 5th by Rev. Thomas Birkby, Mr. William Hatcher and Miss Elizabeth Gregg, both of Loudoun.

Married Thursday, April 7 by Rev. Thomas Birkby, Mr. Benjamin F. Filingame and Miss Elizabeth Jane Thyer [sic] both of Loudoun.

Vol. XV, No. 15 – April 16, 1831

Married at Harper's Ferry on Thursday, March 31st by Rev. Septimus Tuston, Mr. Archibald Robinson of Shepherdstown and Miss Ann Kearsley Mines, eldest daughter of Rev. John Mines of Rockville Md., formerly of Leesburg.

Married on Sunday, April 10 by Rev. Thomas Birkby, Mr. Bailey D. Cockrell and Miss Elizabeth Anderson, both of Loudoun.

Married on Thursday, April 14 by Rev. Thomas Birkby, Mr. James McDonough and Miss Elizabeth Eliza Gardner, both of Fairfax.

Married in Leesburg on April 14 by Rev. Thomas Birkby, Dr. Henry M. Dowling of Hillsborough, formerly of Leesburg, and Miss Harriet Isabella, daughter of the late William Haslett of Philadelphia.

Married on April 14 by Rev. Wm. Wickes, Mr. Israel T. Griffith and Mrs. Sarah E. Weatherill, both of this county.

Vol. XV, No. 16 – April 23, 1831

Died Sunday, April 17, Mrs. Harriet B. Gray, consort of Mr. John Gray of this town. *(communicated)*

Vol. XV, No. 17 – April 30, 1831

Married on 19th inst. by Birkby, Mr. Fielding Tavener to Miss Hannah Tavener, both of this county.

Married on 21st inst. by Birkby, John Fritz to Rebecca Chamblin, both of this county.

Married Tuesday last, by Birkby, Jesse Oxley to Sarah Hesser, both of this county.

Married Thursday last, Joseph Pierpoint to Rue [*sic*] Ann Hogue, both of this county.

Married same day by Rev. Wm. Wickes, Jacob Devine [*sic*] to Elizabeth Dodd, both of this county.

Vol. XV, No. 18 – May 7, 1831

Married 7th April in vicinity of Rock Run, Harford County, William Chesney, 70, and Elizabeth Gilbert, 50, both of Harford Co.

Married 28th ult., John McKeldon to Mary Chell, both fo Washington City.

Married on Sunday morning last by Rev. Bartow, Mr. Wm. Wheeler of Upperville to Sarah Ann Stansbury of Baltimore.

Vol. XV, No. 19 – May 14, 1831

Married on Thursday, May 12 by Rev. Thomas Birkby, Mr. William Jackson and Miss Elizabeth Palmer, both of this county.

Married on 4th inst. at residence of Col. John Stuart, King George Co., Edgar Snowden Esq. of Alexandria and Louisa Jane Grymes, daughter of late Benjamin Grymes of that county.

Vol. XV, No. 20 – May 21, 1831

Married on Tuesday, May 17th by Rev. Chas. A. Davis, Mr. Mahlon S. Lovett, editor of *The Mine* of Frederick *Co.*, and Miss Mary B. Muse, both of Frederick Co., Va.

Vol. XV, No. 21 – May 28, 1831

Married in Georgetown on Thursday, May 19th by Rev. Septimus Tuston of Charlestown, Va., Jno. R. Beall of Jefferson and Miss Martha Luckett of Alexandria.

Died Monday, May 23, at the residence of Mr. Chas. Williams, Ellen Steer, age 17 months, only child of James Gilmore.

Vol. XV, No. 22 – June 4, 1831

Married Thursday, May 26 by Rev. Thomas J. Dorsey, Mr. William T. Cole of Middleburg, Loudoun Co., and Miss Mary E. Talaiferro, of Culpeper Co. Va.

Vol. XV, No. 24 – June 18, 1831

Died at Snickersville, Loudoun Co., Thursday, June 9th, Mrs. Pleasant Conner, age 23 years, wife of Timothy Conner, member of M. E. Church.

Vol. XV, No. 25 – June 25, 1831

Married on Thursday, June 16 by Rev. Morgan, Rev. Thomas H. W. Monroe, Pastor of the Methodist Episcopal Church in Cumberland, Md., and Miss Mary Ann Shuck, only daughter of Mr. Daniel Shuck of the borough of Bedford, Pa. (The Rev. Morgan, professionally a printer, served his time in this office.)

Vol. XV, No. 26 – July 2, 1831

Married on 23 June by Rev. Gilmore, Mr. Samuel Bowles and Miss Amelia Wildman, both of this county.

Vol. XV, No. 28 – July 16, 1831

Married on June 23, Mr. William Hirst and Miss Rebecca Kirk, both of this town.

Married on Tuesday, July 12, Mr. George K. Fox and Miss Frances Edwards, both of Leesburg.

Vol. XV, No. 29 – July 23, 1831

Died July 12, Mrs. Harriett Sim, wife of Dr. Thomas Sim, of Washington City, formerly of Leesburg.

Died in vicinity at his residence on Monday, July 18, Mr. Josiah Hall, age 70 years, member of M. E. Church.

Married at Zanesville, Ohio, on 5th inst., Rev. Wm. Reeves, of Methodist Reformed Church, to Hannah Pearce, late from England.

Died in Alexander, 14th inst., Samuel Snowden, 55 years.

Died on Sunday morning, Mrs. McLeod, consort of Daniel McLeod of Alexandria.

Vol. XV, No. 30 – July 30, 1831

Married on Sunday, July 24, Mr. Geo. Head and Miss Hannah Gover, both of this town.

Vol. XV, No. 31 – August 6, 1831

Married on Thursday, July 28th, Dr. John H. McCabe and Mrs. Margaret H. D. Tebbs, daughter of Chas. Binns, all of this town.

Died, Sunday, 31st ult., Mrs. Sally L. Aisquith, widow of Edward Aisquith, formerly of Baltimore.

Vol. XV, No. 32 – August 13, 1831

Married on Saturday, August 6 by Rev. Wm. Gilmore, Mr. Thos. Edwards and Miss Mary Laurens, both of Loudoun.

Married on Wednesday, August 10th by Rev. Wm. Gilmore, Mr. George D. Smith and Miss Martha L. Gregg, both of Loudoun.

Vol. XV, No. 33 – August 20, 1831

Died on Friday, August 19th Gamaliel Fox, age 9 year son of Mr. Samuel M. Boss of this town. Fell from a roof where he was working, putting shingles on scaffolding.

Vol. XV, No. 34 – August 27, 1831

Died on Friday, August 19th, Mrs. Caroline Mathais, consort of Capt. John J. Mathais of this town.

Died on Monday, August 22, Mary, infant daughter of W. C. Selden of this town.

Vol. XV, No. 35 – September 3, 1831

Died Monday, August 29 of bilious fever, Thomas Carr, son of the late James Carr of this county.

Married in Martinsburg, 23rd ult., the Rev. Wm. Matthews, Presbyterian, to Mary Hunter, daughter of Col. David Hunter of that place.

Died in Baltimore, a coloured woman named Mary Fredericks, at the advanced age of 112 years.

Vol. XV, No. 36 – September 10, 1831

Died Monday, August 29, at her residence in this county, Mrs. Elizabeth Van Pelt, age 69 years.

Died at his residence in Kanawha Co., on 10 August of Apoplexy, Capt. Samuel Washington, about 60 years, an nephew of Gen. George Washington.

Died on Sunday, 14th Aug, Rev. Benjamin Collins, M. E. church, Hunterdon, New Jersey.

Died at Hagerstown, recently, at an advanced age, Benjamin Galloway.

Died at Baltimore, 2nd Sept, Robert Duer Niles, 22 years old, printer, son of Hezekiah Niles, editor of the *Weekly Register.*

Died in Frederick Co., Va. on 3rd inst., Harmon McKnight, 20 years old.

Vol. XV, No. 37 – September 17, 1831

Married on Monday, September 5th by Rev. T. H. W. Monroe, Mr. Henry D. Carleton of Cumberland, Md. and Miss Mary Merryman, of Cumberland, formerly of Leesburg.

Married on September 8th by Rev. William Wickes, Mr. Joseph Carr and Miss Mary Hall, both of Loudoun.

Died on Saturday, September 10th Mr. James White, son of John White Esq., of Short Hill, age 20 years.

Died Thursday, September 8th Samuel Underwood, age 19 years, of Short Hill.

Died Thursday, September 8th Susan Sanders, daughter of Edw'd. Sanders of Short Hill.

Died Sunday, September 11th William Thompson, 22 year old son of James Thompson of Short Hill.

Died Monday, September 12, Morris Osburn, 20 year old son of Richard Osburn of Short Hill.

Vol. XV, No. 38 – September 24, 1831

Married on September 13 by Rev. William Gilmore, John Byrne and Eliza Mathews, both of this county.

Married on September 15th by Rev. William Gilmore, William King and Mrs. Tacy Daniel, both of Loudoun.

Married on Tuesday, September 20th by Rev. William Wickes, Aaron R. Saunders and Miss Ann B. Lee, both of this county.

Died September 9th, Mrs. Catharine Towner, age 60 years, of Leesburg.

Died September 11th, Mrs. Phebe Popkins, age 67 years, of Bloomfield, Loudoun Co.

Died September 18, Mrs. Betsy Surghnor, age 27-4-22, of Leesburg, daughter of Mr. Jesse Dailey and wife of John Surghnor.

Vol. XV, No. 39 – October 1, 1831

Married Thursday, September 22 by Rev. Wm. Wickes, Mr. Samuel Sackman and Susan Mary Hixon, both of this county.

Married on Tuesday, September 27, Mr. W. H. Noland of U.S. Navy and Miss H. M. Armistead of Loudoun.

Vol. XV, No. 41 – October 15, 1831

Died Monday, October 3rd, Miss Elizabeth E. Guest, daughter of Rev. Job Guest of the city of Annapolis, member of M. E. Church. (Communicated)

Died Sunday, October 2, Miss Maria Reed, daughter of Mr. John Reed of this county, age 28 years.

Died Friday, October 7, Mrs. Bethany Monroe, daughter of John Saunders of Leesburg, age 36 years.

Died Wednesday, October 12, Mrs. Sarah Hammett, age 72 years, widow of the late George Hammett of Leesburg.

Died Wednesday, October 12, Mrs. Betsey Murrey, age 70 years, relict of the late Samuel Murrey of Leesburg.

Died Wednesday, October 12, Thomas L. Shortness of Leesburg, age 20 years.

Vol. XV, No. 42 – October 22, 1831

Married on Tuesday, October 18th by Rev. William Wickes, Mr. Thomas S. Hopkins and Miss Sally L. Harris, daughter of Mr. Samuel B. Harris, all of Loudoun.

Married on Tuesday, October 18th by Rev. Robert Wilson, Mr. Creyton Saunders of Leesburg and Miss Catharine Ebersole of Washington Co., Md.

Vol. XV, No. 43 – October 29, 1831

Married on Thursday, October 20 by Rev. Lemon, Mr. George C. Powell of Middleburg and Miss Marietta Fitzhugh, eldest daughter of Thomas Turner Esq. of Kenloch, Fauquier Co., Va.

Died at Hill farm near Middleburg on Monday, October 10, Mrs. Nancy Gibson, consort of David Gibson Esq., age 66 years.

Died on Thursday, October 27, William Nicholas, age 3 months, only son of Mr. Michael Morallee of this town.

Vol. XV, No. 44 – November 5, 1831

Married on Thursday, October 20th by Rev. Collins, Mr. William Harper, editor of the *South Branch Intelligencer*, and Miss Nancy N. Newman, daughter of Dr. Robert Newman of Romney.

Married on Thursday, October 27 by Rev. William Wicks, Mr. Murphy C. Shumate and Miss Margaret Elgin, daughter of Major Gustavus Elgin, all of this county.

Married on Tuesday, November 1 by Rev. William Wicks, Mr. Lewis J. Donohoe and Miss Delilah Hall, both of this county.

Died at St. Helena in September, Mrs. Elizabeth Honoria Frances Lambe, 110 years. She was married eight times.

Married at Black Rock on 20th ult., Geo. Head to Caroline Field, of that place.

Vol. XV, No. 45 – November 12, 1831

Married in Baltimore, Tuesday, November 8 by Rev. Nevins, Lewis M. Goldsborough of U.S. Navy and Elizabeth Gamble Wirt, second daughter of Hon. William Wirt (anti-Masonic convention candidate for the presidency.)

Married on Tuesday, November 1st by Rev. John Henning, Charles G. Eskridge of this town and Miss Margaret P. Hunter, daughter of Gen. John C. Hunter of Fairfax.

Married on November 3 by Rev. William Wickes, Mr. Joseph Grubb and Miss Mary Daniel, both of this county.

Married on Tuesday last, November 8 by Rev. John Swan, Dr. Thomas H. Clagett of this town and Miss Christiana H. Oden, daughter of Benjamin Oden of Prince George Co., Md.

Vol. XV, No. 46 – November 19, 1831

Married on Tuesday, November 1st by Rev. William Gilmore, Mr. James F. Lynn and Miss Violinda Ann Skillman, both of Loudoun.

Married on Thursday, November 3rd by Rev. William Gilmore, Mr. Townshend J. Jury and Miss Mary Ann Drake, both of Loudoun.

Married on Monday, November 7th in Aldie by Rev. Cutler, George G. Armistead of Alabama and Miss Alice Virginia, youngest daughter of the late Carter Fontaine of Prince William.

Married on Thursday, November 10 by Rev. William Gilmore, Mr. Mahlon White and Miss Margaret Wynkoop, both of Loudoun.

Married on Thursday, November 10 by Rev. William Gilmore, Mr. James Merchant and Miss Rebekah Romine, both of Loudoun.

Married on Thursday, November 10 by Rev. William Wickes, Mr. Ignatius Elgin and Miss Mary Ann Lee, daughter of Joshua Lee, all of this county.

Married on Saturday, November 12 by Rev. Thomas Birkby, Mr. John Schooley and Mrs. Sarah Roberts, both of this county.

Married on Tuesday, November 8 by Rev. Thomas Birkby, Mr. Lot Tavener and Miss Phoebe Piggott, both of Loudoun.

Vol. XV, No. 47 – November 26, 1831

Married on Tuesday, November 22 by Rev. Thomas Birkby, Dr. M. C. Klein and Miss Hester B. Janney, both of this county.

Married on Thursday, November 24 by Rev. Thomas Birkby, Mr. Joseph Dixon and Miss Sarah Peacock, both of Loudoun

Vol. XV, No. 49 – December 10, 1831

Died in Hillsborough on December 3, Cornelia Janney, age 22 years.

Vol. XV, No. 50 – December 17, 1831

Married on 1st inst. by Gilmore, Henry Clapper to Miss Zelia Copeland, both of Loudoun.

Married on 8th inst. by Wickes, Lawson Vananda to Miss Susan Clapper, both of Loudoun.

Vol. XV, No. 51 – December 24, 1831

Died on 15th inst. in 17th year, protracted illness, Frances W. Ball, daughter of late Dr. C. B. Ball of this town. (Communicated)

Vol. XVI, No. 2 – January 14, 1832

Married Thursday, December 22, by Rev. Samuel Clark, Joseph Combs and Nancy J. Branham, all of this county.

Married 10 January inst. by Rev. Samuel Clark, William B. Price of Alexandria and Sarah P. S. Martin of Middleburg.

Died in Waterford on 4 January inst., Eliza Dailey, in 17th year.

Vol. XVI, No. 3 – January 21, 1832

Died March 7 at his residence near the German Settlement, Loudoun Co., Daniel Stone, age 62 years.

Died Wednesday last, Rebecca, 6 month old daughter of David Ogden.

Vol. XVI, No. 4 – January 28, 1832

Died in Middleburg on the 15th inst. of the prevailing epidemic 'influenza' at age 54 years, Elizabeth M. Noland, eldest daughter of the late Thomas Noland, Esq. of Noland's Ferry.

Vol. XVI, No. 5 – February 4, 1832

Married on Tuesday last by Rev. Wm. Wickes, George Price of Chambersburg, Pa. and Elizabeth Clapham of this county.

Married Tuesday eve last, Mr. ___ Major and Hannah Ann Harris, both of this town.

Married Thursday last by Birkby, Lee Silkith and Nancy Athey, both of this
county.
Died recently and suddenly at residence of R. Drake in Fallsbury Township,
Licking Co., Ohio, James Drake, about 40 years old, late of Loudoun Co.

Vol. XVI, No. 6 – February 11, 1832

Died in this town Thursday last, John Hammerly, aged about 55 years, confined
by a lingering illness for the last 9 months.

Vol. XVI, No. 7 – February 18, 1832

Married Tuesday, 7th inst. by Gilmore, Presley Orrison and Mary Graham, all of
Loudoun.
Married Wednesday the 8th inst. by Rev. Mr. Dorsey, J. A. W. Smith, Esq., clerk
of Fauquier County Court, and Sarah Hall of Loudoun.
Married Wednesday the 8th inst. by Birkby, John Wren and Elizabeth Hauk, both
of this county.
Married Sunday last by Birkby, Jacob Anderson and Rachel Lafaber, both of this
county.
Married Tuesday last by Birkby, John Moore and Martha Ann Lathrum, all of
Loudoun.
Married Thursday last by Gilmore, Samuel C. Beveridge and Harriet C. Moffett,
all of Loudoun.
Married on Thursday the 9th by Gilmore, James Kittle to Nancy Carr, all of
Loudoun.

Vol. XVI, No. 8 – February 25, 1832

Died on 5th inst. at residence near Hay Market, Prince Wm. Co., Robert Latham
Jr., left young interesting wife and five little promising children.
Died on 14st inst. in Cumberland, Md., Mary Ann Monroe, consort of Rev.
Thomas H. W. Monroe, in the 22nd year of her age.
Died Sunday morn last at age 67 years, George McCabe, "an inoffensive and
worthy citizen of this town."

Vol. XVI, No. 9 – March 3, 1832

Died in Burke Co., NC at his residence on the Catawba on the 19th of January,
James Lack in the 99th year of his age. He was born in Penna, was out [*sic*] a
wagoner in the unfortunate campaign of Braddock. He was among the first
settlers in Burke, participated in the early struggles with the Indians, on this
then frontier country. He was more than once compelled to abandon his
home by their incursion. He was out in Rutherford's campaign and was in the
battle of Kings Mountain.

Vol. XVI, No. 10 – March 10, 1832

Married Thursday, 23rd ult., by Birkby, John Slack and Juliet Lickey, all of
Loudoun.
Married Thursday, March 1st by Birkby, John H. Brown and Susannah Hogue,
both of this county.
Married Thursday, March 1st by Birkby, Samuel Ball and Catharine McPherson,
both of this county.
Married Thursday last by Birkby, William R. Shields and Susan Blaker, both of
this county.

Died in this town on 22nd inst., Pompy, a man of colour. He was born on the 22nd of February 1732 and lived to be exactly 100 years old." [*Cumberland Advertiser*]

Vol. XVI, No. 11 – March 17, 1832

Married Tuesday the 6th inst. by Gilmore, John Curry and Elizabeth Graham, both of this county.

Married Thursday the 8th inst. by Gilmore, Watson Carter and Hannah Marvin, both of Frederick Co. Va.

Married Thursday the 8th inst. by Rev. Wm. Wickes, Robert E. Beale and Susan Wright, both of this county.

Died Sunday the 11th inst. at residence of Richard H. Henderson in town, Mrs. Margaret Moore, widow of Cato Moore dec'd formerly of Shepherdstown, age 76 years.

Vol. XVI, No. 12 – March 24, 1832

Died Saturday eve at Naval Hosp. in Norfolk, Lt. Alexander Eskridge of the Navy, native of Loudoun. Entered Navy a few months before the commencement of the late war with Gr. Britain, midshipman of the *Constitution* when she captured the Gueruere, Java, Cynae Levant ... sank an early victim to his rest.

Died Sunday last, Margaret E. Hughes, age 5 months, daughter of Edward Hughes of Alexandria and formerly of this town.

Vol. XVI, No. 13 – March 31, 1832

Married Thursday the 22nd inst. by Rev. Wm. Wickes, William Hall and Eliza Ann Carr, all of Loudoun.

Died at Haymarket, Prince Wm. Co., on the 10th inst., Mrs. Ann Matilda Tyler, wife of James Monroe Tyler of that place and daughter of William Hebb Esq. of Washington City, in the 26th year of her age leaving husband and three children.

Vol. XVI, No. 14 – April 7, 1832

Mr. Edmund Jennings was born on the 12th day of March 1756, and departed this life on the 11th day of February 1832. He was for many years a resident of Loudoun County, Virginia, where he died. The residence of some of his heirs at law is unknown.

Vol. XVI, No. 15 – April 14, 1832

Married Thursday the 22nd ult. by Birkby, Parkinson L. Lott and Mary Smale, both of this town.

Married Thursday the 29th ult. by Birkby, Samuel Hatcher and Lydia Nichols, both of this county.

Vol. XVI, No. 16 – April 21, 1832

Married at Washington City mansion of President on 10th inst. by Rev. Mr. Hawley, Lucius Polk, Esq. of Tennessee and Mary A. Eastin, member of president's family.

Married at Blenhein B. C. on Thursday the 12th ult. by Rev. Mr. Hamilton, Rev. Dr. Edwin Dorsey of M. E. Church and Matilda H. Price, daughter of Larkin H. Smith, Esq.

Married on Wednesday last by Gilmore, Joseph Blincoe and Lucinda Jones, both of Loudoun.

Married Thursday last by Gilmore, William Taylor and Mary R. Timms, both of
  Loudoun.
Married in New York, by Rev. Henry Anthony, William Weed to Sarah Ann
  Rogers, eldest daughter of the late Joseph & Eliza Rogers, all of that city.

Vol. XVI, No. 17 – April 28, 1832

Died Thursday the 15th ult., Robert Wilson of Baltimore Co., aged 102 years 11
  days.
Died Tuesday last in 13th year, Sarah Catharine, daughter of George Head of this
  town.
Died Wednesday last, Mrs. Lydia Head of vicinity, in 73rd year. Thus has a worthy
  citizen been bereaved of a daughter and a mother in the short space of two
  days.

Vol. XVI, No. 19 – May 12, 1832

Married Thursday last by Birkby, James Woody and Elizabeth Clifford, both of
  this town.
Married Thursday last by Rev. John G. Watt, Lemuel Watson and Lucy H. Birkby.
Died Sunday last, Huldah Ellen, infant daughter of James P. Lovett of this town.
Maried in Palmyra, New York, Thomas Drinkwater (a temperance man it is
  supposed) aged 48, to Miss Joanna Thurston, aged 23.
Died on Friday, 27th ult., at the University of Virginia, Arthur S. Brockenbough
  Esq., formerly a resident of Richmond, and recently proctor to the university.

Vol. XVI, No. 20 – May 19, 1832

Married at Mountain View on Wednesday, the 9th inst., Rev. Dr. Hill, Dr. Joseph
  B. Lacey of Loudoun and Jemina A., daughter of Henry Richards Esq.
Died in York, Pa. on Tuesday the 1st inst., Thomas Wetherald, member of
  Society of Friends, formerly resident of Washington.
Died Sunday the 6th inst. at Union, Loudoun Co., Miss Mary Smith, tedious illness
  of 2 years.

Vol. XVI, No. 21 – May 26, 1832

Married in Janeville, Frederick Co. on Thursday the 17th inst. by Rev. David
  Riddle, Joseph A. Williamson, Atty-at-law of Leesburg, and Miss Mary Mann,
  daughter of Robert Page.
Married on Tuesday last by Wickes, Mr. T. Hempstone of Md. and Mary M. Harris
  of Loudoun.
Married on 1st inst. by Rev. B. Edwards, Dr. Alfred L. Wolf to Miss Rebecca Bear,
  all of Rockingham Co.

Vol. XVI, No. 22, June 2, 1832

Married Thursday the 17th by Rev. John G. Watt, John Norris and Hannah
  Sophia, daughter of Rev. Thos. Birkby.
Married on Thursday the 17th by Rev. Seely Bunn, John Smale of Leesburg and
  Frances Lott of Charlestown, Jefferson Co. Va.
Married May 24 by Rev. John G. Watt, Dr. Wm. F. Simpson and Mary A. Newton,
  all of Leesburg.
Married Thursday, May 24, by Rev. Isaac Robbins, James Fadely formerly of
  Leesburg and Ann Robison of Alexandria, DC.
Married Tuesday last by Rev. Mr. Chamberlain, Samuel Powell, Esq. of
  Upperville and Eliza S., only daughter of Robert Parker of Baltimore.

Vol. XVI, No. 23 – June 9, 1832

Married on Sunday the 3rd inst. by Birkby, Thomas Oden and Mrs. Barbara Drish, both of this county.

Married on Tuesday last the 5th inst., Alfred Bolon and Sarah Roach, both of this county.

Vol. XVI, No. 24 – June 16, 1832

Married on Thursday last by Rev. Wm. Gilmore, Master William C. Galleher, about 16 years old, and Elinor Jane McCormick, about 14 years old, both of Loudoun.

Died on 22nd ult. of scarlet fever in the upper part of Loudoun, Rachel Frances Beavers, 4 year old daughter of Abraham H. Beavers.

Died on 27th ult., Hon. John Rhea, formerly member of Congress from Tennessee, aged 79 years.

Died on 1st inst. at his residence in South Carolina, Gen. Thomas Sumpter, a venerable relic of the revolution.

Vol. XVI, No. 25 – June 23, 1832

Died on the 14th inst. at Mount Vernon in the 43rd year of his age, John A. Washington, Esq., proprietor of that estate.

Married in Belmont, Wm. Melvin, age 90, one who took an active part in destroyig the tea at Boston in 1773, to Sally Parker, 79, widow of M. Parker, who fell at battle of Bennington.

Married on 12th inst., Valentine Miller, age 80, to Miss Jan Duh, aged 18, both of Monroe Co., Va.

Vol. XVI, No. 26 – June 30, 1832

Married Thursday the 21st inst. by Birkby, Jacab Nichols of Frederick and Mrs. Elizabeth Orr of Fairfax Co.

Married Thursday last by Birkby, Enos Potts and Martha Tavener, both of Loudoun.

Married Thursday last by Birkby, Wilson Gregg and Margaret Lightfoot, all of Loudoun.

Vol. XVI, No. 27 – July 7, 1832

Married in Washington on Tuesday the 26th ult. by Rev. O. B. Brown, Isaac Shelby Reed of Mississippi and Ann Laura, daughter of Gen. Duff Green.

Married on Thursday the 28th ult. by Rev. Thomas Dorsey, Thomas Edwin Thompson, merchant of Warrenton, Fauquier Co., and Margaret Mary Ann, daughter of Capt. Notley C. Williams of Loudoun Co.

Vol. XVI, No. 30 – July 28, 1832

Died in vicinity of this town on Monday last, Robert Campbell, aged about 54 years, long a resident of this county, suspected Asiatic cholera tho not so diagnosed.

Vol. XVI, No. 31 – August 4, 1832

Died at residence in West Zanesville, Ohio on Monday, June 11, William Mayne, a native of England some time since a resident of Loudoun County.

Died at late residence in Seviersville, Tennessee on Monday eve, July 9, Spencer Clack, age 96 years 3 months and 11 days. One of the pioneers of the west being among the earliest settlers on Little Pigeon. He was born in

Loudoun Co. 28th day of March 1746, early took part in politics in Tenn, assisted in forming constitution, many years member of Legislature.

Vol. XVI, No. 32 – August 11, 1832

Married Tuesday last by Birkby, John H. Kaighn and Mary E. Triplett, both of this county.

Married Thursday last by Birkby, Thomas B. Walters and Sarah Brown, both of this county.

Died in Fairfax, Culpeper Co. on the 31st ult., James Caldwell, formerly editor of *Culpeper Gazette*.

Vol. XVI, No. 33 – August 18, 1832

Married on the 7th inst. in Richmond Va. by Rt. Rev. Biship Moore, Josiah Babbott, Esq., Jr., Ed. *Richmond Whig*, and Catharine C. Randolph, daughter of the late Harry Randolph of Warwick.

Married on the 7th inst. by Rev. Adie, Francis Elgin of Loudoun and Mary Jane, daughter of Thomas Rogers of Prince William Co. Va.

Vol. XVI, No. 37 – September 15, 1832

Married Thursday the 6th inst. by Rev. Chas. A. Davis, William S. Anderson and Ann M. Gibbons, both of Winchester, Va.

Married Thursday the 6th inst. by Rev. Septimus Tuston, N. H. Swayne, Esq., U.S. Atty Dist. of Ohio, and Sarah Ann S. Wager, daughter of late John Wager, Esq. of Harpers Ferry, Va.

Died on Sunday the 9th inst. at house of Capt. W. C. Palmer, Miss Nodia Weadon.

Died in Baltimore on the 6th inst. at residence on New Church St., Jonathan Ogden "of the prevailing epidemic in the 47 year of his age," "was formerly a resident of Leesburg."

Vol. XVI, No. 38 – September 22, 1832

Married Tuesday the 18th inst. by Wickes, Edwin Rogers, only son of Thomas Rogers of Prince Wm. Co. and Ann, daughter of Walter Elgin, Esq. of Loudoun Co.

Died in this town on Sunday the 16th inst., Ann Peers.

Died on the 13th inst. in Leesburg, Thomas Ludwell Lee, 5 year old eldest child of Rev. Wm. F. Lee.

Died in Washington City on 15 inst., Dr. Thomson Sim, about 56 years, one of the first physicians of that place.

Vol. XVI, No. 39 – September 29, 1832

Married in Knox Co., Ohio on the 6th inst. by Rev. Thos. Rigdon, Samuel Potts and Catharine Templer, both formerly of Loudoun.

Married in Warrenton, Fauquier Co. on Thursday the 20th inst. at residence of T. L. Moore by Rev. Geo. Lammon, Erasmus Helm of this place and Virginia Laura Aisquith, recently of Leesburg, daughter of the late Capt. Edward Aisquith of Baltimore.

Vol. XVI, No. 41 – October 13, 1832

Married Thursday the 4th inst. by Gilmore, Isreal Burke and Elizabeth Garner, both of this county.

Died on the 18th ult., Mrs. Maria Carter Lee Macabe, consort of P. C. Macabe, Esq. of Harper's Ferry. She was a native of Loudoun Co.

Died in Georgetown some few weeks since, of the prevailing epidemic, Matthew Mitchell, aged 62 years, member of Society of Friends, long time resident of Loudoun, removed to D. C., became keeper of the Poorhouse establishment of Georgetown.

Vol. XVI, No. 42 – October 20, 1832
Died on Monday last in neighborhood of Broad Run in Loudoun Co., John Whaley, age about 22, cholera.

Vol. XVI, No. 43 – October 27, 1832
Married in Winchester Va. on the 11th inst. by Rev. Wm. F. Lee of Richmond Va., Dr. Adolphus C. Smith of Upperville, Fauquier Co., and Ellen Powell, daughter of William Chilton, Esq.

Died on 10th inst. at residence in Northumberland Co., Lyttleton Upshur, member of Court and Legislature.

Vol. XVI, No. 44 – November 3, 1832
Married Thursday last by Birkby, John Surghnor and Mrs. Sally Summers, both of this town.

Died in Baltimore of cholera on Tuesday the 23rd ult., Mrs. Cornelia Frye, wife of the Rev. Joseph Frye.

Vol. XVI, No. 45 – November 10, 1832
Married in Alexandria on the 19th ult. by Rev. Wm. C. Walton, Rev. John H. Hargrove and Charlotte E. Rose.

Married on the 1st inst. by Rev. George M. Fry, Alexander Kilgour, Esq. of Rockville, Md. and Margaret Ann Stribling of Loudoun Co.

Married Thursday eve last, Thomas W. Brooks and Sarah Saunders, both of this town.

Died on the 20th ult. in Poolesville, Md., Mrs. Elizabeth B. Matthews, consort of William Matthews, Esq., engineer on C & O Canal.

Vol. XVI, No. 46 – November 17, 1832
Married Thursday the 11th ult. by Rev. Mr. Newman, Richard Van Pelt of Loudoun and Mary Fortune, daughter of late Garner Fortune of Prince William Co., Va.

Died in Middleburg on Sunday the 4th inst. of scarlet fever, Thomas Robbins, 22 month old infant son of Rev. Thomas L. Dorsey, minister of M. E. Church.

Vol. XVI, No. 47 – November 24, 1832
Died suddenly at Brown's Hotel in City of Washington on Monday last, Hon. Philip Dodridge, Rep. in Congress from state of Va., aged about 60 years.

Vol. XVI, No. 48 – December 1, 1832
Married in Anne Arundel, Md. on Tuesday, November 22, by Rev. Mr. Humphreys, John B. Patterson of Georgetown, DC. and Eliza, daughter of the late Joseph McCeney of this county.

Vol. XVI, No. 50 – December 15, 1832
Married on the 4th inst., Thomas Saunders and Mary Mead, both of this vicinity.

Married on the 4th inst. by Gilmore, Wm. Horseman and Sarah Johnson, both of this county.

Married on the 4th inst. by Gilmore, James N. Allnut and Barbara Ann Dawson,
both of Montgomery Co.

Married Tuesday last by Gilmore, Leonard W. Trail and Delias Wailes, both of
Montgomery Co.

Died at Woodgrove, Loudoun Co., after a short illness, Eliza, daughter of S. B. T.
Caldwell, Esq.

Vol. XVI, No. 51 – December 22, 1832

Died Tuesday last, Edward Lewis, infant son of Edward Hammett of this town.

Vol. XVI, No. 52 – December 29, 1832

Died in the town Monday last, Josiah L. Drean, age 30 years. Tribute of
Respect: At a meeting of the Citizen Guards ... the following resolutions: If
having pleased almighty God to remove by death, this esteemed friend and
fellow soldier, Josiah L. Drean, the members of the Citizen Guards have
assembled ... it is therefore Resolved unaminously that in testimony of the
grief felt by the members of the Citizen Guards for the death of this friend and
companion, Josiah L. Drean, they will wear crape on the left arm for thirty
days. Resolved that copies of these resolutions be furnished the editors of
this place, and that they be requests to publish them.

Vol. XVII, No. 1 – January 5, 1833

Married on 16 ult. by Rev. Mr. Dorsey, John Mitchell, age 68 years, and Mrs.
Sally Patterson, age 63 years, both of Fauquier Co. Va.

Married Thursday last week by Gilmore, William Gantt and Chloe Ann Maria
Richardson, both of Fairfax Va.

Married Tuesday last, 1st day of New Year, Ammishaddai Moore of Jefferson Co.
Va. and Mary, daughter of Dr. Brewer of Montgomery Co. Md.

Died on 17 December at Rosehill residence of Rev. John Mines near Rockville,
Md., F. Scott Mines, son of Rev. T. J. Addison Mines late of Philadelphia,
formerly of Leesburg, aged 1 year 4 months.

Died on 28th ult., Mrs. Hannah Ann Majors, aged 20 years.

Vol. XVII, No. 3 – January 19, 1833

Married on Thursday the 27th ult. by Rev. Thos. Burges, Richard H. Toler, son of
the Editor, Lynchburg, Va., and Mary Ann Frances, daughter of Major William
Duvall of Buckingham Co.

Died in Port Tobacco, Charles Co., Md., on the 29th ult., Mrs. Elizabeth Lloyd,
age 25 years, consort of William Lloyd and daughter of Mrs. Frances Bogue
of this town.

Vol. XVII, No. 4 – January 26, 1833

Died on Saturday inst., Samuel Poston, aged about 40 years, was formerly of
Washington City but had resided in this town for the last three years.

Died in town on Tuesday last, Dr. William F. Simpson, 24 years of age.

Vol. XVII, No. 5 – February 2, 1833

Married in Knox Co., Ohio on January 17 by Rev. Thos. Rigdon, Benjamin Smith
and Miss Sarah Brown, formerly of Loudoun.

Vol. XVII, No. 6 – February 9, 1833

Married on Thursday the 31st ult. by Gilmore, Lot Pursel and Hannah Taylor, both
of this county.

Died in vicinity of Bloomfield on 2nd inst., Joshua Fred, age 72 years, "numerous family" and "for sobriety and honesty he was equaled by few."

Vol. XVII, No. 9 – March 2, 1833

Died Saturday morning the 16th ult. at residence of Isaac Cloud, South River, Shennandoah Co., William Gilmore Buck, son of Samuel Buck, aged about 15 years.

Vol. XVII, No. 11 – March 16, 1833

Married in Millford on 21st ult. by Rev. B. Booten, Jacob Hittle, age 80 years of Culpeper, and Mrs. Racheal Wood, relict of late John Wood, age 70 of Page Co.

Married Thursday the 7th inst. by Gilmore, Geo. Fleming and Ann Otley, both of this county

Died at Lucky-hit farm in Frederick Co. on the 28th ult., Richard Kidder Meade, brother of Bishop Meade, in his 50th year.

Died in town on Sunday last, Virginia, infant daughter of Evrit Saunders.

Vol. XVII, No. 13 – March 30, 1833

Married Tuesday last by Gilmore, John H. Hughes and Martha Ann Rogers, both of this county.

Vol. XVII, No. 14 – April 6, 1833

Died at residence in county on Saturday the 23rd ult., Thomas Morris, 52 year native of Charles Co., Md., resident of Loudoun last 26 years. Son James Heaton [Morris] died a few days previously making a loss of eight children – left wife and four living children.

Vol. XVII, No. 15 – April 13, 1833

Married Thursday the 4th inst. by Birkby, John Rinker and Susannah Johnson, both of this county.

Married Sunday last by Birkby, Henry Morrison of Sharpsburg Md. and Mary Ann Reed of this county.

Married Tuesday last by Birkby, William Jackson and Rebecca T. Dulin, both of this county.

Vol. XVII, No. 16 – April 20, 1833

Died on 30th last month at Mill belonging to Joseph Steer in Waterford, Joseph S. Fenton, 6 year old son of John Fenton of Frederick Co. Loaded gun left untended, boy on errand picked up and fired it unintentionally causing fatal accident. Witnessed by a small black boy who went to the mill with Joseph Fenton. Waterford, Va. 4th mo 16th 1833.

Vol. XVII, No. 17 – April 27, 1833

Married on the 14th inst. by Gilmore, John Ellmore and Elizabeth Ann Rose.

Married in Frederick Co. on the 16th inst. by Rev. Saml. Keppler, Capt. Joshua Gore and Margery, daughter of Gen. Lockhart.

Married on the 18th inst. by Gilmore, Thomas M. Humphrey and Lydia Whitacre, both of this county.

Died in Georgetown on the 19th inst., Chas. Hay, 40 year old son of late Judge Hay, Chief clerk of the Navy Dept.

Died in this town yesterday, Daniel Lee, Esq., Clerk District Court 1804 until court abolished 1812, appointed Clerk of Chancery Court for Winchester District, died as President of the Branch of the Farmers Bank, since 1815 in Winchester, Virginia.

Vol. XVII, No. 18 – May 4, 1833
Married on Monday, April 15, by Rev. Mr. Hamilton, Rev. John G. Lyon from this town and Augusta M. Day of Harford Co., Md.

Vol. XVII, No. 19 – May 11, 1833
Married Fairfield Co., Ohio on Tuesday the 23rd ult. by Rev. Saml. Carpenter, Gregory Glasscock of Loudoun Co. and Susan Fristoe, recently of Page Co.
Married on Thursday the 2nd inst. by Rev. Mr. Buck, Daniel Cloud and Mary Elizabeth, daughter of Samuel Buck of Shennandoah Co.
Married Tuesday last by Gilmore, Robert N. Spates and Eliza Ann Hoyl, both of Montgomery Co., Md.

Vol. XVII, No. 20 – May 18, 1833
Married on Tuesday last week at Glenowen by Rev. Mr. Dorsey, William R. Abbot, Esq. of Hagerstown and Ellen J., daughter of Samuel B. Harris, Esq. of Loudoun.

Vol. XVII, No. 21 – May 25, 1833
Married on 7th inst. by Rev. Mr. Johnson, Robert B. Rust of Harper's Ferry and Susan D. Burkhart, daughter of Daniel Burkhart, Esq. of Martinsburg.
Married on the 7th inst. by Rev. Dr. Keith, Major Spencer M. Ball of Fairfax and Mary L. Dulany, daughter of Daniel F. Dulany, Esq. of Oak Mount, Fairfax Co., Va.
Married on the 8th inst. at Oakwood, Fauquier Co. by Rev. Geo. Lemmon, Arthur A. Morson, Esq., atty-at-law of Fredericksburg, and Maria M., daughter of Hon. Judge Scott.
Married Thursday, May 9 by Rev. Thomas McGee, Rev. Thomas H. W. Monroe of the Baltimore Conference and Sarah A. Warfield of Frederick Co., Md.

Vol. XVII, No. 22 – June 1, 1833
Married on April 30 by Rev. Mr. Bond, J. B. Wright, formerly of Harper's Ferry, and Ann V. Jones of Fairfax Co. Va.

Vol. XVII, No. 23 – June 8, 1833
Married Thursday last week by Birkby, Levin Thomas and Rebecca Philips, all of this county.
Married Thursday last week by Birkby, John Lacey and Betsey Ann Van Pelt, all of Loudoun.
Married Tuesday last, Anthony Addison and Mary Thompson, both of this place.
Married in Alexandria on Thursday last, Joseph Birkby of this town and Mary Major of Alexandria.

Vol. XVII, No. 25 – June 22, 1833
Married in Belmont on Thursday, June 6, by Rev. Mr. Lemon, William A. Stephenson of Upperville, Fauquier Co., and Mary D. Grayson, daughter of Benjamin Grayson, Esq. of Loudoun Co.
Married Thursday the 13th inst. by Birkby, John W. Hall and Sarah E. Rice, both of this county.
Married Tuesday last by Birkby, Reuben Cockerill and Mary Eleanor Coe, both of this county.

Died of cholera on May 18 in Vicksburg, Miss, Dr. Robert Braden in 29th year of his age, son of late Major R. Braden of this County. Dr. Braden was a graduate of the U. of Pennsylvania and emigrated to the southwest in 1828.

Vol. XVII, No. 26 – June 29, 1833

Married Sunday last by Gilmore, John Whitacre, aged 70 years, and Mrs. Nancy Hope, aged 55 years, both of Loudoun.

Vol. XVII, No. 29 – July 20, 1833

Died on the 12th inst. at residence in this county, Mrs. Penelope Harrison, age 77 years, consort of Major William B. Harrison.

Vol. XVII, No. 31 – August 3, 1833

Died June 18 last at residence of William Vandeventer in Monroe Co., Mo, John Carr, in 59th year, some time May last left county on journey west.

Died in Rockingham Co. on the 14th ult., Mrs. Frances W. Gray, wife of Wm. H. Gray, Esq., daughter of Col. Wm. Ellzey of Loudoun.

Died on the 14th ult. at residence of her father in Montgomery Co., Miss Correlly Floyd, child of Gov. John Floyd, of scarlet fever.

Died at Alexandria, DC., Dr. Thomas Semmes, 55 year old physician.

Vol. XVII, No. 33 – August 17, 1833

Married on the 16th ult. by Rev. T. W. Newman, Andrew Sale and Lucy Fourtune of Prince William Co.

Married on the 8th inst. by Rev. Mr. Bashair, John Kell of Orange Court House and Lucy Ann Strother of Fairfax.

Married in this town Thursday last week by Rev. George Adie, Gen'l. Thomas Wheeler of Montgomery Co., Md. and Hester Ann McLeod of the city of N.Y.

Married on Thursday last week by Birkby, William Hamilton and Jane Dailey, both of this county.

Married Tuesday last by Birkby, Logan Osburn and Hannah Osburn, both of this county.

Married Wednesday last by Birkby, Jesse Sibbett and Hannah H. Cummings, both of Loudoun.

Vol. XVII, No. 34 – August 24, 1833

Married on the 13th inst. in Upperville, Fauquier Co., William R. Campbell, Esq. of Romney and Mrs. Jane Tapscott, 2nd daughter of William Naylor, Esq. of Romney.

Married on the 15th inst. by Birkby, Reuben Jenkins and Eleanor Ruter, both of Loudoun.

Died in King George Co., Va. on the 14th inst., Passed Midshipman William Fitzhugh Hooe, U.S. Navy.

Vol. XVII, No. 35 – August 31, 1833

Died on the 10th inst. at her residence nr Roseville, Muskingum Co., Ohio, Mrs. Keziah A. McCarty, consort of Mr. Richard C. McCarty, late of Loudoun Co. *Zanesville Gazette.*

Vol. XVII, No. 36 – September 7, 1833

Died in Shepherdstown Va. on Sunday the 25th ult., Mrs. Eliza Lee, wife of Edmund I. Lee Jr., Esq.

Died in this town Tuesday, September 3, Miss Nancy Jordan at advanced age.

Vol. XVII, No. 37 – September 14, 1833

Died at sea near Boston on the 20th ult., Alfred McFarland of this county in the 22nd year of his age.

Vol. XVII, No. 38 – September 21, 1833

Married on the 10th inst. at Christ Church, Winchester by Rev. J. E. Jackson, Rev. Chaplain S. Hedges of Wilmington, Delaware and Mary Robertson Lee of the former place.

Married on the 12th inst. in this town by Birkby, Lorenzo D. Nixon of Rockville Md. and Eliza A. Shaw of this place.

Married on the 12th inst. by Rev. Dr. Roberts, John Warner Niles, son of H. Niles, editor of the *Weekly Register*, and Alisana, daughter of Nixon Wilson, Esq., all of Baltimore.

Died at his residence in Rappahannock Co., Va. on the 31st ult., Dr. Aylett Hawes, age 65 years, 20 yr. in practice, 12 years served in general & state Legislature.

Died on the 5th inst. in Lexington, Ky., John Strother, late of Washington City, Hotel Proprietor.

Died at residence nr Urbana, Ohio on the 6th inst., Andrew Way, Esq., citizen of Washington DC.

Vol. XVII, No. 39 – September 28, 1833

Died in Georgetown, DC. on Sunday the 22nd inst., Stephen B. Balch, D.D., pastor of Presbyterian Church in that place in the 87th year of his age and for the last 55 years pastor of that church of which he also was the founder.

Vol. XVII, No. 40 – October 5, 1833

Married in Columbus, Ohio on the 3rd ult. by Rev. William Preston, Joseph C. Frye from Winchester and Eliza Sterling Wright.

Married on the 12th ult. by Rev. Mr. Gildea, Joseph Ott of Harper's Ferry and Ann Burke of Loudoun.

Married on Thursday the 19th ult. by Birkby, William Gardner of Fairfax and Ann Gover of this town.

Married Monday, the 23rd ult., by Birkby, Henry Oram and Jane Wise, both of this county.

Married Monday, the 23rd ult., by Birkby, Thomas Hogue and Mary Ann Simpson, both of this county.

Married Monday, the 23rd ult., by Birkby, James Skilman and Elizabeth Carter, both of this county.

Died in Washington City on the 23rd ult., Col. John Stanard of Fredericksburg, former Army U.S., lately marshall of the chancery court for the Fredericksburg district.

Died on the 24th ult., Mrs. Anne Maria T. Washington, age 43 years, wife of Bushrod C. Washington, Esq. of Jefferson Co. Va.

Died at Sully, Fairfax Co., on Wednesday, September 25, Mrs. Winifred Brent, consort of William Brent, Richland Co. Stafford, daughter of Col. Thomas Ludwell Lee of Loudoun.

Vol. XVII, No. 41 – October 12, 1833

Married in Boydville on Thursday the 26th ult., by Rev. Mr. Brown, Charles William Faulkner, Esq., atty-at-law, and Mary Waggener Boyd, youngest daughter of Gen. Elisha Boyd, all of Berkeley Co., Va.

Vol. XVII, No. 43 – October 26, 1833

Married Thursday the 17th inst. by Birkby, James Hogue and Miss Phila Holmes, both of Loudoun.

Died in Philadelphia on September 5, Thomas Hagarty, recently a resident of this town.

Died in New Orleans on Thursday the 3rd inst. from prevailing epidemic, Henry Pittman, painter native Alexandria, DC., formerly editor of the *Herald.*

Died in New Orleans on Thursday the 3rd inst., Miss Ann Marks Lewis, daughter of Charles L. Lewis of Albemarle Co., Va., niece of late Pres. Jefferson.

Died in Hillsborough on Tuesday the 8th inst., Mrs. Sarah White, consort of the late Josiah White dec'd in her 52nd year.

Died in Dranesville, Fairfax Co. on Friday the 18th inst., Mrs. Elizabeth Whitehouse, consort of Walter E. Whitehouse, daughter of Nicholas Farr, in her 18th year, left husband, no children.

Died Sunday last near town, John N. Cranwell, about 21 years old.

Vol. XVII, No. 44 – November 2, 1833

Died in Philadelphia on September 5, Thomas Hagerty, resident of this town 43 years, native of Sligo in the west of Ireland. Attended Trinity College, Dublin, taught many abroad and here. Principal of the Leesburg Academy. Left "widow and orphan son are left among us."

Vol. XVII, No. 45 – November 9, 1833

Married Thursday the 24th ult. by Birkby, Middleton Smith and Clarissa Towner of this town.

Married Thursday the 7th inst. by Birkby, Craven Howell and Amy McKnight, both of Loudoun.

Vol. XVII, No. 46 – November 16, 1833

Married the 31st ult. by Gilmore, George Barr and Mary Coe, both of this county.

Died Tuesday last the 5th inst. at father's residence, Robert I. Taylor Jr., 19 year old son of Robert I. Taylor, Esq. of this place, gunshot accident when grounded loaded gun. *Alexandria Gazette.*

Vol. XVII, No. 47 – November 23, 1833

Married Fredericktown, Md. on Tuesday the 12th inst. by Rev. Mr. Johns, Joseph Mead and Jane, daughter of late John Worsley.

Married on Tuesday the 12th inst. by Rev. Mr. Hargrove, Capt. Gabriel Vandeventer and Mary Eleanor Braden, eldest daughter of John Braden, Esq., all of this county.

Died on Saturday last, Micheal Shryock, in 95th year, 60 year resident of Loudoun.

Vol. XVII, No. 48 – November 30, 1833

Married the 21st inst. by Rev. Geo. Adie, Dr. Henry Magill of Frederick Co. and Ann Elizabeth C. Mason, eldest daughter of Wm. T. T. Mason, Esq. of this town.

Married week before last in Shennandoah Co. Va., Daniel Frye, aged about 70 years, and Nancy Roundtree. *Woodstock Sentinel.*

Died Monday morning last at residence of William Grantham of this county, Rev. Seely Bunn of M. E. Church, from severe injuries in gig accident. He was from Charlestown and buried there. Career started at 19, 40 years served in church, both Charlestown and frontier. *Charlestown Free Press*, November 21st.

Vol. XVII, No. 49 – December 7, 1833
Died Thursday the 26th ult. at his seat in Fauquier Co., John Marshall, Esq., aged about 35 years, third son of the Chief Justice of the U.S.

Vol. XVII, No. 51 – December 21, 1833
Died in Baltimore on the 13th inst., Mrs. Mary Dawes, age 93 years.

Vol. XVII, No. 52 – December 28, 1833
Married Tuesday last by Gilmore, Francis Protzman of Washington Co., Md. and Mary Connor of this county.
Died on the 21st ult., Thomas Taylor Sr., 60 years of age, resident of this county many years.

Vol. XVIII, No. 1 – January 4, 1834
Died in Middleburg on Thursday the 26th ult., Mrs. Jane E. McVeigh, consort of Hiram McVeigh, in her 32nd year. Leaves husband and six children.

Vol. XVIII, No. 2 – January 11, 1834
Married in Washington City on the 31st ult. by Rev. J. J. Ungern, Peter Clair, an old Rev. soldier aged about 78 years, and Mrs. Catharine West of Alexandria, age 45 years.

Vol. XVIII, No. 3 – January 18, 1834
Married at the meadows near Winchester, Va. on Thursday the 2nd inst. by Rev. E. Jackson, Col. Thomas G. Gordon of Tallahassee, Fl and Miss Frances E. Magill, youngest daughter of late Col. Charles Magill of Winchester.

Vol. XVIII, No. 4 – January 25, 1834
Married on Tuesday last by Birkby, John Widdicome and Louisa E. Tavenner, both of this county.

Vol. XVIII, No. 5 – February 1, 1834
Married Thursday the 16th ult. by Gilmore, Benjamin Melvin of Jefferson Co., Va. and Isabella Cockrel of Loudoun.
Died in Alexandria, DC., on the 21st ult., Jonah Thompson, in his 77th years, active merchant of Alexandria.
Died at residence in county on the 24th ult., Major Gustavus Elgin, in 80th year of age, gallant officer of revolution.

Vol. XVIII, No. 6 – February 8, 1834
Married on the 14th ult. by Rev. Hargrove, Thomas K. Humphreys of Jefferson Co. and Helen A., daughter of Presley Cordell, Esq. of this town.
Married on Thursday the 30th ult. by Rev. Dr. Dorsey, Noble S. Braden, Esq. of Harper's Ferry and Mary Ann Pusey, daughter of Mr. Joshua Pusey, of Loudoun.
Married on Thursday the 30th ult. by Birkby, Robert J. C. Thompson and Eliza Stedman, both of this town.
Married on Thursday the 30th ult., William F. Carter and Sarah Brown, both of Loudoun.

Died in Albemarle on the 23rd ult., James M. Randolph, 2nd son of late Thomas Mann Randolph, grandson of Mr. Thos. Jefferson.

Died in town on the 31st ult., infant daughter of Thomas Rogers, age 2 years, scalded by overturned teapot, died from complications.

Died on the 31st ult., Mrs. Nancy Rogers of Prince Wm., daughter of Walter Elgin of this county.

Died in Georgetown, DC. on the 2nd inst., celebrated itinerant preacher Lorenzo Dow in the 51st year of his age.

Vol. XVIII, No. 8 – February 22, 1834

Married Thursday the 6th inst. by Rev. Mr. Adie, Henry T. Harrison of this town and Elizabeth Lee of Fairfax Co., Va.

Married the 12th inst. at Clermont, residence of Edward Hall by Rev. Furlong, John Armistead Carter of town and Richardetta Louisa, daughter of late Richard DeButts.

Married Thursday last by Adie, Archibald Henderson of Fairfax Co. and Henrietta, daughter of John Gray of this town.

Married Thursday last by Rev. Levi Reese, James I. Major and Elizabeth B. Crook, all of Alexandria, DC.

Vol. XVIII, No. 9 – March 1, 1834

Married on Thursday, February 6, by Gilmore, David Brown and Kizziah Wiley, both of Loudoun.

Married Thursday, February 20, Uriel Triplett of Fauquier and Sarah Ann Fred of this county.

Died at residence in Washington on Monday last the 24th ult., Col. Henry Ashton, late marshall of DC.

Vol. XVIII, No. 10 – March 8, 1834

Died Tuesday the 18th ult. in Hartford, Conn, Rev. William C. Walton, former pastor of Presbyterian Church in Alexandria.

Vol. XVIII, No. 11 – March 15, 1834

Married in Upperville, Va. on Thursday the 6th inst. by Rev. Henry Slicer, John B. Kerfoot and Mary F. Armistead, eldest daughter of Maj. J. B. Armistead of Fauquier Co.

Vol. XVIII, No. 12 – March 22, 1834

Married Tuesday last by Birkby, Samuel G. Elgin of Loudoun and Susannah Wirts of Md.

Married Tuesday last by Birkby, George W. Mock and Mary Ann Russell, all of this county.

Vol. XVIII, No. 13 – March 29, 1834

Married on the 13th inst. by Gilmore, Joseph Garrett and Elizabeth Harden, both of this county.

Married on the 20th inst. by Gilmore, John Lee and Jane Cecelia Beaumont, both of this county.

Married on the 20th inst. by Gilmore, Samuel Russer and Nancy Turner, all of this county.

Married on the 20th inst. by Gilmore, Simon Mathews and Susanna Fritz, both of this county.

Married in Washington City on the 20th inst. by Rev. T. J. Brooke of Georgetown,
   Capt. Samuel Dawson of Loudoun and Sarah Ann Bayne of Accomac Co.,
   Va.
Married Tuesday last, A. G. Smith of Middleburg and Ann Johnson of this town.

Vol. XVIII, No. 14 – April 5, 1834
Married in Richmond on the 23rd ult. at residence of Gov. Floyd by Rev. Mr.
   O'Brian, Robert B. Randolph, Esq., late U. S. Navy, and Eglantine Beverley
   of Alexandria.

Vol. XVIII, No. 15 – April 12, 1834
Married Tuesday the 8th inst. by Birkby, Curtis R. Saunders of this vicinity and
   Edith Saunders of this town.
Married Wednesday the 9th inst. by Gilmore, John Stevens of Frederick Co. and
   Nancy Steel of Loudoun.
Married Thursday last the 10th inst. by Birkby, Samuel Smith and Hannah L.
   Danniel, all of this county.
Died Sunday, March 30 at Clifton his residence in Loudoun, Joseph Lewis, Esq.,
   aged 62 years, for many years representative in congress from district of
   Loudoun, Fairfax & Prince William.

Vol. XVIII, No. 16 – April 19, 1834
Died on the 29th ult., Miss Eveline Douglas, age 16 years.
Died on the 11th inst., Mrs. Elizabeth Wherry, resident of this town, in 66th year of
   age.
Died on the 14th inst., Hon. Littleton P. Denis, Representative in Congress State
   of Maryland.

Vol. XVIII, No. 17 – April 26, 1834
Died at residence of his father near town on the 19th inst., Thomas Allnut, age 22
   years, cut knee with axe.

Vol. XVIII, No. 19 – May 10, 1834
Married Tuesday last, Wm. Ball of Fairfax and Dorothy McCabe of this town.
Died on the 1st inst. a few miles from Leesburg, Peter Oatyar, age 82 years 9
   months, born New Jersey Aug 1, 1751, soon after marriage removed to this
   county in abject poverty but through industry died in possession of 3000
   acres in Loudoun, much other property and large sums of cash on interest.
   Baptised at 80 years, 3 year member Baptist Church. Widower three years
   plus left offspring up to 4th generation.

Vol. XVIII, No. 20 – May 17, 1834
Married in Greenville, Prince William Co., the 6th inst. by Rev. John Knox, Dr.
   Francis M. Weems and Fanny Elizabeth, daughter of James B. Ewell, Esq.
Died at his residence near Leesburg on the 8th inst., Fayette Ball in 43rd year.

Vol. XVIII, No. 21 – May 24, 1834
Married the 5th inst. by Rev. John S. Lea, Elder William Hill, age 77, and Susan
   Lewis, age 36, all of Prince Edward Co.
Married on the 15th inst. at Mt. Vernon by the Rev. R. Lippett, Dr. William
   Fontaine Alexander of Alexandria and Anna Maria Blackburne Washington,
   daughter of the late John Washington, Esq. of Mt. Vernon.

Vol. XVIII, No. 22 – May 31, 1834

Married in Zanesville, Ohio on 1st inst. by Rev. George C. Sedwick, Robert S. Anderson and Mary C. Hains, both recently of Loudoun.

Married Thursday the 8th inst. by Birkby, James Adams and Jane S. Crawell [Cranwell], both of Loudoun.

Married the 29th inst. by Rev. Wyatt, Thomas Swann Jr., of City of Washington, and Elizabeth Gilmore, daughter of the late John Sherlock, of Baltimore.

Married Thursday last week by Birkby, Horace W. Dowden of Montgomery Co., Md. and Eleanora Smallwood of this town.

Married Thursday last week by Birkby, Craven O. Van Horne and Mary Emberson, both of Leesburg.

Died Monday the 19th inst. in 43rd year, Mrs. Castiliana Griggs, wife of Thomas Griggs of Charlestown, Va., daughter of late David Lacey of Loudoun Co.

Vol. XVIII, No. 23 – June 7, 1834

Married Tuesday the 20th ult. by Rev. Wm. Monroe, George W. Shutt and Eliza S. Bennett, all of Shepherdstown, Va.

Died in this town on Monday last in 3rd year of age, Carolina Eliza, daughter of Samuel M. and Elizabeth Boss.

Vol. XVIII, No. 24 – June 14, 1834

Died Monday last, aged c. 37 years, Samuel Sterrett, apothecary and druggist of this town.

Vol. XVIII, No. 25 – June 21, 1834

Married Tuesday the 17th inst. by Rev. Dorsey, Henry A. Ball and Elizabeth A. Thrift, all of Loudoun Co.

Married Thursday last by Birkby, Nimrod Clasby [*sic*] and Mary Oram, all of Loudoun.

Died Friday last week at residence in vicinity of Leesburg, Capt. Isaac Vandeventer, about 60 years old, long time resident of this county.

Vol. XVIII, No. 26 – June 28, 1834

Married at Llangollen on Tuesday the 17th inst. by Rev. Adie, Dr. Francis Grady and Jane Serene, daughter of Cuthbert Powell, all of Loudoun.

Married in Aldie on Thursday the 19th inst. by Rev. Furlong, Thomas S. Hall, Esq. of Middleburg and Angelina King, daughter of late David Boyle, Esq. of Dumfries, Va.

Vol. XVIII, No. 28 – July 12, 1834

Died on Saturday evening last in attempting to ford Goose Creek, Archibald Henderson, Esq. of Fairfax, son of Richard H. Henderson, Esq. of this town. Buried Epis. Burial Ground. Age 23 years, left widow and parents, brothers and sisters.

Vol. XVIII, No. 29 – July 19, 1834

Married the 16th ult. by Rev. Adie, Samuel Britenbaugh of Harper's Ferry and Maria L. Kline, daughter of Nicholas Kline of Leesburg.

Died on the 4th inst. at Glenora in his 18th year, Thomas Lloyd, eldest son of Col. Lloyd Noland, at Alexandria Boarding School under direction of Mr. Hallowell.

Vol. XVIII, No. 30 – July 26, 1834

Died in Middleburg on the 19th inst. at residence of his aunt Mrs. Jane Love, Peyton Noland, 12 year old only son of Samuel Noland. Mentions 3 cousins, temporarily withdrawn from boarding school by father and guardian Col. Lloyd Noland.

Vol. XVIII, No. 31 – August 2, 1834

Married in Providence, R.I. on 7th ult. by Rev. Dr. Crocker, Joseph T. Daughterty, Esq., attorney of Charlestown, Jefferson Co., Va., and Emily Matilda, youngest daughter of Alexander Jones, Esq. of Providence.

Vol. XVIII, No. 32 – August 9, 1834

Married at Providence, Fairfax, Va., on Thursday, July 31 by Rev. Parkinson, Spencer Jackson and Mary Annett Richardson, both of Fairfax.
Died Saturday last, John B. Rattie, aged upwards of 60 years, long time resident of this town.
Died Monday last, Elijah Brookes, about 65 years.

Vol. XVIII, No. 33 – August 16, 1834

Died in Waterford on the 31st ult., Mrs. Julia Ann, consort of John A. Moore.
Died Monday last at Fairfax Count House, Thomas W. Hewitt, Esq. of Alexandria.
Died Wednesday in vicinity of town, James Thomas, aged about 45 years.

Vol. XVIII, No. 34 – August 23, 1834

Married August 7 at residence of Sydnor Bailey, Esq. of Loudoun by Rev. George Adie, John M. Harrison, Esq. and Susan Bailey.
Married August 13 in Warrenton, Va. by Rev. George Lemmon, Temple M. Washington and Mrs. Mary D. Horner.
Died on the 1st inst. at residence near Lynchburg, Rev. Stith Mead of the M.E. Church, age 68 years, leaving widow and seven children.

Vol. XVIII, No. 35 – August 30, 1834

Married on the 5th inst. by Rev. George M. Frye, John A. Washington and Elizabeth Ann George, all of Loudoun Co.
Married on the 14th inst. by Rev. S. Tuston, William S. Daniel, Esq., attorney at law of Fairfax Co., and Catharine G. D. Hurst, daughter of John Hurst of Jefferson Co., Va.
Married at Hookstown, Baltimore Co. on Thursday the 14th inst. by Rev. Smith, John L. Barry of Baltimore and Mary H, daughter of Rev. James H. Hanson of Georgetown, DC.
Married Tuesday the 19th inst. by Rev. S. Tustin, William D. Beall, Esq. of Georgetown, DC. and Jane Holmes, daughter of Jane Holmes the daughter of Matthew Frame of Charlestown, Va.
Died on Thursday the 7th inst. at Harper's Ferry, Mrs. Ann Wintersmith, wife of Charles G. Wintersmith, daughter of late Robert Gallaher of Martinsburg, Va.
Died on the 15th inst. at residence of son John Jamison in Martinsburg, Mrs. Mary Jamison, age 74 years, relict of Leonard Jamison, Esq. late of Frederick Co., Md.
Died at Gunston, Fairfax Co., on Thursday the 21st inst., George Mason, Esq. of that place.
Died Saturday last at her residence in Loudoun, Mrs. Sarah Saunders, relict of Presley Saunders dec'd, in 78th year of age.

Died Sunday last at his residence in county, Johnson Cleaveland, Esq., aged about 64 years, many years a magistrate of Loudoun.

Vol. XVIII, No. 36 – September 6, 1834

Married in Prince George Co., Md. on Tuesday the 19th ult. by Rev. Francis Henson, Isaac Chapline of Jefferson Co. and Judith S. Latimer, formerly of this place.

Married Thursday the 21st ult. by Rev. S. Tustin, Hamilton Lay and Lydia Mary Deakins, all of Jefferson Co.

Married Sunday eve the 24th ult. by Rev. S. Tustin, Henry Lenhort and Mrs. Sarah B. Myers, both of Harper's Ferry.

Married Tuesday the 26th ult. by Rev. Alex Jones, John H. Little and Margaret F. Hammond, daughter of late Thomas R. Hammond, all of Jefferson Co.

Died at his residence in Accomack Co., Va., on the 11th ult. in his 80th year, Capt. Samuel Waples, native of Sussex Co., Delaware. Capt. Waples entered army of U.S., in the Revolutionary War as a Lt. in the 9th Va. Regt. and marched from Accomack County in late 1776. At Brandywine and Germantown, taken prisoner 1st year, confined at Philadelphia, escaped disguised as Quaker. Secreted by a widow Jones with whom he boarded as apprentice prior to war. Reached Valley Forge and there sent home on recruiting service, served out war. After war settled in Accomack County and lived to a good old age.

Died __ in Augusta Co., Va., in 7th year, Elizabeth, daughter of Rev. Francis McFarland, granddaughter of Lemuel Bent, Esq. of Winchester, Va.

Died on Monday the 1st inst., Laban Lodge, aged 34 years. "On his way from the camp meeting in the German Settlement, to a friend's house, horse bolted and threw him against a tree causing severe head wound. Taken to house of David Copeland and died 9 hours after incident. Left mother."

Vol. XVIII, No. 37 – September 13, 1834

Married Tuesday, September 2 in Pleasant Valley, Fauquier Co., Va. by Rev. John Ogilvie, Dr. J. Willet Leach and Jane R., daughter of Major Charles Hunton, all of Fauquier Co.

Died on the 22nd ult., Marguerite Chichester, consort of George Chichester, Esq. of Fairfax Co. and youngest daughter of Dr. Valentine Peyton, late Stafford Co., in 37th year of age. Left husband and four young children.

Died Thursday, August 28, Mrs. Elizabeth Newton, 72 year old widow of Ignatious Newton, who died 3rd September 1833. They were married 8 September 1777 and lived together nearly 56 years.

Died on Saturday the 6th at Waterford, Daniel W. Thomas in the 74th year, formerly of Winchester, Va. and late of Fredericktown, Md. Member of M. E. Church, husband and father of 11 children.

Vol. XVIII, No. 38 – September 20, 1834

Married Thursday the 11th inst. at 1st Presbyterian Church in Baltimore by Rev. Nevus, Fleming H. Hixon of Leesburg and Elizabeth W. Braden, daughter of late Major Braden of Loudoun.

Married at same time and same place, Willis L. Williams, Esq. of Tennessee and Sarah M., youngest daughter of Thomas Phillips of Waterford, Loudoun Co.

Married Brooklyn, Connecticut, Mr. William Lloyd Garrison, Editor of *Boston Liberator*, and Miss Helen Eliza Benson [a white woman.]

<u>Vol. XVIII, No. 39 – September 27, 1834</u>

Married in Washington City on Thursday the 18th inst. by Rev. S. Bryson,
 Stephen W. McCarty and Elizabeth Ann Francis, only daughter of Enoch
 Francis of Loudoun Co.

Died at Palestine, Crawford Co., Illinois on Friday, August 29, Dr. Richard H.
 Mauzy, formerly of Culpeper Co. Va.

Died at Stafford Co., Va. on the 11th inst., Capt. William Ford, age 46 years,
 officer in late war and aide to Gen. Porter, represented his county in
 legislature.

Died at residence of Mordecai Throckmorton, Esq. in Loudoun on Friday the 12th
 inst., Mrs. Maria M. G. Hooe, wife of John Hooe Jr., Esq. of Locust Grove,
 Prince Wm. Co., only daughter of late Robert Gaines Beverly of King George
 Co.

Died Friday the 12th inst. in Georgetown, DC., Zachariah Smart, elderly stroke.

Died in Alexandria, DC. on the 20th inst., Joshua Yeaton, merchant there.

Died on the 4th inst. at residence near Leesburg, Robert Wade, in 73rd year. "He
 was a soldier of the revolution," elder of Presbyterian Church in Leesburg.

<u>Vol. XVIII, No. 40 – October 4, 1834</u>

Married in Warrenton, Va. on the 17th ult. by Rev. Geo. Lemmon, Richard Payne,
 Esq. and Alice Dixon, daughter of late Turner Dixon, both of Warrenton.

Married Tuesday, September 23, by Rev. Mr. Broadus, William H. Rogers and
 Mary Jane, daughter of Hugh Rogers, Esq., all of Middleburg.

Married Thursday, September 18, Henry F. Schenk of Jefferson Co. and Mrs.
 Agnes E. Dowell, daughter of late Sylvester Welsh, Esq., of Fauquier Co.

Died at residence of son-in-law E. W. Coleman of Loudoun Co. on the 4th ult.,
 Mrs. Ann Wilson of Georgetown, DC., in her 66th year.

Died in town on the 23rd ult., Alvin Summerfield, infant son of James Brady.

Died in town on the 25th ult., Sally Ann, infant daughter of William Torreyson.

<u>Vol. XVIII, No. 41 – October 11, 1834</u>

Married on the 25th ult. by Rev. Mr. Kalbfus, Robert S. Ashby, Esq. and Lucy S.
 Ashby, both of Fauquier Co. Va.

Died in Covington, Ky in hotel of E. Garnett on the 15th ult., Elias Bowman, aged
 about 40 years. No papers but by conv. understood he claimed a wife and
 son in Loudoun Co., had been engaged in or about Nashville and
 Plaquemine, Louisana and referred to a Mr. Foster or Dr. Dickenson and that
 he was worth about $20,000, left in possession of Mr. Garnett between 6-7
 hundred dollars, and a valuable gold watch. Was attended by Dr. Drake of
 Cincinnati.

<u>Vol. XVIII, No. 42 – October 18, 1834</u>

Married at Christ's Church in Winchester on Tuesday the 7th inst. by Rev. J. E.
 Jackson, E. C. Breedin, Esq. and Lucy P., daughter of late Gen. James
 Singleton.

Married on Tuesday the 7th inst. in Alexandria by Rev. Elias Henderson, Hon.
 William B. Shepard of N.C. and Charlotte Casanove, daughter of A. C.
 Cazanove, Esq. of Alexandria.

Married in Philadelphia on the 9th inst. by Rev. H. J. Morton, Samuel B. Larmour
 of Alexandria, DC. and Anna, daughter of John Worrall, formerly of Penn.

Married Tuesday last in Waterford by Elder Trott, George L. Moore and Ann
 Amanda Russell, both of Loudoun.

Died at residence near Fairfax Court House on September 29, Doct. William Gunnell, in 49th year of his age.

Died in Shepherdstown, Va. on the 1st inst., James Forman of Berkeley.

Died at residence in county on Monday last, Jesse Oxley, many years resident of Loudoun, from injuries sustained from a free mulatto man about a week or 10 days prior to his decease.

Vol. XVIII, No. 43 – October 25, 1834

Married in Funkstown, Md. on the 16th inst. by Rev. Baker, David Miller and Margaret S. Cridler, both of this town.

Died in Bladensburg on the 9th inst., Alexander Evans, age 56 years.

Died on Monday the 20th inst., Byran Hampson in his 77th year, merchant of Alexandria, DC.

Died on the 4th ult., Mrs. Ann Brown, age 64 years, wife of John Brown, Esq. of Loudoun.

Died on the 4th inst., Joshua B. Overfield of Loudoun, about 25 years old.

Vol. XVIII, No. 44 – November 1, 1834

Died on Saturday the 18th ult., Mrs. Sarah Nixon, wife of James Nixon of Shepherdstown, in her 84th year.

Died on the 16th ult., John Brown Jr. of Loudoun, aged about 25 years.

Vol. XVIII, No. 45 – November 8, 1834

Married on Thursday the 30th ult. by Rev. Smith, John S. Horner, Esq. of Va. and Miss H. L. Watson, daughter of late James Watson, Esq. of Washington City.

Married Tuesday the 28th ult. in Albemarle Co. by The Rev. Wadsworth at residence of William L. Craven, Samuel Sinclair and Euphemia H. Craven, both of Loudoun.

Married here on the 28th ult., Samuel Jackson and Margaret Donohoe.

Married in Fairfax Co. on Thursday the 30th ult. by Rev. Professor Lippitt, Rev. William Johnson of Beaufort, S.C. and Flora Love, eldest daughter of Richard H. Love, Esq. of Leesburg.

Married Sunday last by Birkby, Miller Downing and Sarah G. Mount, both of this county.

Married Thursday last by Birkby, Samuel T. Canby and Julietta Cookus, both of this county.

Died in Alexandria, DC. on Saturday the 25th ult., Charles T. Chapman, aged 58 years.

Died on Sunday the 19th ult. at Winsor Mills in Middleburg, Loudoun Co., Mrs. Gwen Handey, age 75 years.

Died Thursday the 29th ult., Bernard Hough, long time resident of Leesburg.

Died Sunday last, Mrs. Mary Norris, consort of Ignatius Norris.

Vol. XVIII, No. 46 – November 15, 1834

Married in Washington on Thursday the 23rd ult. by Rev. Mr. Sergeant, Legran I. Luckett, printer, and Minerva T. Downer, daughter of Joel Downer, formerly of Charlestown, Jefferson Co., Va.

Married Thursday the 23rd ult. by Rev. Alex Jones, Madison Odies and Eliza Ann Hall, daughter of the late Levi Hall of Harper's Ferry.

Married Thursday the 30th ult. by Rev. Dan'l. J. Hauer, Daniel Deaver and Catharine Kitchie [*sic*, Ritchie], both of this county.

Married on the 5th inst. by Rev. Walls, John Davenport, Esq., atty at law of
   Charlestown, Jefferson Co., Va., and Elizabeth Catharine Heaton, daughter
   of Col. Geo. Orrick [*sic*] of Winchester.
Died on the 24th ult., Mrs. Eliza Maria Selden, consort of William Selden and only
   child of Dr. John T. Swann of Richmond.
Died on Sunday the 26th ult. near Petersville, Alexius Boone of Frederick Co.
   Md., in 28th year.
Died on Tuesday the 28th ult., Stuart Gaither, late merchant of Frederick Co. Md.,
   age 44 years.
Died at his residence in Union, Loudoun Co., on Wednesday evening, October
   29th, Isaac Brown Sr, in the 73rd year of his age after a short but agonizing
   illness.

Vol. XVIII, No. 47 – November 22, 1834
Married at Friends Meeting House on Courtland St, Baltimore on the 7th inst.,
   Andrew Scholfield and Catha. Wilson of Alexandria, DC.
Died on the 8th inst., Mrs. Mary Carbery, consort of Capt. Thomas Carbery of
   Washington.
Died in Georgetown, DC. on the 17th, Bvt. Brig. Gen. James House, Col. 1st U.S.
   Military.

Vol. XVIII, No. 48 – November 29, 1834
Married in Georgetown, DC. on Tuesday the 18th inst. by Rev. Hanson, William
   Davies of Alexandria and Amelia Virginia, youngest daughter of late Rev.
   Zebulon Kankey of Pr. Wm. Co., Va.
Married Thursday the 20th inst. by Birkby, Samuel B. Taylor and Sarah E. Hogue,
   both of Loudoun.
Married Thursday last by Birkby, Benjamin Saunders and Mary Catharine Blaker,
   both of Loudoun.
Married Thursday last by Birkby, Elam C. Veale and Mary E. Hough, all of
   Loudoun.
Married Thursday last by Birkby, Bernard R. Atwell and Jane A. Hammerly, both
   here.

Vol. XVIII, No. 51 – December 20, 1834
Married Thursday the 27th ult. by Rev. J. H. Jones, Joseph C. Offutt and Letha M.
   Clagett, all of Montgomery Co. Md.
Married Thursday the 27th ult., Cephas Hempstone of Montgomery Co., Md. and
   Mary E. Belt of Loudoun.
Married Thursday the 11th inst. by Birkby, John Orrison and Sarah Sherb, both of
   Loudoun.
Married Saturday the 13th by Birkby, Absolam Beans and Maria Goodin, both of
   Loudoun.
Married Thursday last by Birkby, Nelson Fisher and Mahuldah Brooks, both of
   Loudoun.
Died Thursday the 13th ult., Lavinia, age 13 years. Died Saturday the 15th ult.,
   Penelope, age 15 years. Died Monday the 17th ult., Churchill, age 18 years.
   Children of Richard Rixey, of Fauquier Co.
Died Monday the 8th inst. at residence of Andrew Hunter of Charlestown, Mrs.
   Mary Stubblefield, age 55 years, consort of Col. James Stubblefield of
   Winchester.

Vol. XVIII, No. 52 – December 27, 1834

Married Tuesday even the 16th inst. by Rev. Dan'l Hauer, Seth D. Robinson and Christiana Mason, all of this county.

Married on Thursday the 18th, Leonard Frye and Susanna, daughter of Jacob Spring of this county.

Vol. XIX, No. 1 – January 3, 1835

Married Sunday the 21st ult. by Rev. Daniel I. Hauer, Josiah Ullum and Elizabeth, daughter of Jacob Waters, Esq., all of Loudoun.

Married in Philadelphia on Wednesday the 24th ult. by Rev. Mr. Coskrey, Edward L. Fant of Fairfax Co. and Mary A. R. McQuinn of Baltimore.

Died on Friday the 12th ult., Dr. John Briscoe of Shepherdstown, Va., age 46 years.

Died on Sunday the 21st ult. in Washington Co. Md., Mrs. Susannah McLaughlin, age 92 years, left 8 children, 52 grandchildren and 58 great-grandchildren.

Died at residence here Tuesday last, Caleb C. Sutherland, aged about 30 years.

Vol. XIX, No. 2 – January 10, 1835

Married Monday the 15th ult. by Rev. Dr. McNeill, David Swively, Esq. and Catharine Arts, all of Shepherdstown.

Married at Woodbury residence of Hon. Henry St. George Tucker on Thursday the 18th ult. by Rev. Sept. Tuston, John T. Cookus of Shepherdstown and Sophia Abert [*sic*] of Jefferson Co.

Married the 23rd ult. by Rev. John P. Daggy, Jacob Clayton Jr. of Pendleton Co. and Marianne, only daughter of Mr. M. Hartman of Loudoun.

Married Thursday the 25th ult. at residence of Mrs. Jenna Arundell by Rev. C. Parkinson, John H. Gossom and Mary Ann Bradley, all of Fairfax Co.

Married Thursday the 1st inst. by Gilmore, Caleb Aduddell [*sic*] of Ohio and Ann Wilson of this county.

Married Thursday the 1st inst. by Gilmore, Moses Thomas of Fairfax and Ann Fox of this county.

Died Wednesday the 10th ult., Jacob H. Manning of Jefferson Co., Va., age 23 years.

Died at his residence in Pr. Wm. Co. on the 24th ult., Mr. William Ashmore, age 82 years.

Died Sunday the 28th ult., Henry Krebs, longtime resident of Fredericksburg, formerly of Leesburg.

Died New Years day at his residence in this county, Peter Benedum in 83rd years, member M. E. Church, buried Methodist Church yard by Rev. Dorsey.

Vol. XIX, No. 3 – January 17, 1835

Married at Stoney Point near Hillsborough on Tuesday the 30th ult. by Rev. Wickes, Hiram McVeigh, merchant of Middleburg, and Mary Elizabeth McIlhaney, daughter of John White, Esq.

Married at Mt. Airy near Middleburg on Tuesday the 1st inst. by Rev. Kalbfus, Joshua Gibson of Upperville and Mary Ann McVeigh, daughter of Jesse McVeigh, Esq.

Married Thursday the 8th inst. at residence of Benjamin Cross by Rev. C. Parkinson, Enoch Money and Nancy Cross, all of Fairfax.

Married Thursday the 8th inst. by Rev. Charles B. Kalbfus, Dr. David H. Lovett and Jane L., daughter of Rev. Dr. John C. Green, all of this county.

Vol. XIX, No. 4 – January 24, 1835

Married Thursday the 15th inst. at house of Mrs. Arundell by Rev. C. Parkison, Addison Keene and Elizabeth Arundell, all of Fairfax.

Married Thursday the 15th at house of Mrs. Arundell, George Fugitt of Loudoun and Catharine Arundell of Fairfax, third union by same family since Xmas.

Died at home of father in Harrisonburg, Rockingham Co., Va. on Monday the 12th inst., John W. Gray in his 18th year.

Died on the 14th inst., Mrs. Harriet Lewis, about 35 years old, consort of Daniel Lewis of here.

Died Wednesday last at residence here, Mrs. Lucy Cartlich, age 78 years.

Died Friday the 9th inst. at residence near Woodgrove, James Best, age 94 years, member of M. E. Church 50 years or more, 11 years crippled from stroke.

Vol. XIX, No. 5 – January 31, 1835

Married on the 25th ult. by J. Jackman, Esq. [*sic*] Thomas W. Collier, printer formerly of this town, and Eliza Barrett, all of Carroll Co., Ohio.

Married Thursday the 8th inst. by Rev. Thos. Buck, Major Byran H. Henry of Shennandoah and Sarah Ann Allen of Front Royal, Va.

Married Sunday the 18th inst. by Rev. Thos. Buck and Rev. Wm. Ryland, Henry G. Rind, editor of *Columbian Gazette*, Georgetown, and Rebecca Ann Rowzee of Fairfax Co.

Married Tuesday the 13th inst. by Rev. Dalvol, Bazil Spaulding of Pleasant Hill, Charles Co. Md. and Charity Ann Jenkins, daughter of late Edward Jenkins of Baltimore.

Married on the 21st inst. by Rev. S. Tustin, Joseph Nichols of Loudoun and Mary Ann McPherson, youngest daughter of Daniel McPherson, all of Jefferson Co., Va.

Married Thursday at Episcopal Church by Rev. Adie, Bushrod C. Washington of Jefferson Co. and Maria P. Harrison of Loudoun.

Died at residence in Fairfax Co. on Wednesday the 21st, William Moss, Esq., in his 57th year, many years held office of Clerk of Superior &Inferior Courts.

Vol. XIX, No. 6 – February 7, 1835

Died Friday the 16th ult. at Oak Hill family residence in Fairfax Co., Benjamin F. Higgs, Esq.

Died in Fairfax Co. Va. on the 27th ult. by Mrs. L. Gunnell, wife of Col. George W. Gunnell, in her 34th year.

Vol. XIX, No. 7 – February 14, 1835

Married Thursday the 5th inst. by Rev. Mr. Dana, Sidney S. Lee, Esq. of the U.S.N. and Ann M. Mason, daughter of Gen. John Mason of Clermont, Fairfax Co.

Married Tuesday last by Birkby, Sanford Cockrell of Fairfax Co. and Nancy Shryock of Loudoun.

Died in Baltimore on Saturday the 7th inst., William Patterson, Esq., in his 83rd year.

Died in Woodgrove in Loudoun Co. on the 21st ult., Benjamin Frank, age 23 years, arrived there 27 December seeking employment as journeyman tailor in company with a young man of same profession. They obtained employee with Geo. W. Noland. Shortly became ill developed typhus fever, living till 21 January. Hailed from Breckenridge Co. Ky., had relatives, no parents living.

Vol. XIX, No. 8 – February 21, 1835

Married Tuesday the 8th inst. by Rev. Dan. I. Hauer, Clauson Bond and
Susannah C. Bowles, all of this county.

Married Thursday the 5th inst. by Rev. S. Tuston, Jas. Caten and Ann Lindsay,
both of Harper's Ferry.

Married Thursday the 5th inst. by Rev. Staley, John Russell and Jane Wade, all of
Shepherdstown, Va.

Died Monday last at age 43 years, John M. Broome, merchant of Winchester.

Vol. XIX, No. 9 – February 28, 1835

Married Thursday the 12th inst. by Rev. Nevins, George B. Stephenson of
Jefferson Co. and Augusta Virginia Levering, daughter of Nathan Levering of
Baltimore.

Married Thursday the 12th inst. by Gilmore, Benjamin Newman and Eliza
Newman, both of Loudoun.

Died at his farm in vicinity of Waterford on the 20th inst., Andrew Shankland
Anderson, of quinsy of most violent form.

Vol. XIX, No. 10 – March 7, 1835

Died at Warrenton on February 22, Nathaniel Tyler, Esq., formerly of Leesburg,
more recently member of bar of Fauquier Co., aged about 32 years. Court,
bar and citizens of Warrenton resolved to wear crepe on left arm for 30 days.

Died here Saturday the 28th ult., Major William B. Harrison, aged c. 76 years,
veteran of Revolutionary war, interred with military honors.

Died Sunday last, Jacob Hoffman of Raspberry Plain in vicinity, aged 70 years.
Former mayor of Alexandria, DC., removed to Loudoun Co. some 6 or 7
years since, interred in Baltimore.

Vol. XIX, No. 11 – March 14, 1835

Married Thursday the 5th inst. by Rev. Daniel I. Hauer, George Kabrick and Jane
Morrisson, both of this county.

Died near Hillsborough Saturday the 28th ult., Mrs. Rachel Janney, consort of
Capt. Mahlon Janney, member Methodist Episcopal Church.

Vol. XIX, No 12 – March 21, 1835

Married Thursday the 5th inst. by the Rev. Thomas Birkby, John Carruthers and
Malinda Elizabeth, daughter of Joel Nixon, all of this county.

Married Tuesday the 10th inst. by Rev. Evans, Colin Mortimer Cordell, formerly of
Leesburg, and Miranda, daughter of Jos. Crandall of Washington City.

Married Tuesday the 10th inst. by Rev. Post, Dr. A. H. Sanders of Occoquan, Pr.
William Co., and Ellen M. Moore, daughter of late Thomas Moore of
Alexandria, DC.

Died at Big Cacapon, Hampshire Co., Va. on the 24th ult., William Carlyle, age 96
years.

Died Saturday last at residence in vicinity, Dr. Wilson C. Seldon, "Rev. Patriot",
member of Protestant Episcopal Church.

Died Monday last, Elizabeth D., 8 year old daughter of Charles Shepherd of this
town.

Vol. XIX, No. 13 – March 28, 1835

Died, Nathaniel Tyler Esq. of Fairfax Co., resolves by bench and bar.

Died on the 14th inst. at Exeter, his residence near Leesburg, at age 74 years, Dr.
Wilson Cary Selden. Entered the Revolutionary War as surgeon under

auspices of brother-in-law Dr. McClurg Senr., at hospital at Hampton and
Cordonia Campaign captured by British on sea trip, imprisoned at Antigua.
Before war resided at Elizabeth City, Va.

Vol. XIX, No. 15 – April 11, 1835
Died here on Thursday last week, Miss Cassandra Hamilton.

Vol. XIX, No. 16 – April 18, 1835
Married Tuesday the 7th inst. by Birkby, Samuel Hough and Mary Smallwood,
both of Waterford.
Married Thursday last, Burr Piggot and Hannah J. Nichols, all of this county.

Vol. XIX, No. 17, April 25, 1835
Died in Washington the 17th inst., Isaac S. Craven, native of Loudoun Co. and
last 7 or 8 years a citizen of Washington. Left wife and two children.
Died on Friday the 17th inst. at Belmont, his late residence, in Loudoun, Benjamin
Grayson, in his 72nd year. Left a wife and large family.

Vol. XIX, No. 18, May 2, 1835
Married at Butler's Union Hotel in Washington City on Friday the 24th ult. by Rev.
Clarke, Charles W. Rose and Mrs. Ann Cox, both of Fredericksburg, Va.
Died on Saturday the 25th ult., George Holtzman, 60 year old long time residence
of Georgetown, DC.

Vol. XIX, No. 19, May 9, 1835
Married in Winchester on April 23rd by Rev. Alex Jones, Rev. William M. Jackson
and Mary H. Hopkins, daughter of the late John Hopkins, Esq. of Frederick
Co. Va.
Died of consumption in Raleigh, N.C. on Saturday the 25th ult., Jonathan P.
Cushing, President of Hampton Sidney College, Va.
Died on Sunday the 26th ult., Mrs. Timms, consort of Jesse Timms of this county.

Vol. XIX, No. 20 – May 16, 1835
Married in Crawfordia [sic] on Thursday the 30th ult. by Rev. S. Tuston, Nathanial
Greene North, one of the editors of the *Virginia Free Press*, and Mary Morrow
Worthington, daughter of Robert Worthington, Esq., all of Charlestown,
Jefferson Co., Va.
Married in Baltimore on May 1st by Rev. Henshaw, Sidney Smith Gallaher of
Charlestown, Va. and Jane Amanda Howard, great-granddaughter of the late
Samuel Howard of Jefferson Co.
Married on the 5th inst. at Oakhill, Montgomery Co., Md. by Rev. Gillis, James
Stephenson of Loudoun and Elizabeth C. Beall, daughter of late Major Lloyd
Beall of the U.S. Army.
Married on the 6th inst. by Rev. Drane, Samuel H. Williams and Mary E.
Marmaduke, all of Jefferson Co.
Married here on the 7th inst. by Rev. Geo. Adie, Dr. Francis W. Powell and
Harriet, daughter John I. Harding, Esq., merchant, all of this place.
Married in Fairfax Co. on the 7th inst. by Rev. Tippet, Dr. John Hunter of
Washington and Anna T. Dulany, daughter of Daniel F. Dulany, Esq. of
Fairfax Co.
Died at residence in Leon Co. near Tallahassee, Fla. on the 15th ult., Mrs. Mary
Elizabeth Cleland Eppes, wife of Francis Eppes, Esq., formerly of Virginia.

Died on Saturday the 2nd inst. at age 61 years, John Diffenderffer, merchant of Baltimore.

Died in Washington City on Wednesday the 6th inst., Thos. L. Martin, age 45 years, hatter, many years inhabitant of Alexandria.

Vol. XIX, No. 21 – May 23, 1835

Married Tuesday the 12th inst. by Rev. McGee, William Weber, editor of *Hagerstown Mail*, and Mary Philips of Frederick City, Md.

Married Tuesday the 12th inst. by Rev. Matthews and immediately after by Rev. Hawley, Wm. B. Hill of Prince Georges Co., Md. and Catharine B. Smith, daughter of Richard Smith, Esq. of Washington.

Married at Goose Creek Meeting house on last fifth day, Thomas Nichols and Nancy Dillon, youngest daughter of late Abdon Dillon.

Died on the 9th inst. at residence Vaucluse, Fairfax Co., Va., Albert Fairfax, age 34 years.

Died on the 15th inst. in Washington, Mrs. Anne Lucinda Jones, consort of Gen. Walter Jones.

Married at Cedar Grove (near Norfolk) on 13th inst. by Rev. Mr. Smith, Charles H. Poor, of U.S. Navy, to Mattie L., second daughter of Dr. Robert B. Stark.

Vol. XIX, No. 22 – May 30, 1835

Married on the 19th inst. by Rev. Swan, William J. Berry and Sarah Eliza, daughter of Thomas Clagett, all of Prince Georges Co., Md.

Married at Claren, Fairfax Co., on Thursday the 21st by Rev. E. R. Lippett, Rev. Charles C. Pinkney of S.C. and Nancy F. R. McKenna, daughter of James L. McKenna.

Vol. XIX, No. 23 – June 6, 1835

Died at Bloomsbury, Fauquier Co., at his residence on the 21st ult., William Steuart, age 74 years.

Died here Sunday last, William Leven Powell, age about 7 years, son of John Cridler.

Married in Marcellus, Onondaga Co., on 4th ult., Orlando Beach to Miss Julia Herring.

Vol. XIX, No. 24 – June 13, 1835

Married Thursday the 4th inst. by Rev. Daniel Hauer, Solomon Everhart and Mary Ann Wenner, daughter of William Wenner, all of this county.

Died on the 26th ult. at residence of his son, Col. Wm. C. Preston, of Columbia, S.C., General Francis Preston of Abington, Va., age 70 years.

Vol. XIX, No. 25 – June 20, 1835

Died at Annington, Montgomery Co. on the 10th ult., Mrs. Ann Belt, wife of Doct. S. H. C. White, in 31st year.

Died Tuesday, June 2, at residence near Georgetown, Col. Edmund Brook, age 74 years, one of the surviving officers of the revolutionary army, interred at Snow Hill, Prince William Co. Va.

At West Point on 9th inst. by Rev. Wm. Jackson of New York, Lt. Francis H. Smith and Sarah [Henderson], Lt. Seth Eastman to Mary [Henderson], daughters of Dr. Thomas Henderson of U.S. Army.

Vol. XIX, No. 26 – June 27, 1835
Died in Richmond, Va. on the 13th inst., Mrs. Lucy S. Munford, 24 year old wife of George W. Munford, Esq.

Vol. XIX, No. 27 – July 4, 1835
Married Wednesday the 24th ult. by John Swift, Esq., Mayor of Philadelphia, John Leadbeater of Baltimore and Mary P. Stabler of Alexandria, DC.

Married in Philadelphia on Wednesday the 24th ult. by Rev. Albert Barnes, Inman Horner, Esq. of Va. and Anna Marie Peace, daughter of the late Joseph Peace, Esq. formerly of Charleston, S.C.

Died the 25th ult. near residence in Fauquier Co., Col. Turner Ashby.

Vol. XIX, No. 28 – July 11, 1835
Died in Richmond, Va. on the 30th ult., Major James Gibbon of Stony Point Memory in 77th year of his age, for past 35 years collector for the port of Richmond. The major was a Lt. at the attack upon Stony Point.

Died in Baltimore a few days since, Isaiah Thomas, aged about 70 years, son of the late Isaiah Thomas, known as the father of printing in the U.S., native of Mass.

Vol. XIX, No. 29 – July 18, 1835
Died Saturday the 4th inst. at Llangollen, seat of her son-in-law Cuthbert Powell, Mrs. Nancy Douglas Simms, relict of late Col. Charles Simms of Alexandria DC., in the 75th year of her age.

Vol. XIX, No. 30 – July 25, 1835
Died on the 17th inst. at West End near Alexandria at residence of his son-in-law, Eli Legg, 61 years old of Prince William Co.

Vol. XIX, No. 32 – August 8, 1835
Married Thursday, July 30, by Rev. J. T. Johnston, Charles M. Conrad, Esq. of New Orleans and Mary Elizabeth Angela Lewis of Woodlawn, Fairfax Co., residence of father Major Lawrence Lewis.

Vol. XIX, No. 33 – August 15, 1835
Married Thursday the 6th inst. at residence of Presley Saunders by Gilmore, Joseph Hawkins Jr. and Mary Ann King, both of this county.

Died Friday the 7th inst. at residence of Presley Saunders near this town, Mr. James S. Triplett of Fleming Co. Ky in his 37th year.

Vol. XIX, No. 35 – August 29, 1835
Died in Waterford of bilious cholic on Tuesday last, John Paxson, about 35 years old.

Died on 15th inst. at house of Mrs. Lyle in Staunton, Judge Sample of Williamsburg.

Vol. XIX, No. 36 – September 5, 1835
Married at Christ Church in Alexandria at 11 o'clock on Tuesday the 25th ult. by Rev. C. B. Dana, John Waddell, Esq. of Louisianna and Lucia Chauncey, daughter of late Capt. John Porter, U.S.N.

Married Thursday the 27th ult. in Georgetown by Rev. Lucus, Major John W. Minor of Alexandria, D. C. and Ellen Maria, daughter of late Francis Diggs of Charles Co. Md.

Married the 27th ult. by Rev. Wm. Monroe, Herod Osburn and Prisilla Osburn, both of Loudoun.

Died recently, Col. John Strickland of Harper's Ferry, age 58 years. He was one of the oldest inhabitants engaged in the armory 27 years, no known relatives.

Died of bilious fever at age 17 years at residence of Hugh Cox in Charles Co. Md. on visit, Margaret E. Swann, oldest daughter of Thomas Swann Jr. of Alexandria.

Vol. XIX, No. 37 – September 12, 1835

Married in Georgetown on the 1st inst. by Rev. Porter, William McPhail of Baltimore and Sarah Ann Oard [*sic*] of this county.

A new series started with the next issue as B. W. Sowers' son became the new publisher for several issues. when it was taken over by George Richards he picked up the volume and number carried on by B. W. Sower.

The Genius of Liberty

Published by Brook W. Sower, Jr.

Vol. XIX, No. 38 – September 19, 1835

Died on Tuesday, September 15, Rev. Christopher Frye, age 57 years, "while attending to the operations of a threshing machine, his right foot was caught in the machine, and before it could be stopped the left limb had been drawn in, the thigh bone broken and forced through the flesh. This dreadful and most painful incident brought on a violent paroxysm of a long constitutional malady he had long suffered (angina pectoris) which terminated his life in a few hours." Member of M. E. Church.

Died at Raymond, Miss on August 5th in his 21st year, Enoch McKnight, native of Loudoun Co., had but a few weeks prior emigrated to Miss., settled in Raymond.

Vol. XIX, No. 39 – September 26, 1835

Married at Southport, Conn. on Monday the 7th inst. by Rev. N. E. Cornwall, E. I. Lee Jr., Esq. and Henrietta Bedinger, daughter of late Daniel Bedinger, Esq., both of Jefferson Co. Va.

Died in Mississippi on August 20th, Dr. Thompson Bennet of Waterford, Loudoun, Co., former resident of Washington City.

Died at Warrenton, Fauquier Co. Va. on the 12th inst., Margaret Ann Lee, 18 month old daughter of Dr. George Lee, formerly of this town.

Died here on Wednesday last, Ann Elizabeth, infant daughter of Dr. John H. McCabe.

Vol. XIX, No. 40 – October 3, 1835

Married at house of Mrs. Wiggington, Culpeper, the 15th ult., Samuel Campbell of Leesburg and Martha Francis Thompson, 2nd daughter of William P. Thompson.

Married on Thursday the 17th ult. by Rev. Alex Jones, Capt. Hierom L. Opie Jr., son of Senator Opie of Jefferson, and Ann S. Locke, daughter of late Meveral Locke, Esq. of Martinsburg.

Married on Thursday the 17th ult., Dr. Sydenham Hereford, eldest son of T. P.
Hereford, M.D. of Haymarket, Va. and Lavinia Flowerree, daughter of Daniel
Flowerree, Esq., all of Fauquier Co.
Married Thursday the 24th ult. by Rev. White, Alexander Johnson, grocer of this
town, and Miranda Craven, daughter of James Craven of this county.
Married Thursday eve the 24th ult. by Rev. Henry Slicer, Rev. Richard Brown of
Baltimore Annual Conference and Matilda Ridgeley, youngest daughter of
late Major Philip Hammond of Anne Arundel Co. Md.

Vol. XIX, No. 41 – October 10, 1835
Married on the 1st inst. by Gilmore, Richard W. A. Power and Susanna E. Davis,
both of this county.
Married Thursday last by Rev. White, John M. Moran of Leesburg and Drusilla
Ann Luck of Loudoun.

Vol. XIX, No. 42 – October 17, 1835
Married Tuesday, September 15, by Birkby, John Littleton and Rebecca Elgin,
both of this county.
Married Thursday last by Gilmore, James West and Miss Judah Jackson, both of
Loudoun.
Died at residence in this county Monday last, Charles B. Hamilton, aged 40
years.
Died here Monday last, Mrs. Mary Catharine Kline, age 69 years. Mrs. Kline was
a native of Hanover, Germany and emigrated to this county while an infant.
Born 1766, removed to Loudoun in 1766.
Died Thursday, September 10, at St. Aubyns residence of Geo. G. Armistead,
Cornelius M. Brocchus, in 18th year. Born Alexandria, DC. and removed to
this county in fall '34. *[Florence (Alabama) Gazette]*

Vol. XIX, No. 43 – October 24, 1835
Married in Washington City on Sunday the 4th inst. William Emmons, biographer
of Col. Johnson, and Ann Royal, editress of the "Paul Pry."
Married Stafford Co. Va. on Thursday the 8th inst. by Rev. E. C. McGuire,
Thomas H. C. Daniel and Eliza Mason Bronaugh, daughter of late John W.
Bronaugh.

Vol. XIX, No. 44 – October 31, 1835
Married Tuesday the 20th inst. at Milford, Pr. Wm. residence of William I. Weldon
by Rev. Trout, Henry C. Dye of Fairfax and Emily Jane Fouche, daughter of
late Thompson Fouche of Loudoun.
Married Thursday the 22nd inst. by Birkby, Henry Grimes and Ann Elizabeth
Cridler, both of Leesburg.
Died in Alexandria on the 20th inst., Henrietta Maria, 5 month old daughter of
Rev. E. C. Dorsey of that place and recently Leesburg.
Died here Tuesday last, Matthew Gates, aged about 30 years.

Vol. XIX, No. 47 – November 21, 1835
Married on the 5th inst. at Col. Lloyd Noland's near Middleburg by the Rev. Geo.
Adie, Doctor William B. Cochran and Miss Catharine P. Noland.
Married the 12th inst. at Clifton by the Rev. Geo. Adie, George Carter Esq. of
Oatlands and Mrs. Elizabeth O. Lewes.
Died Wednesday morn the 18th inst., Mrs. Eleanor Drish, age 65 years, relict of
Mr. John Drish, formerly of Leesburg.

<u>Vol. XIX, No. 48 – November 28, 1835</u>
Married in Philadelphia on Wednesday the 18th inst. by Rev. Dr. Cayler, Albert G. Waterman, formerly of town, and Miss Emelie, only daughter of James S. Spencer, Esq. of Philadelphia.
Married Tuesday the 16th inst. at Thoroughfare, Prince Wm. Co. by Rev. Mr. Slaughter, H. C. Williams, Esq. of Georgetown, DC. and Miss Frances A., daughter of the late George Chapman, dec'd.
Married in Georgetown on the 19th by Rev. Dr. Hawley of Washington, William Hunter Jr., Esq. of the State Dept. and Salley H., daughter of General W. Smith, all of Georgetown.
Died at residence of his son James A. Tait in Wilcox Co., Alabama on the 7th ult., Hon. Chas. Tait in 68th year.

<u>Vol. XIX, No. 49 – December 5, 1835</u>
Col. Wm. Ellzey, age 71 years, died Monday eve the 30th ult. At 16 while at school remote from family, he was drafted and went with Va. troops who served at York in fall of 1781. Present as ensign in taking of Cornwallis. Made several expeditions to Ky. & Ohio. Settled permanently in Loundoun County. Representative 1799-1800 and later, 1828-29 acting Justice of Peace 35 or 40 years. Member of Board of Public Works several years... [long obit]

<u>Vol. XIX, No. 51 – December 19, 1835</u>
Died at his residence near Leesburg on Saturday the 12th inst., George M. Chichester, Esq., age 43 years.
Died on Monday the 7th inst. at residence of her father, Wm. Darnes Esq. of Montgomery Co. Md., Mrs. Maria Lacey, wife of Robt. A. Lacey of the Post Office Dept.

<u>Vol. XIX, No. 52 – December 26, 1835</u>
Died at his residence in this county Thursday the 17th inst., John West in his 84th year. The deceased was a Revolutionary War soldier.

<u>Vol. XX, No. 1 – January 2, 1836</u>
Married Wednesday the 23rd ult. in Leesburg by Rev. Mr. White, Algernon S. Tebbs, Esq. of Fairfax and Miss Julia, daughter of late Wm. Coleman of Loudoun Co.

<u>Vol. XX, No. 2 – January 9, 1836</u>
Married Tuesday eve the 22nd ult. at Llangollen, the residence of Mr. Cuthbert Powell, by the Rev. Charles W. Andrews, Rev. George Adie of this place and Mrs. Mary E. Powell, daughter of Mr. Cuthbert Powell.
Married Tuesday the 15th ult. by Rev. Mr. Campbell, Mr. S. George W. Shuman and Miss Harriett Peyton Harrison, eldest daughter of Mr. James Surghnor of Middleburg.

<u>Vol. XX, No. 3 – January 16, 1836</u>
Married Thursday the 7th inst. by Birkby, Amos W. Maginis and Susan Copeland, both of this county.
Married Thursday the 31st ult. by Gilmore, Mandley Iden and Elizabeth Pierce.
Married Thursday the 31st ult. by Gilmore, George N. Brown and Julia Ann Saffle of Fauquier Co. Va.

<u>Vol. XX, No. 5 – January 30, 1836</u>
Died on Monday morn the 25th inst., Mrs. Sarah Pyott, consort of Mr. John Pyott
   of this county, member of M. E. Church, left husband and "several fond
   children."
Died at Beverly, Randolph Co., Va. on December 24, Mr. Robert McCrum, aged
   44 years, formerly of this place.

<u>Vol. XX, No. 7 – February 13, 1836</u>
Married by Birkby on Tuesday the 9th inst., George W. Hunter Esq. of Fairfax
   Court House, Va. and Mary A. Conrad of Waterford.
Died on the 31st ult., Margaret, daughter of James McIlhaney, Esq. of this county,
   between 4 and 5 years of age.

<u>Vol. XX, No. 9 – February 27, 1836</u>
Died on Sunday, February 14th at his residence in Leesburg, John M. Edwards,
   aged 39 years, formerly of the U.S. Army.

<u>Vol. XX, No. 10 – March 5, 1836</u>
Married Thursday the 25th ult. by Gilmore, Willis B. Clark of Frederick Co. Va.
   and Emily Pierce of Fauquier Co.
Married in Norfolk on the 4th ult. by Rev. Thitselberger, Henry B. Reardon, Esq.,
   merchant of that borough, and Elizabeth B., 3rd daughter of the late Nath'l
   Manning, Esq. of Loudoun.

<u>Vol. XX, No. 11 – March 12, 1836</u>
Married Thursday the 3rd inst. by Rev. Morgan, Charles Greenlease of Loudoun
   and Adelaide Withers of Fauquier Co.
Died on Tuesday the 8th inst., Ann Hamilton Fox, 19 years old, only daughter of
   George K. Fox.

<u>Vol. XX, No. 13 – March 26, 1836</u>
Married Tuesday eve last by Birkby, Addison Osborne and Lydia Ann Osborne,
   both of this county.

<u>Vol. XX, No. 14 – April 2, 1836</u>
Died at Waterford on Sunday the 27th ult., John Minor, infant son of Dr. Charles
   G. Edwards, aged about 8 months.
Died Wednesday nite the 23rd ult. at his residence in the county, Ludwell Lee
   Esq., age 76 years ... oldest son of Richard Henry Lee, served Lafayette
   Staff, became lawyer but withdrew at an early period, became disting.
   member of Va. Legislature, Pres. of Senate. Retired at Belmont. [long eulogy]

<u>Vol. XX, No. 17 – April 23, 1836</u>
Died the 13th inst. at residence of his mother in this town in the 30th year, Mr.
   Edmund W. Coleman, third and only son of late Capt. William Coleman.

<u>Vol. XX, No. 21 – May 21, 1836</u>
Married by Gilmore on the 12th inst., John Crain and Elizabeth Wornell, all of this
   county.

<u>Vol. XX, No. 22 – May 28, 1836</u>
Married Thursday eve last by Rev. Geo. Adie, Algernon S. Gray of Rockingham
   Co. and Anna Henderson, daughter of Richard H. Henderson, Esq.

Married Tuesday eve last by Rev. A. W. Campbell at residence of Mrs. Stone, Wm. Graham and Sarah Stone, both of this county.

Married Wednesday last at the house of Dr. L. Klein by Rev. A. W. Campbell, Daniel Miller of Lovettsville and Mary A. Klein of Waterford.

Vol. XX, No. 23 – June 4, 1836

Died near Russellville, Logan Co. Ky on May 12th near this place, Rev. John Littlejohn, M. E. Minister, at a very advanced age, and minister of M. E. Church upwards of fifty years.

Vol. XX, No. 28 – July 9, 1836

Died on the 17th ult. at Farmer Repose residence of her father Mr. Reuben Hutchinson, Mrs. Lucy Bayly, young consort of John Bayly Jr.

Died at residence of his father-in-law Dr. John C. Green of Frederick Co. on the 1st day of this month, David H. Lovett, M. D., son of Daniel Lovett of Loudoun, in the 27th year of his age.

Died June 9, Lancey G. Lovett, infant son of Dr. Lovett, aged about 6 months.

Vol. XX, No. 33 – August 13, 1836

Married Tuesday the 9th inst. by Rev. George Adie at house of her mother in Leesburg, Rev. Wm. N. Ward of the Bowling Green and Miss Mary Blincoe.

Vol. XX, No. 35 – August 27, 1836

Married Monday eve the 22nd inst. by Gilmore, George W. Taverner and Leah Ewers, both of Loudoun Co.

Vol. XX, No. 36 – September 3, 1836

Married the 1st inst. by Gilmore, Leven P. Hereford and Louisa M. Powell, both of Loudoun Co. Va.

Died at his farm near Leesburg on August 9, Walter Elgin, in 81st year. Lived at his residence in Loudoun for 78 years. During Revolutionary War took part and was non-commissioned officer in Loudoun Militia. [long obit]

Vol. XX, No. 43 – October 22, 1836

Died Monday last the 10th inst. at residence of Thos. J. Randolph, Mrs. Martha Randolph, daughter of Thomas Jefferson.

Vol. XX, No. 44 – October 29, 1836

Married the 20th inst. by Birkby, Presley Parker and Lucy Ellen Parker, both of this place.

Married the 20th inst. by Gilmore, Jonathan Ewers and Pheobe Gregg, both of Loudoun.

Vol. XX, No. 46 – November 12, 1836

Married Tuesday last at Llangolen, Loudoun Co., by the Rev. Geo. Adie, Wm. H. Gray, Esq. and Ellen D., daughter of Cuthbert Powell, Esq.

Vol. XX, No. 47 – November 19, 1836

Married at Mt. Pleasant, Fairfax Co. by Rev. E. Vietch, Wm. B. Peake, Esq. of Berryville, Clarke Co., and Miss Jane E., daughter of the late Joseph Powell, Esq.

<u>Vol. XX, No. 48 – November 26, 1836</u>
Married the 25th ult. by Rev. Wm. Monroe, Mahlon James and Rachel Ann Paxson.
Married the 27th ult. by Rev. Wm. Monroe, Andrew H. Kalb and Ann James.
Married the 27th ult. by Rev. Wm. Monroe, Richard Tavenner and Miss Sidney Copeland, both of Hillsborough.
Married the 3rd inst. by Rev. Wm. Monroe, Samuel Brown and Mary Jane Bradfield, both of Snickersville.
Married the 15th inst. by Rev. Wm. Monroe, Samuel Tavenner and Sarah Jane McRea, all of this county.

<u>Vol. XX, No. 49 – December 3, 1836</u>
Married Tuesday the 22nd ult. by Gilmore, William Coe of Loudoun and Mary Jane Read of Fauquier.
Married Thursday last by Birkby, Harrison Cummings and Miss Ansey Cummings, both of Loudoun.
Died in Brooklyn, N. J. at residence of her son Rev. B. C. Cutler, Mrs. Sarah Cutler, relict of late Benjamin Clarke Cutler of Boston, Mass, at 75 years. She was a native of Georgetown, DC. and daughter of Esther the only sister of Gen. Francis Marion.
Died recently in Miss while on visit, Rev. Albert G. Burton of Va. Conf of M. E. Church.
Died at St. Chester, Morris Co. N. J. on the 9th ult., Keturah, consort of John Burnett, age 51 years. Died on the 13th, Howell B., age 18 years. Died on the 17th, Richard B. age 18 years. Died on the 12th, Harrison B., age 25 years. Died on the 24th James, age 30 years. All of dysentery and sons of John Burnett of that place.

<u>Vol. XX, No. 50 – December 10, 1836</u>
Married Sunday the 4th inst. by Gilmore, Luke S. Forest, of Maryland and Mrs. Mary Ann Middleton of Loudoun Co.

<u>Vol. XX, No. 52 – December 24, 1836</u>
Married Thursday inst. by Birkby, Jonah Steer and Mrs. Mary E. Brown.
Married Thursday inst. by Birkby, Samuel Laycock and Matilda Blaker.
Married Tuesday the 20th by Birkby, Mahlon Taylor and Amanda M. Gore.
Married Thursday last by Birkby, John Sexton and Alcinda Parker, all of this county.

<u>Vol. XX, No. 53 – December 31, 1836</u>
Married the 8th inst. by Rev. Wm. Monroe, Wm. T. Hart and Emeline F. Thatcher.
Married the 21st by Rev. Wm. Monroe, Sam Evans and Mary Ann Myers.
Married the 22nd by Rev. Wm. Monroe, Josiah Bennet and Elizabeth Ann Lowe, all of this county.
Married the 20th by Rev. J. White, John L. Parsons and Jane Timms.
Married the 22nd by Rev. J. White, James Feagans and Mary A. McCrae.
Married the 27th inst. by Rev. J. White, Manly Mead and Mary Ann Nichols, all of this county.
Married the 22nd by Wm. Gilmore, Richard Triplett and Sarah Taverner.
Married the 27th by Wm. Gilmore, Thos. Muse and Miss Sydney J. Havener, all of this county.

Died at Belmont, Loudoun Co. on Sunday morn the 18th inst. at 18 years, Eliza
   Contee, daughter of John Contee, Esq. of Prince George Co., Md. Student of
   Belmont Seminary.

Vol. XXI, No. 1 – January 7, 1837
Married nr. Memphis Tenn on the 17th November last, Alfred H. Powell Esq., atty
   at law of Marshall Co. Miss, and George Ann, 2nd daughter of Judge
   Humphreys of Tenn.

Vol. XXI, No. 2 – January 14,1837
Married the 29th ult. by Birkby, Lawson Kelly and Amanda J. Clowe, both of
   Loudoun.
Married the 5th inst. by Gilmore, Joel White and Harriet Blaker, both of Loudoun.
Married the 3rd inst. by Rev. Wm. Monroe, Thomas Leman and Maria Bodine of
   Waterford.
Married the 5th inst. by Rev. Wm. Monroe, Stephen Marlow and Tacy Watkins,
   both of Clarke Co.

Vol. XXI, No. 3 – January 21, 1837
Married the 12th inst. by Rev. Wm. Gilmore, John Brown and Margaret Whiting,
   both of Loudoun.
Died in Leesburg on Wednesday the 18th inst., John Nicholas Kline, age 73
   years, removed to Leesburg from Penna some 36-37 years ago. Rev. Soldier
   in Penna Militia, pensioner act 1832.

Vol. XXI, No. 4 – January 28, 1837
Married Thursday the 19th inst. by Birkby, Eli F. Cooper and Susan Commerel,
   both of this county.

Vol. XXI, No. 5 – February 4, 1837
Married Thursday the 9th ult. by Rev. G. W. Humphreys, Rev. Alfred A. Eskridge
   of the Baltimore Conference and Isabella Margaret, daughter of John
   Buchanan of Rockbridge.
Died of croup on the 29th ult., Charles Temple, 3 year old child of Dr. H. D. Magill.
Died the 30th ult., Mary Wood, widow of the late Mark Wood, aged 66 years.
Died on eve of 31st ult., Lewis Hole, aged 22 years.
Died at Ft. Washington on the 17th ult., Eliza North, 5 year 10 month old daughter
   of Major H. Saunders, U. S. Army.

Vol. XXI, No. 6 – February 11, 1837
Married Sunday the 5th inst. by Gilmore, Wesley White of Fauquier and Jane
   Hardin of Loudoun Co.

Vol. XXI, No. 7 – February 18, 1837
Married the 14th inst. by Gilmore, Milton M. Bussard and Mary Ann Reece, all of
   this county.
Died the 31st ult. at the Glebe, John Aldridge, Esq., age 68 years, formerly of
   Maryland but for last 7-8 years a highly respected farmer of this county.
Died Monday, February 13, Thomas Watson, 4 year old son of Lemuel Watson.

Vol. XXI, No. 8 – February 25, 1837
Died at Oatlands Farm on Tuesday eve the 21st inst., Mr. Jesse Timms, age 67
   years. Monday the 20th while conversing with son, gun slipped and accidently

exploded shattering his left arm and shoulder in a shocking manner, arm amputated but mortification set in and he died 24 hours later. Commissioner of the Revenue of Loudoun Co. for last 37 years. For many years Steward for Geo. Carter, Esq. of Oatlands.

Vol. XXI, No. 9 – March 4, 1837
Married at Cedar Grove, Charles Co. Md., Thursday the 2nd inst. by Rev. Simon Willmore, Henry M. Hannon and Julia Longden, all of that place.

Vol. XXI, No. 10 – March 11, 1837
Married the 2nd inst. by Rev. Mr. Broadus, W. H. Cassidy and Mary Jane Denham, all of Loudoun Co.

Vol. XXI, No. 11 – March 18, 1837
Married the 9th inst. by Birkby, John Williams and Miss Pleasant H. Brown, all of Loudoun.
Married Monday last by Birkby, Hugh Rutter and Elizabeth Rivers.
Married Monday, March 13, by Rev. Birkby, Richard L. Hipkins and Elizabeth Jacobs, all of Loudoun.
Married Wednesday last by Rev. John Allemong, Rev. Samuel D. Rice of M. E. Church and Miss Mary, daughter of Mr. Randolph Rhodes of Loudoun Co.
Died Tuesday the 28th ult., Mrs. Margaret Shumate, consort of M. C. Shumate of this county. Left husband and two little children, joined Baptist Church under Rev. T. Herndon.

Vol. XXI, No. 12 – March 25, 1837
Died at his residence in Loudoun Co. on Thursday the 8th inst., Valentine Purcell, aged about 40 years.
Died in this town on the 17th inst., Mrs. Susan Wright, wife of Isaac Wright, member M. E. Church.
Died near Poolesville, Montgomery Co., Md. on the 17th inst., Miss Henrietta E. Dawson, in 18th year.
Died the 15th inst. at residence of Henry Stevens her son-in-law, Mrs. Anna Barker, formerly of Fairfax, 76 years old, member Baptist Church.
Died the 11th inst. at her residence in Loudoun, Mrs. Margaret McIlhany, age 78 years.

Vol. XXI, No. 13 – April 1, 1837
Married the 28th ult. by Gilmore, John Vermillion and Hannah Pomroy, both of Loudoun.
Married Thursday the 16th ult. by Birkby, Jacob Nichols and Ianthe Smith.
Married Thursday the 16th ult. by Birkby, Fenton M. Love and Elizabeth Morris.
Married Thursday the 16th ult. by Birkby, Matson James and Hannah Thomas.
Married the 29th ult. by Birkby, John Pyott and Mrs. Ann Nixon, all of this county.
Died Thursday the 16th ult., Valentine V. Purcell, 41 year old merchant. Left wife and four children. [long obit]
Died on the 23rd ult., Caroline Mary Louisa, daughter of John Barrett, age 7 years 11 months.

Vol. XXI, No. 15 – April 15, 1837
Died in this town on the 13th inst., Mrs. Mary T. Ball, consort of the late Fayette Ball, Esq.

Vol. XXI, No. 16 – April 22, 1837

Married Thursday the 13th inst. by Birkby, Richard Adams and Anna Dyer.

Married Thursday the 13th inst. by Birkby, Marcus Anderson and Mary Ann Brown, all of this county.

Married the 22nd ult. in Millwood, Frederick Co. Va. by Rev. Stringfellow, Dr. Peyton R. Berkeley of Prince Edward Co., Va. and Frances A. B., daughter of Dr. Little of former place.

Died in Fairfax Co. on the 14th inst., Major James Saunders, 52 years old, officer in U.S. Army during War of 1812. Served on borders of Canada. Appointed Aide to Gen. Parker later Inspection General of the troops at Norfolk. Left army at rank of Major, entered as ensign. Left widow and four children.

Vol. XXI, No. 18 – May 6, 1837

Married on Monday last by Birkby, Eli C. Albaugh and Sarah Ann Gray, all of Waterford.

Vol. XXI, No. 20 – May 20, 1837

Married on the 9th inst. at Wellburn Hall seat of John P. Dulany, Esq. of Loudoun by Rev. J. A. Collins, Richard H. Carter, Esq. and Mary W. DeButts, daughter of late John DeButts, Esq.

Vol. XXI, No. 21 – May 27, 1837

Died, John R. Key, Esq. of DC., attorney at law and son of Francis S. Key, Esq. *National Intelligencer.*

Vol. XXI, No. 23 – June 10, 1837

Died nr Snickersville on Sunday the 4th inst., Mrs. Margaret Chew, age 75 years, wife of John Chew, Esq.

Died on the 6th inst. at Welburn Hall, Selina Dulany, daughter of John P. Dulany, age about 13 years.

Vol. XXI, No. 27 – July 8, 1837

Died in this town on the 3rd inst., James W. Fox, 19 year old son of George K. Fox.

Vol. XXI, No. 28 – July 15, 1837

Married on the 4th inst. in Montgomery Co. Md. by Rev. Mr. Jones, Dr. Stephen N. C. White and Elizabeth, daughter of Capt. Wm. Chiswell.

Married eve of the 6th inst. by Rev. E. P. Phelps, Norman R. Davis, Esq. and Mary Jane Wren, all of Fairfax.

Married at Winchester the 6th inst. by Rev. Job Guest, Andrew K. Smith and Elizabeth, daughter of Rev. David Steele of Methodist Episcopal Church.

Died in this town on Saturday eve the 8th inst., Lloyd S. Birkby, infant son of Joseph Birkby, age 9 months.

Died on the 7th inst., John MaCarty Mason, U.S. Navy, eldest son of Geo. Mason, Esq., late of Gunston Hall, Fairfax Co., Va. Local boating accident from skiff in Pohick Creek in saving a young cousin 12 years old proceeding toward residence of his relative Wm. MaCarty, Esq. Accident occurred near Gunston Hall. *National Intelligencer.* [long obit]

Died at his residence on June 29 in his 83rd year, Nathaniel Macon, of North Carolina. Legislator from formation of present government to 1829.

Vol. XXI, No. 29 – July 22, 1837
Married Thursday the 13th inst. by Rev. J. Mason, John Rhind of the Chesapeake & Ohio Canal and Eliza Snyder, daughter of Anthony Snyder of Washington Co., Md.

Vol. XXI, No. 30 – July 29, 1837
Died on the 25th inst. at residence of Capt. John Rose, Major John Alexander Binns, son of the late Charles Binns, Esq., age 42 years old.
Died on the 20th inst. in Snickersville, John Chew, son of Mr. Alfred Glasscock, aged 6 months 15 days.

Vol. XXI, No. 31 – August 5, 1837
Died in Waterford on the 31st ult., Ellen, consort of Rev. J. Berkley and daughter of T. Cromwell of Md. Buried in Episcopal burying ground.
Died the 10th ult. at residence of her father in Millwood, Clarke Co., Va., Miss Elizabeth Little, member of Prot. Epis. Church. Victim of parylisis January last. [*Southern Churchman*]

Vol. XXI, No. 33 – August 19, 1837
Married Tuesday eve last by Gilmore, Wm. H. Francis and Mary E. Glasscock, all of this county.

Vol. XXI, No. 34 – August 26, 1837
Married Tuesday, August 1st, by Birkby, Bernard Hough of Hillsborough and Sarah Ann, daughter of Wm. Clendening of this county.

Vol. XXI, No. 37 – September 16, 1837
Married Thursday, August 31, by Gilmore, Armistead Quick and Margaret A. Powell, all of this county.

Vol. XXI, No. 38 – September 23, 1837
Married Tuesday last by Gilmore, Elisha Chamblin and Mahala Romine, all of this county.
Died in this town the 19th inst., Mary Elizabeth Smale, age 13 months 15 days.
Died on the 27th ult. at residence in Hereford, Baltimore Co., Rev. Andrew Hemphill, eminent itinerant minister of M. E. Church, age 60 years old.

Vol. XXI, No. 39 – September 30, 1837
Married Thursday the 21st inst. by Gilmore, John McCarty and Emily Jane Coe, all of this county.
Died Friday, September 22nd, Albert Vandeventer of Loudoun Co., age 19 years. Died at Baltimore after two weeks residence. *Baltimore American*.

Vol. XXI, No. 40 – October 7, 1837
Died on Friday, September 22nd, Albert Vandeventer of Leesburg, age 18 years 6 months, left widowed mother. (Communicated)
Died 16th ult., Douglas McLean at New Orleans, 22 year old son of late Dan McLean of this town. [*Alexandria Gazette*]
Died in this town [Romney, West Virginia], Mr. John Jack, cashier of Bank of the Valley, 75 years old. Lived in Romney last 49 years.

Vol. XXI, No. 41 – October 14, 1837
Married in Martinsburg, Va. on the 4th inst. by Rev. E. P. Phelps, Rev. B. N.
  Brown of Washington City and Ellen Small, daughter of James Small, dec'd.
Died at New Orleans of prev. epidemic on September 14th R. Meredith Ratcliffe,
  late of Fairfax Co.
Sudden death, Nicholas Bryan of New Brighton *[Fallstown (Pa.) Gazette]*

Vol. XXI, No. 42 – October 21, 1837
Married Thursday the 28th ult. by Birkby, John McKimmy and Sarah Waters [*sic*].
Married Thursday the 5th inst. by Birkby, Joseph Carr and Martha Carr.
Married Monday the 9th inst. by Birkby, Jason Wilmarth and Mary Ann P. Rutter.
Married Tuesday the 10th inst. by Birkby, William Weedon and Lavinia Wiley.
Married Tuesday the 10th inst. by Birkby, Hiram McKenna and Amanda Fichter,
  all of Loudoun.

Vol. XXI, No. 43 – October 28, 1837
Died suddenly at Hamilton, Loudoun Co., in 34th year, Mary Amelia, consort of
  James H. Bennett, Esq., daughter of late Lawrence Hoff of Alexandria.

Vol. XXI, No. 46 – November 18, 1837
Married Tuesday eve last by Rev. Samuel Keppler, Francis M. Weadon of
  Warrenton and Sarah Jane Briscoe of this place.
Married Thursday, November 9, at Union by Rev. John A. Collins, Dr. Theoderic
  Leith and Veturia A. Plaster, daughter of Henry Plaster Jr., all of Loudoun Co.
Died at Haymarket, Prince William Co. on 5th inst., Mrs. Elizabeth Hereford, wife
  of T. P. Hereford, M.D.
Died on 28th Sept last at residence of her husband, Muskingham County, Ohio,
  Mrs. Elizabeth Munroe, wife of Rev. William Munroe, formerly of this county.
  Sister of Mr. B. T. Towner of Shepherdstown.

Vol. XXI, No. 48 – December 2, 1837
Married Tuesday eve last by Birkby, Mason James and Patience Nichols, all of
  this county.

Vol. XXI, No. 49 – December 9, 1837
Married Thursday, November 30, by Gilmore, Joseph Davis and Amey Powell.

Vol. XXI, No. 50 – December 16, 1837
Died at Vicksburg, Miss on the 22nd ult., Mrs. Mary Ellen Wallace, wife of David
  M. Wallace and daughter of Wm. Johnson of this place. Died from cold on trip
  to Vicksburg. Member of M. E. Church.
Married Dec 7 at Aldie at residence of Edmund Tyler by Rev. George Adie,
  William Gadsby of Washington, DC. to Miss Jane K. Smith of Richmond,
  daughter of late James Smith.
Married on Tuesday evening last by Rev. Samuel Keppler, Murphy C.
  Shumate, Esq. to Miss Diadama, daughter of late Walter Elgin, Esq., all of
  Loudoun County.

Vol. XXII, No. 2 – January 13, 1838
Married Thursday the 4th inst. by Rev. Samuel Keppler, Cyrus Burson and Miss
  Ansey Thompson, all of Loudoun.

Vol. XXII, No. 3 – January 20, 1838

Married Tuesday last by the Rev. Mr. Gilmore, James Skinner of Fauquier Co. and Jane Elizabeth Turner of Loudoun Co.

Married in Baltimore on the 21st December ult. by Rev. Dr. Watt, Brook W. Sower Jr., formerly of this town, and Harriet Elvira, first daughter of late James DeBaufre, Esq. of Baltimore.

Vol. XXII, No. 4 – January 27, 1838

Died morn of 15th inst. in Middleburg, Loudoun Co., Mrs. Elizabeth Broun, consort of Mr. Edwin C. Broun in the 36th year of age. Methodist, interested in Oregon Mission. Mother of 9 children most small, only daughter of aged widowed mother. Companion of a delicate afflicted husband. Entombed at Middleburg. [long obit]

Died at residence in Marion Co., Ohio on the 20th ult., John Irey, aged nearly 81 years. About 9 years ago moved to Ohio, resident of Loudoun 56 years. In early life served 3 successive tours of duty in Army of Rev., present at surrender of Cornwallis at Yorktown October 1781.

Vol. XXII, No. 5 – February 3, 1838

Married Wednesday, January 17, by Birkby, Jonas Potts and Amanda Silcott.

Married Thursday, January 25, by Birkby, Wm. H. French and Mary Ann Hanes, all of this county.

Died Saturday last about noon at Rose Hill residence of father near Rockville, Rev. T. J. Addison Mines.

Died in Texas November last, John J. Mathias, 42 years old, former Surveyor of Loudoun Co.

Vol. XXII, No. 6 – February 10, 1838

Married Thursday the 1st inst. by Gilmore, Isaac G. Nichols and Louisa White, all of Loudoun.

Vol. XXII, No. 7 – February 17, 1838

Married the 6th inst. at Spring Hill, Stafford Co., by Rev. G. C. Brooke, Rev. Nelson Head and Margaret U. W. Morton, daughter of late Richard Morton of said county.

Vol. XXII, No. 8 – February 24, 1838

Married Thursday the 15th inst. by Gilmore, Wm. O'Neale of Alexandria, DC. and Harriett Triplett of Fauquier Co.

Vol. XXII, No. 9 – March 3, 1838

Married the 22nd ult. by Rev. James Berkley, Wm. Sullivan and Susan, daughter of Mr. Wm. King of this town.

Fatal accident – John Workman killed by a team running away with him. About 25 years old, native of Virginia. *[New Carlisle, Clark Co., Ohio]*

Vol. XXII, No. 10 – March 10, 1838

Died at residence in Middleburg on the 25th ult., James Surghnor, age 53 years.

Died the 28th ult. near Salisbury, Somerset Co., Md., Rt. Rev. Wm. Murry Stone, D.D., Bishop of Prot. Epis. Church, Md.

Vol. XXII, No. 11 – March 17, 1838

Married Wednesday the 14th inst. by Birkby, James M. Carr and Elizabeth Cost, all of this county.

Married in Washington the 7th inst. by Rev. Mr. Hawley, Lt. John Navarre Macomb, U.S. Army, and Czarina, daughter of Major Gen. Alex Macomb.

Died 12th inst. at residence of George C. Washington, Heights of Georgetown, Major John Peter, of Jefferson Co., Va., 56 years old.

Vol. XXII, No. 13 – March 31, 1838

Married Tues inst. by Birkby, Warner Holmes and Elizabeth Smith.

Married Wednesday last by Birkby, Edward Green and Malinda Darne, all of Loudoun.

Died in Middleburg on Tuesday the 27th Mrs. Jane Love.

Vol. XXII, No. 14 – April 7, 1838

Married on the 20th ult., Frederick A. Frazier of Kent Co. and Elizabeth C. George of Queen Ann Co., Md., daughter of late Bishop George.

Died on the 29th ult. at residence of mother, Elisha Janney, age 22 years.

Died ___, Hon. Isaac McKim, Member of Congress, Representative for Maryland.

Vol. XXII, No. 15 – April 14, 1838

Married Thursday, March 29, by Birkby, Joseph Rhodes and Mary Ann Brown, all of this county.

Vol. XXII, No. 16 – April 21, 1838

Married the 12th inst. by Rev. Samuel Keppler, John D. Hope and Lydia C. Reed, all of Loudoun.

Married Thursday the 12th inst. by Rev. John Bear, Robert White, merchant of Georgetown, DC., and Sarah Adelaide Hunter, daughter of Gen. John C. Hunter of Fairfax Co.

Vol. XXII, No. 17 – April 28, 1838

Married Thursday inst. by Birkby, Wm. H. Fridly and Elizabeth McCormick, of Clarke Co.

Married Thursday inst. by Birkby, Presly Beech and Frances Lane of this county.

Died the 23rd inst. at Glen Ora, Fauquier Co., Anna Lloyd Noland, age 3 years, daughter of Col. Lloyd Noland.

Vol. XXII, No. 20 – May 19, 1838

Married in Washington on the 8th inst., John S. Edwards, Esq. of Leesburg and Miss Susan Washington, daughter of the late Joseph S. MacPherson of the U.S. Navy.

Vol. XXII, No. 21 – May 26, 1838

Married Wednesday eve the 16th inst. by Rev. Mr. Taylor, Fairfax Catlett of Texas and Esther Ann, daughter of Henry Laverty, Esq. of N.Y.

Vol. XXII, No. 22 – June 2, 1838

Married Thursday last by Birkby, Wm. H. Rice and Jane, daughter of Mr. George Rhodes.

Died on May 24 at Llangollen, residence of her brother Cuthbert Powell, Mrs. Sarah H. Chilton, 62 years old, member of Pres. Church.

Died at residence near Snickersville, John Chew, age 90 years.

Died May 21st at Mill Park, Prince William Co., Va., Mrs. Sarah Tyler, in 72nd year, relict of Charles Tyler, deceased.

Vol. XXII, No. 23 – June 9, 1838
Died at Washington on the 31st ult., Rev. Joseph Rowen of the M. E. Church, buried from Alexandria meeting house. *Alexandria Gazette.*

Vol. XXII, No. 24 – June 16, 1838
Married May 31 last by Rev. Mr. Gilmore, Henson Allnutt of Loudoun Co. and Elizabeth Jane Allnutt of Montgomery Co., Md.

Married the 5th inst. by Rev. Mr. Gilmore, Richard Carter of Loudoun Co. and Hannah E. Rust of Fauquier Co., Va.

Died in this town Wednesday night the 13th inst., Jacob Towner.

Died Sunday morn last at residence of Rev. Joshua Wells, Baltimore Co., Md., Rev. Thomas J. Dorsey. Member of Baltimore Annual Conference of M. E. Church and lately General Agent of Md. Temperance Society.

Vol. XXII, No. 25 – June 23, 1838
Married the 5th inst. by Gilmore, Richard R. Carter of Loudoun Co. and Hannah E. Rust of Fauquier Co., Va.

Married at Locust Hill on Thursday eve the 7th inst. by Rev. A. H. Boyd, Philip Pendleton of Martinsburg, Va. and Virginia M. Tutt.

Married at Lexington, Ky, Hon. T. M. Hickey and Mrs. Catharine A. Barry, widow of late Post Master General Barry.

Vol. XXII, No. 26 – June 30, 1838
Married Tuesday eve June 19 by Rt. Rev. Dr. Moore, William M. McCarty of Fairfax and Mary B. Burwell, daughter of late Col. Burwell of Gloucester Co.

Vol. XXII, No. 29 – July 21, 1838
Died at Baltimore on Wednesday, July 12, Henry Louis, infant son of George & Margaret Cridler, age 5 months.

Vol. XXII, No. 31 – August 4, 1838
Died Friday morn, July 27, Louisa Ellen, infant daughter of C. R. Dowell.

Died in Hagerstown, Md. on the 23rd ult., Dr. Samuel Young, in his hundredth year.

Died a few week hence near Mercersburg, Pa, Mrs. Hornbaker from Washington Co., Md., aged 110 years.

Vol. XXII, No. 32 – August 11, 1838
Died at Oxford, Ohio on March 28, Laura Eugenia, daughter of Mr. Cyrus Yemans, aged 5 years 6 months.

Died May 1838, Miss Elizabeth Clapper formerly of Loudoun Co. [*Clifton, Ohio*]

Vol. XXII, No. 33 – August 18, 1838
Died at residence of Eli Janney in Loudoun Co. on the 9th inst., Miss Mary Vandevanter, youngest daughter of late Capt. Isaac Vandevanter of this county, age 17 years.

Died on the 21st ult. at residence near Newtown, Frederick Co., Dr. John B. Tilden, age 78 years. Officer in War of Independence, physician, Minister Methodist, Frederick Co. as early 1799 appointed magistrate of Frederick until last illness except for two years when he was the high sheriff.

<u>Vol. XXII, No. 36 – September 8, 1838</u>
Married on the 28th ult. by Rev. S. Tuston, Valentine Surghnor of Middleburg and M. E. L. Brashears of Fauquier Co.
Married on the 30th ult. by Birkby, Samuel Young, Esq. of Montgomery Co., Md. and Sophia V. Craven of this county.
Married Monday last the 3rd inst. by Birkby, John Cross and Elizabeth Burgess, both of this county.
Died in town the 4th inst., Ann Sutherland, daughter of late Alexander Sutherland, Esq.
Died in town the 4th inst., Thomas L. Darby, age 17 years.

<u>Vol. XXII, No. 37 – September 15, 1838</u>
Married in town Thursday eve by Rev. Mr. White, Charles A. Johnston and Miss Mary Rebecca, daughter of Samuel M. Boss Esq.
Died on the 2nd inst. near Rockville, Montgomery Co., Md., Dade Peyton Noland, Esq., 54 years old, leaves widow & 7 children.
Another Soldier of the Revolution has descended into the tomb. Died suddenly of apoplexy on Saturday, September 1, at Difficult Hill, Fairfax Co., George Sommers, age 76 years. Enlisted army when young. Was at battle of Guilford Court House, Ninety Six, Eutaw Springs and served throughout Southern Campaign under General Greene.

<u>Vol. XXII, No. 39 – September 29, 1838</u>
Married on the 2nd inst. by Rev. Deems, Rev. William Monroe, of Ohio formerly of Jefferson Co., and Mary T. Welsh of Berkeley Co. Va.

<u>Vol. XXII, No. 40 – October 6, 1838</u>
Died at Harper's Ferry Thursday last, Patrick C. McCabe, Esq., 47 years old, attorney at law, native of Ireland, resident of Harper's Ferry last 14 years.
Died at his residence at Page Brook, Clarke Co., Monday eve the 17th inst., John Page Sr., Esq. *Winchester Republican.*

<u>Vol. XXII, No. 43 – November 3, 1838</u>
Married on Sunday, October 28, by Gilmore, Mr. Albert (torn)ing [Harding] and Miss Ellen E. Fox, all of Loudoun Co.

<u>Vol. XXII, No. 45 – November 10, 1838</u>
Died at sea October 10 on passage to Tallahesee for rest of health, Mrs. Elizabeth W. Hixon, wife of Fleming Hixon, Esq., daughter of late Major Robert Braden.
Died at Alexandria, DC. the 3rd inst., Rev. Thomas Jackson of Episcopal Church, 57 years old.

<u>Vol. XXII, No. 46 – November 17, 1838</u>
Married in Washington the 8th inst. by Rev. John Owen, Lt. Th. Jefferson Page, U.S. Navy, and Benjemima Price, youngest daughter of Benjamin Price of Va.
Married October 23rd by Rev. M. M. Marshall, Byrd Douglas of the house of H. & B. Douglas and Martha R. Bright, third daughter of James Bright, Esq., all of Lincoln Co., Tennessee.
Died 23 Oct last at Oatlands, residence of her son-in-law, George Carter, Mrs. Nancy Grayson, 75 years old, member of Protestant Episcopal Church.

Vol. XXII, No. 48 – December 1, 1838

Married Tuesday eve last by Gilmore, Griffith E. Thomas and Rebecca B. Wright, all of Loudoun.

Married Thursday eve the 22nd inst. at Orchard Grove, Fauquier Co. by Rev. Thaddeus Herndon, James H. Hathaway and Sarah Frances Weeks, both of Fauquier.

Vol. XXII, No. 50 – December 15, 1838

Died on Monday the 2nd inst. at his residence in Loudoun Co., Samuel Beavers in the 62nd year, farmer, member of Methodist Episcopal Church.

Vol. XXII, No. 51 – December 22, 1838

Married Tuesday, November 27, by Rev. Converse, Maj. Abraham Van Buren, eldest son of President of U.S., and Sarah Angelica Singleton, youngest daughter of Richard Singleton, at her father's house, Sumptor District, S.C.

Vol. XXII, No. 52 – December 29, 1838

Married Tuesday inst. by Birkby, James A. Cox and Lydia Garner.

Married Tuesday eve, December 18, by Gilmore, Perry L. Trundle and Barbary E. Dawson, all of Montgomery Co., Md.

Married Thursday, December 20, by Gilmore, Otho W. Trundle and Sarah White, all of Montgomery Co., Md.

Died Wednesday eve last, Jotham Wright, tailor, old and respectable inhabitant.

Died yesterday afternoon, Hon. Thomson F. Mason, Judge of Criminal Court, DC. [*obit - Alexandria Gazette*]

Died Sunday eve last, Jonathan Janney, merchant of Leesburg. [*Alexandria Gazette*]

Vol. XXIII, No. 1 – January 5, 1839

Died the 1st inst. at Waterford, Anna Ball, in 61st year, member of Society of Friends.

Vol. XXIII, No. 2 – January 12, 1839

Died at residence in Hampshire Co., Va. on December 23, John Davy, 103 years old. Dec'd came to this county as a drummer with Gen. Wolfe in the great battle fought at Quebec between British & French. He served also in the American Army during the war of the Rev. [*Romney Intelligencer*]

Vol. XXIII, No. 3 – January 19, 1839

Married Tuesday eve the 8th inst. by Birkby, Richard Francis and Miranda Jane Lewis, all of Loudoun.

Vol. XXIII, No. 4 – January 26, 1839

Married Thursday the 17th inst. by Birkby, John Tavener and Rebecca M. Nichols, all of Loudoun.

Married Tuesday the 22nd inst. by Birkby, Temple Fouch and Rebecca Torrison, all of Loudoun.

Vol. XXIII, No. 5 – February 2, 1839

Married Thursday the 24th ult. by Birkby, Elisha Holmes and Hester Thomas.

Married Tuesday the 29th ult. by Birkby, Lewis Thompson and Elizabeth Ann Burke, all of this county.

Married Thursday, January 24, by Rev. Samuel Keppler, Philip Houser and Elizabeth Baughters [*sic*] [Vaughters], both of Loudoun.

Vol. XXIII, No. 6 – February 9, 1839
Married the 31st by Rev. Gilmore, Josiah Burke and Lucinda Davis, all of this county.

Vol. XXIII, No. 7 – February 16, 1839
Married the 5th inst. by Rev. Edwin Dorsey, Rev. French S. Evans of Washington, DC. and Susan P. Gover of Baltimore.

Married the 7th inst. by Rev. W. Gilmore, Philip Vauters and Eliza J. Fling, all of this county.

Married the 9th inst. by Rev. W. Gilmore, James F. Timms and Lydia Ann Head, all of this county.

Vol. XXIII, No. 9 – March 2, 1839
Died yesterday morning at 8 o'clock in position as Doorkeeper, Senate Chamber, Mr. Edward Wyer, aged about 62 years, served in Navy when young. Native of Boston. [*National Intelligencer*]

Vol. XXIII, No. 10 – March 9, 1839
Married at Prospect Hill, Va. on Thursday the 28th ult. by Rev. James Curley of Georgetown College, Henry W. Thomas, Esq., atty at law in Fairfax Co., and Julia M. Jackson, youngest daughter of late Richard Jackson, Esq., of said county.

Married Monday eve last at Parsonage M. E. Church by Rev. Saml. Keppler, James H. Chamblin, Esq., of Loudoun Co., and Octavia, youngest daughter of John Keppler, Esq., of Carlisle, Pa.

Married Thursday the 28th ult. by Rev. Wm. Gilmore, Dr. Samuel G. Buck of Leesburg and Sarah C. Hall of Warren Co.

Vol. XXIII, No. 11 – March 16, 1839
Married at Locust Hill on Thursday the 14th inst. by Rev. Mr. Boyd, John Throgmorton, Esq. and Mary B., daughter of late Charles Pendleton Tutt, Esq.

Died in town Tuesday the 12th inst., Mrs. Margaret Garner, wife of Mr. James Garner, aged 66 years.

Died in Georgetown on Thursday the 7th inst., Clement Smith, Esq.

Vol. XXIII, No. 12 – March 23, 1839
Married January 29th last in St. Louis, Mo, Wm. W. Kitzmiller, formerly of Leesburg and Margarette Mitchell of Indiana.

Married in Maryland at residence of Joshua Chilton, Esq., on Thursday the 14th inst., George Rhodes, Esq. of Leesburg and Mrs. Jane Green.

Vol. XXIII, No. 13 – March 30, 1839
Died in town Thursday the 28th inst., Fayette W. Ball, son of late Dr. Charles B. Ball, age 19 years.

Vol. XXIII, No. 15 – April 13, 1839
Died at his residence on Friday, April 5, Eli Hunt, in 54th year, left wife and large family of children, member Methodist Episcopal Church.

Vol. XXIII, No. 16 – April 20, 1839

Married the 16th inst. by Gilmore, Sydnor B. Johnson of Fauquier Co. and Rosanna R. Heskit of Loudoun.

Married Tuesday last by Birkby, William K. Hoge and Sarah Ann Janney, both of Loudoun Co.

Died in town on Monday eve the 15th inst. at residence of Fleming Hixon, Esq., Mrs. Mahala J. Paxson, aged about 30 years.

Vol. XXIII, No. 17 – April 27, 1839

Married Tuesday last in Montgomery Co., Md. by Rev. Thos. Birkby, Zadock Talbert of Prince George Co., Md. and Henrietta Benson of former place.

Married Tuesday the 23rd inst. by Rev. George Adie at Friendship residence of Charles Gassaway, Esq., David W. Porter, Esq. of Montgomery Co., Md. and Mary E. Catlett of Loudoun.

Married Wednesday the 10th inst. at N.Y. by Rt. Rev. Bishop Onderdonk, N.Y. Diocese, Rev. Lewis P. W. Balch, rector of St. Bartholomew's Church, N.Y., and Anna, eldest daughter of the Hon. William Jay.

Vol. XXIII, No. 18 – May 4, 1839

Died the 26th ult., Mrs. Elizabeth Maffett, in 62nd year.

Vol. XXIII, No. 19 – May 11, 1839

Married the 6th inst. by Rev. James Berkeley, Henry Carter and Mary Jane Eaches, all of Loudoun Co.

Died in town on the 3rd inst., Mrs. Elizabeth Hilliard, in 86th year, relict of John Hilliard, dec'd, a soldier of the army of the Revolution.

Died within a few hours on Thursday the 2nd inst., Virginia and Elizabeth, daughters of Capt. Gustavus Elgin. This disease was scarlet fever in its most malignant form.

Vol. XXIII, No. 20 – May 18, 1839

Married Tuesday the 14th inst. by Rev. Thos. Birkby, John W. Woody of this town and Mary A. McKnight.

Vol. XXIII, No. 21 – May 25, 1839

Married at Shoal Creek, Dorchester Co., Md. on Thursday the 16th inst., Philip Pendleton Dandridge, Esq. of Jefferson Co., Va. and Caroline Fitzhugh Goldsborough, daughter of late Gov. Charles Goldsborough.

Died in Carrollton, La on 6 April, William Jones Jr., formerly of Loudoun Co.

Vol. XXIII, No. 23 – June 8, 1839

Died at York England at 115 years, Henry Brough. This patriarch was born of Dutch parents at N.Y. He was formerly in the army and was in the battle of Bunker's Hall. He also served in Holland under the Duke of York.

Died late, Adam Boss, native of Lancaster Co. Pa, last 57 years a resident of Baltimore. Volunteered very young and took his father's place, who was drafted to go with Penna troops. With Gen'l. Washington at capture of the Hessians when they were secured and marched to Lancaster jail and he was one of the band that formed the guard. He was also with the American army at Yorktown. At close of Rev. the company now called the First Baltimore Light Infantry then called the Light Blues was under Capt. Mackenheimer. Mr. Boss was one of its first members. A 50 year member of Prot. Ch., left 6 children and many grand and great-grandchildren. His remains were followed to the tomb by a large number of relatives, friends, etc. Sunday last also by the First Baltimore Light Infantry Co. who performed on solemn occasion, the duty of guards. [*Baltimore Patriot,* May 21]

Vol. XXIII, No. 25 – June 22, 1839

Married on the 5th inst. by Rev. Morrison, Henry Bedinger, Esq. of Jefferson Co. and Margaret E., daughter of General George Rust of this county.

Died at residence in Fauquier Co. on Tuesday the 4th inst., William Hampton, native of Fairfax Co., 4th 100th birthday.

Died the 16th inst. Charles P. Janney, youngest son of late Elisha Janney of Hillsboro, in 21st year.

Vol. XXIII, No. 26 – June 29, 1839

Married June 20th inst. by Rev. Mr. Adie at Greenway, Loudoun Co., Major John West Minor of Alexandria, DC. and Louisa Fairfax Catlett, daughter of Charles I. Catlett of the first named place.

Married Wednesday, June 19, by Rev. Wm. Wickes, Samuel P. Thompson and Elizabeth, daughter of Wm. Hough Sr., both of Loudoun Co.

Vol. XXIII, No. 28 – July 6, 1839
[Incorrectly numbered, should be No. 27]

Married Tuesday the 2nd inst. by Rev. Wm. Gilmore, William Weedon and Mary Wright, both of Loudoun Co.

Died yesterday after 79 years, Mrs. Winifred Gales, consort of Joseph Gales, Esq., of this city (late of N.C.,) mother of one of the editors of the *National Intelligencer*. Native of Newark, England emigrated to this county with her surviving husband and her then living children in 1795. Residence in Philadelphia until 1799, remainder of time except for past 6 years in N.C. [*National Intelligencer,* June 27]

Vol. XXIII, No. 28 – July 13, 1839

Died at residence in county on 27th ult., Enoch Francis, in 73rd year, admitted member of Baptist Church North Fork, baptised by Rev. W. Gilmore on 13 May 1827, blind many years.

Died at his residence in Loudoun Co. on the 7th inst., Samuel Welby DeButts, age 25 years, neighborhood of Hillsborough will long hold in remembrance the virtues of Samuel Welby DeButts.

Died in Hannibal, Mo on May 21, Col. John B. D. Smith, formerly a delegate in Virginia Legislature from Frederick Co., aged about 45 years.

Vol. XXIII, No. 32 – August 10, 1839

Married 1st inst. by Rev. Andrew H. H. Boyd, Robert Wade and Amelia Ann Myers, daughter of late Thomas Myers, all of Loudoun Co.

Vol. XXIII, No. 33 – August 17, 1839

Died Thursday, July 18, at Needwood, Frederick Co., Md., Archibald Lee of Montgomery Co., in 59th year. At 18 entered Army U.S. stationed on frontier. Officer under late Col. Gaither of Revolutionary War memory, repeatedly elected to State Legislature.

Died Saturday the 10th inst., Edwin C. Broun, Post Master at Middleburg.

Vol. XXIII, No. 34 – August 24, 1839

Married the 20th inst. by Gilmore, Scott Veirs and Lydia Dyson, all of Montgomery Co., Md.

Died in Ohio on the 11th inst., John Parsons, aged 40 years, formerly of this county.

Vol. XXIII, No. 35 – August 31, 1839

Died in Bedford Springs, Va. on the 10th ult., where he had gone for benefit of his health, Morris Osburn of this county, aged 70 years.

Died Sunday morn the 25th inst., Commodore Daniel T. Patterson, U.S. Navy and Commandant of the Navy Yard and Station in Washington, DC.

Vol. XXIII, No. 37 – September 14, 1839

Married August 20 by Rev. Thaddeus Herndon, William M. Prosser of Kentucky Co. and Mary Ish of Loudoun Co.

Married Tuesday, September 10, by Rev. Mr. Boyd, Isaac Vandeventer and Caroline Braden, daughter of Mr. John Braden, all of Loudoun Co.

Vol. XXIII, No. 39 – September 28, 1839

Died September 9th in 18th year, Miss Margaret McIlhany, daughter of Mortimer McIlhany, of this county, on visit to Kentucky at time, at residence of Mr. A. D. Offutt.

Vol. XXIII, No. 40 – October 5, 1839

Died at his residence in county on Tuesday the 1st inst., George Apsey, highly respectable citizen.

Name changed to *The Leesburg Genius of Liberty*

Vol. XXIII, No. 41 – October 12, 1839

Died at his residence in Fairfax Co. on Wednesday the 2nd inst., Thomas Moss, Clerk of the County Court, in 60th year of age.

Vol. XXIII, No. 42 – October 19, 1839

Body of John Hunton found murdered in vicinity of Washington, Georgetown. His own son has been arrested as murderer!

Vol. XXIII, No. 43 – October 26, 1839

Married by Rev. Gilmore Thursday the 17th inst., Thomas Smitson and Eliza A. Campbell, all of Loudoun.

Married by Rev. Gilmore on Tuesday the 22nd inst., V. W. Linthicum and Mary Jane Hoyle, both of Montgomery Co., Md.

Died at his residence near Middleburg on Monday the 12th inst., Major Burr Powell in 73rd year of age.

Vol. XXIII, No. 44 – November 2, 1839

Died in town Tuesday the 29th ult., Mrs. Anne Roszell, widow of late Stephen C. Roszell, Esq.

Married Tuesday the 22nd ult. at Unity Hill by Rev. Mr. Quigley, Wm. Norris Berkley of Alexandria, DC. and Emily W., daughter of James Pattison of Dorchester Co., Md.

Vol. XXIII, No. 45 – November 9, 1839

Married the 29th ult. in Middleburg by Rev. Mr. Broadus, Dr. T. P. Hereford of Haymarket, Va. and Matilda W. Lacey, eldest daughter of Dr. Elias Lacey of Laceyville, Loudoun Co.

Vol. XXIII, No. 46 – November 16, 1839

Married Tuesday the 12th inst. by Gilmore, P. L. Bussard and Caroline Amanda Sheid, all of Loudoun Co.

Died at Baltimore on Sunday morn the 10th inst., Luke Tiernan, age 81 years, native of Ireland, 60 years a merchant in Baltimore.

Vol. XXIII, No. 47 – November 23, 1839

Died in town on the 21st inst. Asa Peck, age about 45 years.

Died the 3rd inst., Dr. Carter Berkeley of Edgewood, Hanover Co., in 72nd year. Graduate of Edinburgh School, distinguished physician.

Vol. XXIII, No. 48 – November 30, 1839

Died at his residence near this place yesterday the 20th inst., William Daniel, Esq., many years Judge of General Court of Va. Member Va. Legislature, memorable session 1798-99, zealous advocate of Madison's report & resolution. Left wife & 4 children. [*Lynchburg Virginian* Nov. 21]

Vol. XXIII, No. 49 – December 7, 1839

Died in town Thursday the 5th inst., John Adams, Esq., age 69 years, eighteen months near Leesburg, formerly many years at Middleburg. Member M. E. Church for upwards 30 years.

Vol. XXIII, No. 50 – December 14, 1839

Married the 28th ult. by Rev. Mr. Packard, Henry T. Harrison, Esq. of this town and Mary E. Jones, daughter of Gen. Walter Jones of Washington City, DC.

Married Thursday the 5th inst. by Gilmore, Charles Wm. Simpson and Emily M. Luck, all of this county.

Vol. XXIII, No. 51 – December 21, 1839

Died Sunday morn the 15th inst. at residence of his father in this place, Mr. William Ault Jr, age 20. Member Loudoun Volunteers – leaves resolved to wear crepe on the left arm for the space of 30 days in testimony of their regard.

Vol. XXIII, No. 52 – December 28, 1839

Died on the 23rd inst., Mrs. Margaret Tucker, in 50th year.

Vol. XXIV, No. 1 – January 4, 1840

Married Thursday, December 26, by Gilmore, Lorenzo D. Thompson and Martha Francis Feagins, all of Loudoun.

Vol. XXIV, No. 2 – January 11, 1840

Died at residence at Broad Run Bridge on Friday the 3rd inst., William Whaley, about 40 years of age.

Vol. XXIV, No. 3 – January 18, 1840

Married Norristown the 8th by Rev. Mr. Stem, Samuel Nixon, M.D. of Caddo Parish, Louisana, and Emily, daughter of Edwin Magee, Esq. of former place.

Vol. XXIV, No. 4, January 25, 1840

Married Tuesday the 21st inst. by Rev. Wm. Gilmore, Benjamin B. Benson & Mrs. Matilda Williams, both of Montgomery, Md.

Married Tuesday the 21st inst. by Rev. Wm. Gilmore, David T. Jones and Mary Ann Dawson, both of Montgomery Co., Md.

Married January 2nd at residence of Felix Seymour, Esq., Hardy Co., Va. by Rev. J. A. Collins, Rev. Maybury Goheen and Jane McNeill, daughter of Daniel McNeil, Esq.

Died Saturday, the 18th inst., John A. Divine, 3 month old infant son of James F. Divine.

Vol. XXIV, No. 5 – February 1, 1840

Died Thursday the 23rd ult. at her residence in this town, Mrs. Anna Rose, wife of John Rose. Mrs. Rose last child of the late Col. George Beall of Georgetown, D. C. Residence of Loudoun since her marriage in 1792. Member of M. E. Church 30 years. Aged about 68 years. [long obit]

Vol. XXIV, No. 7 – February 15, 1840

Married Thursday the 6th inst. by Gilmore, Mr. Thomas Claxton of Montgomery Co. and Miss Caroline Fichter of Loudoun Co.

Died Wednesday the 5th in 81st year, Mrs. Mary Mead, relict of late William Mead, at house of son Joseph Mead. Buried Friends burying ground, Waterford, next to husband. Native of this county. Brother Benjamin Shreve, parents Episcopal, made no profession herself. [long obit]

Died at her residence near Hillsborough the 9th inst., Mrs. Albina Summers, member Friends Society, consort of William Summers. Left husband and bereaved children. [long obit]

Vol. XXIV, No. 9 – February 29, 1840

Married Tuesday the 25th inst. by Gilmore, Ishmael Dove and Mary Whaley, both of Loudoun Co.

Married Thursday the 20th inst. by Gilmore, Benjamin Hummer and Emily Havener, both of Loudoun.

Died Thursday the 27th inst., Henry D. Magill, 2 year old child of Dr. H. D. and Ann E. Magill.

Vol. XXIV, No. 10 – March 7, 1840

Married Tuesday the 31st inst. by Rev. Joseph White, Dr. Richard H. Edwards and Ann Eliza, daughter of Dr. Charles G. Edwards of Loudoun Co.

Married Thursday the 20th ult. by Birkby, Fenton Johnson and Elizabeth J. Stephenson, both of this county.

Married Tuesday the 25th ult. by Birkby, John R. Skinner and Sarah B. Stover, both of this county.

Married Wednesday the 26th ult. by Birkby, Garrett B. Walker and Adeline V. Skinner, both of this county.

Died at residence near Leesburg on Sunday the 1st, James Greenlease, age 70 years.

Vol. XXIV, No. 11 – March 14, 1840

Married February 10 by Rev. Samuel Gover, William Myers and Miss Mary Donaldson, all of this county.

Died at residence in county on Tuesday the 9th ult., John Brown, age 73 years. Left family, was churchman.

Vol. XXIV, No. 12 – March 21, 1840

Died in Loudoun Co. on Sunday, February 16, of dropsy, Mrs. Anna Lafferty, former consort of Thomas Backhouse, at age 65 years 2 months 16 days, Not church member, but partial to Society of Friends.

Died in Alexandria on Sunday the 15th inst., Colin Auld, Esq. age 74 years. Native of Scotland, 41 years at Alexandria.

Died March 13, James Johnston, native of Alexandria, Va., aged 43 years.

Died on 25th ult., Jeanette White, 17 years old, Millersburg, Ohio.

Vol. XXIV, No. 13 – March 28, 1840

Died Monday eve the 23rd inst., Nicholas Fry, a soldier of the Army of the Revolution and Pensioner of the U.S., age 95 years. Member of M. E. Church, consigned to tomb with military honors.

Vol. XXIV, No. 15 – April 11, 1840

Died on the 6th inst. at age 42 years, Margaret Hannah Douglas, wife of Doct. John H. McCabe, daughter of late Charles Binns, Esq. 16 years past member of Protestant Episcopal Church, 4 years under ministry of Rev. Charles B. Tippet, then stationed in this borough, she attached to M. E. Church. [long obit]

Vol. XXIV, No. 16 – April 18, 1840

Died in Baltimore, Md. on March 31 at age 6 years, Mary Anna Lavinia, only daughter of William & Ruth B. Woody.

Married the 12th inst. by Rev. Samuel Gover, Isaac L. Mock and Elizabeth S. Paxson, all of this county.

Married Georgetown, DC. on Thursday, April 9th, by Rev. Mr. Johns, His Excellency Alexander DeBodisCo. Chamberlain, of his Majesty, Emporer of all the Russias, his Actual Council of State, Envoy Extraordinary and Minister Plenipotentiary to U.S. and Miss Harriet Williams, daughter of Brooke Williams, Esq.

Vol. XXIV, No. 17 – April 25, 1840

Married the 16th inst. by Rev. Sam. Gover, Samuel Dixon and Eliza Smitly, all of this county.

On same day, Jacob D. Lemon and Mary Jane Bodine, all of this county.

Married the 16th inst. by Rev. Thos. Birkby, George W. McKim and Miss Martina Merchant, both of this county.

Vol. XXIV, No. 19 – May 9, 1840

Married Tuesday the 28th ult. by Rev. Septimus Tuston, Thomas H. Fowke, Esq. late of Prince Wm. Co. and Anne Weaver, daughter of Joseph Weaver of Fauquier.

Vol. XXIV, No. 20 – May 16, 1840

Married Thursday the 12th inst. by Rev. Mr. Boyd, James Graham and Catherine Klein, both of Lovettsville.

Died on 5th of April last, at Holly Spring, Miss., Alfred H. Powell, Esqr. Ntaive of Loudoun, went to west to pursue his profession. [long obit]

Vol. XXIV, No. 21 – May 23, 1840

Married the 14th inst. by Rev. Wm. Gilmore, Emanuel Vansickler and Mary Jane Coe, all of Loudoun.

Married the 19th inst. by Rev. Wm. Gilmore, Nimrod Triplett of Frederick Co., Md. and Susanna E. Saffer of Loudoun Co.

Married the 19th inst. by Rev. Wm. Gilmore, Luke Fields and Catharine Shell, all of Loudoun.

Vol. XXIV, No. 22 – May 30, 1840

Married the 28th inst. by Rev. Samuel Gover, James G. Otlay and Louisa Hope, all of this county.

Died in town on Tuesday inst., Mrs. Emily Cornelia Smart, wife of John P. Smart, aged 29 years.

Died on the 27th inst., Micheal M. Morallee, aged 43 years.

Vol. XXIV, No. 23 – June 6, 1840

Married the 3rd inst. by Rev. Gilmore, Robert P. Hutchinson and Virginia Bayley, both of Loudoun.

Married Thursday the 28th ult. by Rev. J. T. Johnson, George Davis and Hannah Ann Allen, both of Alexandria.

Vol. XXIV, No. 24 – June 13, 1840

Married the 4th inst. by Rev. Birkby, Wm. M. Collier and Mrs. Mary Styles, both of Loudoun.

Married the 4th inst. by Gilmore, Wm. Thomas and Elizabeth Stewart, both of Loudoun.

Vol. XXIV, No. 25 – June 20, 1840

Married in town Wednesday the 17th inst. by Rev. George Adie, Robert W. Gray, Esq. and Mary Elizabeth, daughter of Robert Bentley, Esq.

Vol. XXIV, No. 26 – June 27, 1840

Married in town Tuesday the 23rd inst. by Birkby, Frederick A. Crissey and Mary Elizabeth, daughter of John Surghnor.

Married Sunday the 14th inst. at Waterford by Rev. Samuel Gover, Andrew M. Cridler and Rachel Smallwood, both of that town.

Married in Washington City on the 16th inst. by Rev. John Davis, James H. Boss, Esq. and Ann S. Benson.

Died at residence in county on Monday the 22nd inst., Charles Chamblin, age 72 years.

Died in Washington on Friday the 19th inst., Alfred Newman Balch, age 19 years, only son of Judge Alfred Balch of Florida.

Vol. XXIV, No. 28 – July 11, 1840

Died on the 2nd inst. in 54th year, Sarah, wife of Anthony P. Gover, daughter of late Elisha Janney, formerly of this town. *Alexandria Gazette.*

Vol. XXIV, No. 29 – July 18, 1840

Died in county Monday the 13th inst., Adolphus S. Hart, nearly 7 years, son of Edward & Eliza Hart.

Vol. XXIV, No. 31 – August 1, 1840

Married Thursday last in this city by Rev. Geo. G. Cookman, James Harvey
Monroe and Maria E. Berkeley of this city. *Alexandria Gazette, July 24.*

Vol. XXIV, No. 32 – August 8, 1840

Died in this town on Tuesday the 4th inst., Charles S., 14 month old only son of
Charles A. & Mary R. Johnston.

Vol. XXIV, No. 33 – August 15, 1840

Died at Bolington in this county on Monday the 3rd inst., Mrs. Eleanor Boland,
wife of Daniel Boland, in 32nd year.

Died in this town Friday the 7th inst., John C., 2 year old youngest son of James
& Sarah Littleton.

Died at Oatland in Montgomery Co., Md. on the 22nd ult., Mrs. Margaret C.
Bowie, relict of Washington Bowie, formerly of Georgetown, DC., in 67th year
of her age.

Notice by Jacob Gideon, townsman and fellow soldier, Sgt. Lawrence Everhart,
died Sunday last at Middletown, Frederick Co. at his residence at age 85
years. Dist. service 1776 – Germantown & Brandywine, Guilford Courthouse,
Camden Meadows & Cowpens, captured twice for brief period, refused
commission under Col. William Washington in troop of Cavalry. *National
Intelligencer.* [long obit]

Vol. XXIV, No. 34 – August 22, 1840

Married the 13th inst. by Rev. S. Gover, John E. Fulton and Massey Warner, all of
this county.

Married Thursday the 20th inst. by Gilmore, Thomas I. Brabham and Martha
Stephenson, all of this county.

Married Thursday the 13th inst. by Gilmore, Phineas Gibson of Loudoun and
Harriet A. Lanham of Fauquier Co.

Another Revolutionary Hero Gone. Died near Middleburg on the 6th inst., Edward
Harvin, aged about 88 years. He was a private during all the war of the
Revolution, fought at the Battle of the Cow Pens [*sic*], Camden and Guilford
Court house and was wounded in three places. He applied for a pension in
1820 but justice was never awarded him until the year 1833, when he last
obtained a pension. He was emphatically an honest man, the noblest work of
God.

Vol. XXIV, No. 36 – September 5, 1840

Died in town Sunday the 30th ult., Mrs. Matilda Mason, consort of Richard B.
Mason of Georgetown, DC.

Died the 8th ult. at No. 6, residence of late John Carter, Mrs. Harriet W. Chilton,
wife of Wm. O. Chilton, Esq. of Miss. *Alexandria Gazette.* [obit]

Vol. XXIV, No. 38 – September 19, 1840

Married the 13th inst. by Rev. S. Gover, William Lamb and Elizabeth Gregg, all of
Loudoun.

Died at his residence in Clarke Co., Va. Thursday last, Judge Richard E. Parker,
Court of Appeals of Virginia.

Vol. XXIV, No. 39 – September 26, 1840

Married Wednesday the 23rd inst. by Rev. Samuel Gover, William Riggs and
Caroline Woodward, all of this county.

Vol. XXIV, No. 40 – October 3, 1840
Died Monday the 28th ult., John W. Coe, in 57th year.
Died Wednesday the 30th ult., John Chamblin of a tumour of the paroted gland. Left wife and six children.

Vol. XXIV, No. 41 – October 10, 1840
Married the 8th inst. by Gilmore, William D. Vermillion and Jane Smitzen, both of this county.
Died in this town Wednesday eve the 7th inst., Isaac Harris, in 70th year, member M. E. Church, long ill 16 years.
Died Sunday the 4th inst. in Alexandria, DC., Robert I. Taylor, Esq., in 63rd year.
Died Baltimore on Thursday at Wilk St. Parsonage, Virginia Waring, eldest daughter of Rev. Samuel Keppler, aged 7 years 7 months 26 days.

Vol. XXIV, No. 42 – October 17, 1840
Married Thursday, October 8, by Birkby, Henry Williams and Rebecca E. Johnson.
Married Thursday, October 8, by Rev. Samuel Gover, Uriah Stedman and Louisa Carpenter, both of this place.
Married Tuesday the 13th inst. by Rev. Thomas Birkby, John D. Baldwin and Susan H. Love, both of this county.

Vol. XXIV, No. 43 – October 24, 1840
Married Thursday the 15th inst. by Rev. S. Gover, William Jackson and Julia Ann Woodard, both of this county.
Married Thursday the 15th inst. by Birkby, John Wynkoop and Mary Campbell, both of this county.

Vol. XXIV, No. 44 – October 31, 1840
Died of croup on Sunday, October 27, Armistead Mason, youngest son of Col. Benjamin Shreve, age 1 year 10 months 18 days.
Died at residence near Middleburg on the 20th inst., Capt. John Beveridge, in 65th year, at death weighed 450 lbs, left wife and no children.
Died on the 3rd inst. at Rox Hill, Montgomery Co. Md., Eliza, wife of Rev. Mines, in 56th year, from ruptured blood vessel.

Vol. XXIV, No. 47 – November 21, 1840
Married on Wednesday the 28th ult. at residence of Rev. J. G. Watt in Loudoun Co. by the Rev. N. J. B. Morgan, Rev. Elisha D. Phelps of the Baltimore Conference and Mary W. Bennett, daughter of Charles Bennett, Esq. dec'd.
Married Thursday the 13th inst. by Birkby, John Arnet and Mary Elizabeth Reed, both of this county.
Married Tuesday the 17th inst., John Turner and Juliet Ann Wildman, both of this county.
Died at Charlestown, Va. on the 8th inst., Mrs. Elizabeth Noland of Loudoun Co., age 59 years.

Vol. XXIV, No. 48 – November 28, 1840
Died in town on the 23rd inst., Mrs. Susan Fortney, age about 80 years, widow of the late George Fortney.

Vol. XXIV, No. 49 – December 5, 1840

Married Thursday, December 3, by Gilmore, Joseph Thompson and Susannah Gregg, both of Loudoun.

Died Sunday, November 29, near Snickersville, Loudoun Co., Mrs. Rachel Wornel, consort of John Wornel, in 40th year of her age. Left husband and large circle of friends.

Died at Monroe Township (Ohio) on the 14th ult., George Downs, age 68 years. [*Knox Co. (Ohio) Republican*]

Vol. XXIV, No. 51 – December 19, 1840

Married Tuesday the 15th inst. by Gilmore, Erasmus Perry of Montgomery Co., Md. and Adeline M. Sheid of Loudoun Co.

Vol. XXIV, No. 52 – December 26, 1840

Married on the 3rd inst. at Lowndes Co., Ala. at residence of Dr. F. L. Lee by Rev. Wm. Johnson, __ Bedford, Esq., atty at law of Montgomery, Ala., and Ellen A. Lee, formerly of Loudoun Co., daughter of late Ludwell Lee, Esq. of this county.

Married Tuesday the 22nd inst. by Rev. S. Gover, Braxton B. Jeffries and Miss Tacy H. Daniel, both of this county.

Vol. XXV, No. 2 – January 9, 1841

Married December 31 by Rev. S. Gover, Augustine McDaniel and Elizabeth Lamb, both of this county.

Died October 26 at his residence, Green Wood, Caddo Parish, La, Dr. Samuel Nixon, in 34th year of age, leaving wife and mother.

Vol. XXV, No. 3 – January 16, 1841

Married Tuesday eve the 5th inst. by Rev. Birkby, James T. Vermillion and Nancy Cruthus [*sic*] [Carruthers], both of this county.

Died in Washington City the 7th inst., Col. William Lawrence, late U.S. Army, age 60 years old. Native of Calvert Co., Md. Platoon Officer, 1808 promoted to Col. "by reg promotion." Comm. Ft. Boyer or Mobile Pt. September 1814 as Major attacked by British navel force under Commodore Nichols and land forces of Marines and Indians under notorous Captains Woodbine, Ashethnot and Hombrister. ... Served as Col. 5th regt. for 5 or 6 years, pension for work at Ft. Boyer. [long obit]

Vol. XXV, No. 4 – January 23, 1841

Died in town on Wednesday the 20th inst., Ann Divine, 64 years old, wife of Aaron Divine.

Married Thursday the 14th inst. by Rev. S. Gover, Richard W. Wade and Mary E. Myers, both of this county.

Married Thursday the 14th inst. by Birkby, Wm. H. Schooley and Hanna Stocks, both of this county.

Vol. XXV, No. 5 – January 30, 1841

Married Monday last by Birkby, George W. Bruerd and Jane Stream, both of this county.

Married Tuesday last by Birkby, Harman J. Gregg and Anna Maria Janney, both of this county.

Died in town Saturday the 23rd inst., Mrs. Christiana H. Clagatt, wife of Dr. Thomas H. Clagett, daughter of late Benjamin Oden, Esq. of Prince George Co., Md. [long obit]

Died on October 26 at his residence in Caddo Parish, Louisiana, Dr. Samuel Nixon, formerly of Loudoun Co. April 1834 graduate of Jefferson Medical College, practiced in Loudoun, ever in poor health, moved to Louisiana September. Left mother, brother and sister.

Died Wednesday the 20th inst. at residence near Warrenton, Fauquier Co., Richard Weadon, in 82nd year.

Died Thursday the 21st inst. at residence in Navy Yard, Commodore Thomas H. Stevens, Commandant, Navy Yard, Washington City, age 47 years.

Vol. XXV, No. 6 – February 6, 1841

Died Sunday, January 31, Eliza, wife of Daniel Smith, long of this place.

Died the 31st ult., Louisa, only child of Eliza Ann & Wm. W. Divine, age 5 weeks 3 days.

Vol. XXV, No. 7 – February 13, 1841

Died the 8th inst. at residence in Leesburg, Richard H. Henderson, atty at law, aged 59 years. Leaves large family...resident of Leesburg more than 30 years long. Attorney for the Commonwealth in the Superior and Inferior Courts of the County. [long obit]

Vol. XXV, No. 8 – February 20, 1841

Married Tuesday the 9th inst. by Birkby, Hannibal James and Elizabeth P. Bradfield, both of this county.

Vol. XXV, No. 9 – February 27, 1841

Died the 13th inst. at 5 years old, Delia, daughter of John L. Powell of this county.

Married on Tuesday 23rd inst. by Gilmore, Richard Alexander to Mary Elizabeth Brabham, both of Mt. Gilead, Loudoun County.

Vol. XXV, No. 11 – March 13, 1841

Married on the 10th inst. by Rev. S. Gover, Daniel Monday and Mary Ann Taylor, both of this county.

Died January 1841, Mary Beacham of this county of Northumberland, born 1812. Mother member of Baptist Church, father died in her infancy.

Vol. XXV, No. 12 – March 20, 1841

Married the 11th inst. by Rev. S. Gover, William Rian and Elizabeth Yabower, all of this county.

Married the 11th inst. by Gilmore, John W. Stallings and Mary A. Dickey, all of this county.

Married Monday the 8th inst. by Birkby, Isaac Moore and Catharine Ann Kent, all of this county.

Married the 12th inst. by Birkby, Jas. Bowley and Nancy Updike, both of this county.

Vol. XXV, No. 13 – March 27, 1841

Married Thursday the 18th inst. by Rev. Samuel Gover, James H. Muse and Ann Eliza Seeder, both of this place.

Married Thursday the 18th inst. by Birkby, Thos. Cornelle and Harriet Ann Hawes, both of this county.

Married Thursday the 18th inst. by Birkby, Bernard Charlton and Mary Mills, both of this county.

Died on 11th inst., Mr. John Johnson, native of Ireland, resident of Alexandria, leaves wife and 5 children. *[Alexandria Gazette,* Mar 19]

Died at Dover, Loudoun County on Friday 19 March, Mrs. Elizabeth Rogers, wife of William Rogers, in the 42nd year of her age.

Vol. XXV, No. 15 – April 10, 1841

Died on the 3rd inst. at residence in Waterford, Thomas Philips, age 66 years, member of Society of Friends.

Vol. XXV, No. 16 – April 17, 1841

Died Friday the 9th inst. in 49th year, Mrs. Anna Cecelia McKenna, wife of J. L. McKenna, daughter of late Ludwell Lee, Esq.

Died the 11th inst. at residence of son Major William Fulton, Robert Fulton, Esq., at nearly 78 years. Predicted 30 years ago he would die in 78th year.

Vol. XXV, No. 17 – April 24, 1841

Married Tuesday, April 8, by Birkby, Henry Milhollen and Charlotte Walker, both of this county.

Married Tuesday, April 20, by Birkby, Joseph Wildman and Charlotte Turner, both of this county.

Died in Florence, Ala. on March 29, Mrs. Mary L. Pope, wife of Willis Pope, born Loudoun Co., 1801 member Presbyterian Church.

Vol. XXV, No. 18 – May 1, 1841

Died at Mt. Gilead, Marion Co., Ohio on April 7, Mary Van Horn, relict of James Van Horn, age 74 years.

Died at Cumberland, Md. on April 22, Alice Janney, daughter of Samuel H. & Mary E. Williams, age 3 years.

Died Thursday the 22nd ult. in Alexandria, DC., Rev. Jas. Berkely [*sic*] of Baltimore Annual Conference, age 40 years.

Vol. XXV, No. 19 – May 8, 1841

Died in town at residence of Dr. Jno. H. Kaighn, her son-in-law, on Friday the 30th ult., Mrs. Eleanor Triplett, wife of late Simon Triplett, aged 59 years.

Died Friday the 30th ult. at residence near Union, Thomas M. Colston, Esq.

Died Monday the 3rd inst. near Leesburg, Garret Wynkoop.

Vol. XXV, No. 20 – May 15, 1841

Died at Harper's Ferry on the 25th ult., Otho Barron, "gallant soldier in the last war, and lately in the Florida service." Served twenty-five years.

Vol. XXV, No. 21 – May 22, 1841

Married Thursday the 6th inst. by Birkby, William H. Wey and Permelia A. Wilkerson, both of this county.

Married Thursday the 13th inst. by Birkby, Logan Osborne and Miss Margaret C. Osborne, both of this county.

Married in New Albany, Ind. on April 13 by Rev. Enoch Woods, Thomas C. Shively of that city and Susan B. Shaw of Loudoun Co.

Died at residence in this town on Friday, May 14, Rev. Stephen George Roszell, native 53 years, M. E. Minister, died in 73rd year. 51 year member of Baltimore Conference, oldest itinerate M. E. preacher. [long obit]

Vol. XXV, No. 22 – May 29, 1841

Married Tuesday eve last by Gilmore, Thomas Glasscock and Emily Ann
Fletcher, daughter of Dr. Fletcher, all of Fauquier Co.

Vol. XXV, No. 23 – June 5, 1841

Married the 25th ult. by Elder R. N. Herndon, Parkinson D. Shepherd of Clarke
Co. and Mrs. M. A. Margaret Jennings of Loudoun.
Married by same on the 27th ult., James Alder Jr. and Amanda Elizabeth Marshall
of Snickersville.
Married in New Albany, Ind. on the 20th ult. by Rev. Enoch G. Wood, Joseph
Gray and Mary B. Shaw, formerly of this town.

Vol. XXV, No. 24 – June 12, 1841

Married Thursday the 3rd inst. by Birkby, Samuel A. Tillett and Caroline S.
Dennis, all of this county.
Married Thursday the 3rd inst. by Birkby, Hezekiah Davis and Francis Brooks, all
of this county.
Died the 31st inst., Mary Jane, consort of Rev. Samuel Keppler of Baltimore
Annual Conference, daughter of Basil & Elizabeth Waring of city. [*National
Intelligencer*, June 5. See also 28 August 1841]

Vol. XXV, No. 25 – June 19, 1841

Married Thursday the 10th inst. by Rev. S. Gover, Absolom Johnson and Louisa
J. Hough, both of this county.

Vol. XXV, No. 26 – June 26, 1841

Married Thursday the 17th inst. by Birkby, Wm. Poulton and Anna Jared, both of
this county.

Vol. XXV, No. 28 – July 10, 1841

Married Tuesday, June 29, by Revd. R. N. Herndon, John L. Gill and Mary Todd,
all of Loudoun Co.

Vol. XXV, No. 29 – July 17, 1841

Died at residence of mother in Fairfax Co., Va. on Friday, July 2, George W.
Smith, aged 30 years. Accidental death. Left mother, brother, sister.

Vol. XXV, No. 31 – July 31, 1841

Died in Aldie on Sunday the 25th inst. Lewis Ellzey, Esq. Interred at family estate
at Mount Middleton where he was born April 1780. Mr. Ellzey was only
surviving brother of late Wm. Ellzey of Loudoun Co.

Vol. XXV, No. 32 – August 7, 1841

Died at residence at Laceville, Loudoun Co. on the 30th ult., Sarah Lacey, in 80th
year.

Vol. XXV, No. 33 – August 14, 1841

Married at Georgetown on Wednesday the 4th inst. by Rev. Wm. Edwards, Hugh
Divine of Leesburg and Mary Elizabeth Rollins of former place.
Married the 5th inst. by Gilmore, James F. Walden and Ann M. Vauters, all of
Montgomery Co., Md.

Married the 5th inst. by Rev. Sam Gover, Charles William Schooley and Mary Hough, both of this county.

Died at Snickersville on Saturday, August 7, James E. Chew, Esq., age 21 years. Left sister.

Died at Aldie on 6th inst. at age 5 years, Betty Burwell, youngest child of Lewis Berkeley, of that place.

Vol. XXV, No. 34 – August 21, 1841

Died Saturday, July 18, at residence of husband Wm. H. Day, Esq. in Smithfield in 23rd year, Mrs. Phoebe S. Day, daughter of Wm. Chilton, Esq. of Loudoun Co. Left son, member of Presbyterian Church. [*Richmond Enquirer*]

Vol. XXV, No. 35 – August 28, 1841

Died at Washington City on June 3, Mary Jane, consort of Rev. Sam'l Keppler of Baltimore Annual Conference, at age 30 years. Joined M. E. Church. 1829 1831 married, had children, lost two, left children at death. [long obit] [*Christian Advocate & Journal*. See also June 1841]

Vol. XXV, No. 36 – September 4, 1841

Married at Rosemont on the 31st ult. by Birkby, Beverly T. Gill of Fredericksburg, Va. and Emily E. Summers, daughter of late Dr. Samuel Summers of Salem, Fauquier Co.

Married in town Thursday the 2nd inst. by Rev. Wm. Wickes, James H. Benedum and Sarah, daughter of Edward Hammett.

Died at Raleigh, North Carolina on 24th inst., Joseph Gales, father of one of the editors of this paper and of the wife of the other. [long obit]

Vol. XXV, No. 37 – September 11, 1841

Married Thursday the 2nd inst. by Birkby, William Silcott and Frances Eliza Downs, both of this county.

Married Monday the 6th inst. by Rev. Wm. Wickes, Leander Carter and Elizabeth Beatty, both of Loudoun.

Married Tuesday eve last by early candlelight by Rev. Wm. Gilmore, Sydnor B. Wilson and Henrietta Chiles, both of Fauquier Co.

Married in this town Wednesday the 8th inst. by Wickes, Edgar L. Bentley, Esq. and Helen Mary, daughter of late Dr. Isaac Wison [*sic*] [Wilson].

Died in Louisville, Ky on Tuesday, August 3, Arthur Lee, 26 year old grandson of Hon. Richard Henry Lee. Had been in Kentucky but a few years.

Died on the 11th ult. at residence in Mount Stuart, King George Co., Va., Dr. Robert O. Grayson, age 53 years. *[Richmond Enquirer]*

Vol. XXV, No. 38 – September 18, 1841

Married Tuesday the 14th inst. by Rev. Geo. Adie, James Minor, son of Col. George Minor of Fairfax Co. and Ann E., daughter of Capt. Benjamin Shreve of Loudoun Co.

Died at West Point on the 9th inst. in 16th year, Cadet Thompson F. Mason of Alexandria, son of the late Judge T. F. Mason of Alexandria.

Vol. XXV, No. 39 – September 25, 1841

Married in town on Sunday eve the 19th inst. by R'd. William Wickes, John War and Caroline Emberson, both of this county.

Vol. XXV, No. 40 – October 2, 1841

Married Thursday the 23rd ult. by Gilmore, Robert C. Bowman of Shennandoah Co. and Hannah P. Glasscock of Loudoun.

Married Tuesday the 28th ult. by Gilmore, Wm. Burke and Mrs. Mahala Wright, of this county.

Died of apoplexy on Tuesday the 27th ult., Mrs. Ann Nixon, consort of John Nixon, about 50 years of age.

Died at his residence in county on Monday, September 27, Stephen Joseph Donohoe.

Died in Nashville, Tenn on the 16th ult. at age 60 years, Newton Cannon, ex-Gov. of the State, formerly one of its Representatives in Congress.

Vol. XXV, No. 42 – October 16, 1841

Married Wednesday the 13th inst. by Revd. Geo. Adie, Jno. P. Smart, Esq. and Mary E., daughter of late Silas Wherry, Esq. of Loudoun Co.

Died at residence near West Union Parke, Ind., of fever on September 20, Humphrey Milbourn, formerly of Loudoun Co.

Died at Hagerstown, Md. on the 7th inst. in 49th year, William D. Bell, Esq., senior editor of the *Torchlight*.

Vol. XXV, No. 43 – October 23, 1841

Died at Princeton, Ky. on September 15, Abelino Hole, aged 33 years, formerly of Leesburg.

Vol. XXV, No. 45 – November 6, 1841

Married October 21 by Rev. J. G. Watt, Lambert Myers and Rachel Eveland.

Married on the 26th ult. by Rev. E. P. Phelps, Sydnor Bennet and Sarah E., daughter of Henry Russell, Esq.

Married the 3rd inst. by Rev. J. A. Collins, Rev. S. A. Roszell and Louisa H. D., daughter of late Dr. T. F. Tebbs.

Died Sunday the 24th ult., General Elisha Boyd of Martinsburg, Va., 70 years old. Served in Legislature and was Commander of Militia Norfolk.

Vol. XXV, No. 46 – November 13, 1841

Died at Wheeling on Wednesday the 13th ult. in 28th year, Rev. John Brice McCoy, Pastor of Presbyterian Church, Hookstown, Brook Co., Va.

Vol. XXV, No. 47 – November 20, 1841

Married Saturday the 30th ult. by Rev'd Mr. Camden, Rev. Job Shepherd of Maryland to Nancy Roszel, of this county, sister of the Rev. Stephen G. Roszel, dec'd.

Married on Tuesday the 9th inst. by Rev. Jas. Ryder, John Tayloe, of Virginia to Imogene, daughter of late James Mosher Jr. of Georgetown.

Vol. XXV, No. 48 – November 27, 1841

Married at Colross near Alexandria on November 17 by Rev. C. B. Dana, St. George T. Campbell and Sarah Elizabeth, daughter of late Hon. Thompson F. Mason.

Married at Front Royal, Va. on the 16th inst. by Rev. Robt. Cadden, E. C. Broun, postmaster of Middleburg, and Catharine B. Hopkins.

Married in town Thursday the 25th inst. by Rev. Wm. Wickes, Benjamin D. Rathie and Sarah D. M., daughter of Jacob Fadely, Esq.

Married Wednesday, November 17, by Birkby, John L. Tillett and Harriet A.
Poulton.
Married Thursday, November 18, by Birkby, William Caruthus [*sic*] [Carruthers]
and Louisa White, all of this county.

Vol. XXV, No. 49 – December 4, 1841

Married Thursday the 18th ult. by Rev. Wm. Evans, Wm. Clendining and
Elizabeth Ann Thompson, both of this county.
Married Tuesday the 23rd ult. by Rev. Wm. Evans, Joseph Mock and Mary
James, both of this county.
Married Tuesday the 23rd ult. by Rev. Wm. Wickes, Lewis D. Means and Alcinda
A. Paxson, both of this county.
Died Tuesday the 30th ult., James Mortimer, eldest son of James & Margaret
McIlhaney, aged 4 years.
Died at Champaigne Co., Ohio, Thomas Tipton, soldier of Revolution, aged 111
years.
Died at Urbana, Ohio on the 9th ult., Frederick Rump, a Rev. soldier age 107
years. Was German, lost father on journey over, twice married, had 18
children, 14 still alive. Upon beginning of war enlisted as dragoon in Penna,
served most of war. Removed at early day to Ky and to Ohio in 1807.

Vol. XXV, No. 50 – December 11, 1841

Married Sunday the 5th inst. by Rev. Wm. Evans, Benjamin Hough and Rachael
Lambaugh, both of this county.

Vol. XXV, No. 51 – December 18, 1841

Died at St. Louis, Mo on the 25th ult. of fever, Townsend Heaton of this county,
third son of late Dr. James Heaton, in 36th year. Deprived of father, left
mother, brothers and a sister. [long obit]
Married on the 25th ult. by Birkby, John J. Hogeland and Jane F. Ayres, both of
this county.
Married Thursday the 9th inst. by Birkby, George W. Ryan and Catharine Dorrell,
both of this town.
Married Tuesday the 7th inst. by Rev. Wm. Wickes, Wm. S. Gray and Sarah Ann
Orrison, both of this county.
Married Thursday the 9th inst. at Methodist Parsonage in this town by Rev. Wm.
Wickes, John Randolph White and Sarah Gover Janney, both of this county.

Vol. XXV, No. 52 – December 25, 1841

Married Thursday the 16th inst. by Birkby, Robert James and Winefred Simpson,
both of this county.
Married Thursday the 16th inst. by Birkby, Landon Jones and Sarah E. Wynkoop,
both of this county.
Died at Wheatland on the 20th inst., Mrs. Margaret, consort of John Wright, in her
61st year.

Vol. XXVI, No. 2 – January 8, 1842

Died at residence near this town on the 30th ult., John F. Barrett.

Vol. XXVI, No. 3 – January 15, 1842

Died on 10th inst. at Oatlands residence of his brother-in-law George Carter,
Richard O. Grayson, age 38 years. Left 6 children (lost bro. Dr. Grayson,
King George Co., lost wife.) [long obit]

Died Tuesday the 11th inst. at age 67 years, Mrs. Mary McCormick, relict of the late John McCormick, Esq., of Leesburg, member of Presbyterian Church.

Vol. XXVI, No. 4 – January 22, 1842

Married at Rockville, Md. on the 11th by Rev. Mr. Gilliss, Dr. J. D. Heaton and C. M. Stribling, both of Loudoun Co.

Died at Snickersville on Sunday the 2nd inst., James Stephenson, left widow and 4 children.

Died Thursday the 13th inst. at Waterford, Mrs. Elizabeth Bond, wife of Edward Bond.

Died Thursday the 13th inst. at Waterford, Mrs. Ellen Moffatt, wife of Mr. Robert Moffatt.

Vol. XXVI, No. 5 – January 28,1842

Married Monday the 24th inst. by Rev. Mr. Rich, Levin M. Powell, Lt. U.S. Navy, and Jeanette C. Thruston, daughter of Hon. Judge Thruston, of this county.

Died Wednesday the 19th inst. at Upperville in house of her uncle Wm. A. Stephenson, Ellen R. Grayson, daughter of late Richard O. Grayson, Esq., of Belmont in Loudoun, in 6th year of age.

Vol. XXVI, No. 6 – February 5, 1842

Married Thursday the 6th ult. by Rev. Wm. Evans, John W. Win [*sic*] and Mary A. Derry.

Married Tuesday the 11th ult. by Rev. Wm. Evans, Edward Owens and Eliza Jeffers, both of this county.

Married Tuesday the 18th ult. by Rev. Wm. Evans, Charles Paxson and Eleanor Hough, both of this county.

Married Tuesday the 18th ult. by Rev. E. P. Phelps, Charles F. Anderson and Mary Frances Hough, daughter of B. Hough, Esq.

Married Wednesday the 2nd inst. by Rev. Wm. Wickes, John A. McDonough and Elizabeth King, both of this place.

Vol. XXVI, No. 7 – February 12, 1842

Married Thursday last by Rev. John C. Smith, Rev. John Mines, D.D., pastor of Presbyterian Churches at Rockeville and Bethesda and Mary, daughter of late James Dunlop of Montgomery Co., Md.

Vol. XXVI, No. 8 – February 19, 1842

Died Sunday the 13th inst. at residence of James McIlhany, Esq., Mary Garnett, daughter of late Richard H. Henderson, in 16th year.

Died November last, Richard B. Mason, many years resident of the District, age 50 years, drowned in fall from steamboat when boarding at Alexandria. *[National Intelligencer]*

Died Saturday afternoon, Jane Gadsby, consort of Wm. Gadsby, in 32nd year. *[National Intelligencer]*

Vol. XXVI, No. 10 – March 5, 1842

Married Thursday the 3rd inst. by Birkby, Colvin F. Beales and Martha Ann Ruse, all of Loudoun.

Died at Baltimore on the 22nd ult., William M. Worthington, Esq., lately member New Orleans bar but formerly of Georgetown, DC.

Vol. XXVI, No. 11 – March 12, 1842
Married Tuesday the 8th inst. by Rev. Wm. Gilmore, Thomas B. R. Massie of
Shenandoah and Catharine C. Hicks of Fauquier.

Vol. XXVI, No. 12 – March 19, 1842
Married Sunday the 6th inst. by Elder R. N. Herndon, Armistead Hough and
Harriet E. Elliott, both of Loudoun Co.
Married the 3rd inst. by Rev. E. P. Phelps, George W. Johnson and Nancy Wright.
Died at residence of Samuel M. Boss, Esq. on the 19th inst., Mrs. Ann Wright,
widow of late William Wright, aged about 93 years, resident of Leesburg near
40 years, member M. E. Church.

Vol. XXVI, No. 13 – March 26, 1842
Married Thursday, March 17, by Gilmore, Henry H. Nichols and Maria White, all
of this county.

Vol. XXVI, No. 15 – April 9, 1842
Married Wednesday the 30th ult. by Rev. L. R. Ruse, Samuel Smart of Loudoun
Co. and Martha Ann Streeks of this place. [*Georgetown Advocate*]

Vol. XXVI, No. 16 – April 16, 1842
Married Thursday the 7th inst. by Rev. Wm. Wickes, Mahlon Tavener and Susan
Ann Nichols, both of this county.
Married the 12th inst. by Rev. Wm. Gilmore, William H. Hittaffer and Sarah E.
Powell, both of Fauquier Co.
Married Wednesday the 13th inst. by Wickes, Washington Vandeventer and
Cecelia E. Braden, both of Loudoun Co.
Married Thursday, March 31, by Rev. J. T. Massey, Thomas Jinkens [*sic*]
[Jenkins] of Clarke Co. and Eleanor Jinkens of this county.
Died at Woodville residence of her father D. Buckhart near Martinsburg, Va. on
Sunday the 27th ult. of dropsy, Mrs. Susan D. Rust, age 25 years, consort of
Robt. B. Rust of Post Office Department.

Vol. XXVI, No. 17 – April 23, 1842
Married Thursday the 14th inst. by Birkby, John Athey and Ann E. Edwards, all of
this county.

Vol. XXVI, No. 19 – May 7, 1842
Married Tuesday the 26th ult. by Rev. Samuel Gover, William V. Casey formerly
of Baltimore and Sarah Virginia Perry of Loudoun Co.

Vol. XXVI, No. 21 – May 21, 1842
Died in town on the 20th inst. Dr. Henry Clagett, age 70 years.

Vol. XXVI, No. 22 – May 28, 1842
Married May 25 at Middleburg by Rev. Mr. Slaughter, Dr. William Gibson, Prof.
surgery at U. of Phila., and Sarah Noble Smith, neice of Col. N. Beveridge.
Died Friday the 20th inst., Dr. Henry Clagett, in 71st year, resident of Leesburg
upwards 35 years, more partial to Protestant Episcopal Church, but
broadminded to all denominations. [obit]
Died on Friday the 20th inst., Sarah D. H., 1 year 7 month old daughter of Dr.
Charles G. and Margaret Eskridge.

Vol. XXVI, No. 23 – June 4, 1842

Died of scarlet fever on the 20th ult., William C. Saunders, [child] only son of Aaron Saunders of Loudoun Co.

Died Monday the 30th inst. at her late residence of Leesburg, Mrs. Julia A. Wilson, in 55th year of age. [obit]

Died in town on the 26th ult., Caroline Perry, 22 year old daughter of John & Sarah Perry.

Died at residence in county on the 29th ult., Mrs. Martha Carr, widow of late James Carr.

Vol. XXVI, No. 24 – June 11, 1842

Died at residence in town on the 2nd inst. at age 76 years, James McDonough Sr., native of Ireland, 50 year resident, member M. E. Church, 25 years hence. *Spirit of Democracy.*

Vol. XXVI, No. 25 – June 18, 1842

Married on the 9th inst. by Rev. Mr. Lewis, John C. Bronaugh of Washington and Sarah B. Tyler, daughter of late John Tyler of Prince William Co., Va.

Vol. XXVI, No. 28 – July 9, 1842

Married Thursday, June 30, by Gilmore, James W. Hummer and Frances Rollison, both of this county.

Vol. XXVI, No. 29 – July 16, 1842

Married Tuesday the 12th inst. by Rev. S. Gover, Cylus H. Feagans and Sarah J. Wilder, both of this county.

Vol. XXVI, No. 31 – July 30, 1842

Died in town on Sunday the 24th inst., Jacob Fadely, age 71 years, among oldest inhabitant, years member M. E. Episcopal Church.

Vol. XXVI, No. 32 – August 6, 1842

Died at Bolington on the 5th ult., Eliza Eleanor, third daughter of Wm. & Catharine Jacobs, age 5 years 1 month 25 days.

Vol. XXVI, No. 33 – August 13, 1842

Married Tuesday the 9th inst. by Rev. Gilmore, David Alexander and Sarah Susannah Brabham, both of Mt. Gilead, Loudoun Co.

Vol. XXVI, No. 34 – August 20, 1842

Married Thursday, July 28, by Birkby, David Ruse and Catharine Wynkoop, both of this county.

Married Thursday, July 28, by Birkby, John J. Wynkoop and Matilda J. Simons, both of this county.

Vol. XXVI, No. 35 – August 27, 1842

Died on the 20th inst. at residence of uncle John Keene of Clarke Co. where he had gone to visit for his health, Newton Oldham, b. Co. Northumberland 1816.

Vol. XXVI, No. 37 – September 10, 1842

Married in town on Wednesday the 7th inst. by Wickes, Charles Fenton Fadely and Orra Moore, daughter of Wm. P. Drish.

Died at Woodbury his late residence in Fairfax Co., Va. on Tuesday the 23rd, Dr. Mottrom Ball, in 75th year. Born Northumberland Co., Va., sent to Scotland, educated at Glasgow & Edinburgh. Proff. William Hambleton major influence, returned to U. S. c. 1790. Commenced practice of Medicine. Practiced 24 years. 1814 his property being devasted by the British left Northumberland and settled in Fairfax [obit]

Vol. XXVI, No. 38 – September 17, 1842
Died at residence of son near Waterford, Rachel Phillips, member Society of Friends, in 60th year.
Married in town Wednesday the 14th inst. by Rev. Wm. Wickes, James S. Harris and Mary Ann, daughter of the late Alexander Sutherland, Esq.
Married on Thursday the 8th inst. by Rev. Thos Birkby, Mathias Prince to Mary Merchant, both of this county.
Married on Tuesday the 13th inst. by same, Henry Virts to Esther R. Brown, both of this county.

Vol. XXVI, No. 39 – September 24, 1842
Married near Bloomfield in Loudoun Co. on the 13th inst. by Rev. J. T. Massey of Middleburg, Matthew W. Royston and Minerva C. Carpenter.
Married in Clarke Co. by Rev. J. T. Massey on the 15th inst., Lewis H. Bennett and Sarah Catharine Royston.
Married Thursday the 22nd inst. by Rev. Wickes, Samuel Beans and Hannah Newhouse, both of this county.
Married Thursday the 1st inst. at Green Level in Prince William Co. by Rev. Dr. Dorsey, Rev. Layton I. Harnsberger and Martha T. French, 2nd daughter of late William French.
Died at residence of her son near Waterford, Rachel Phillips, member of Society of Friends, in 60th year – 9 mo 10th, 1842.
Died on Friday the 26th ult. at her residence in this county, Mrs. Elizabeth Daniel, consort of Eli Daniel, formerly of Loudoun County, in her 39th year.
[Martinsburg Gazette]

Vol. XXVI, No. 40 – October 1, 1842
Died at Upperville on Friday the 23rd ult., Rev. John Gill Watt of Methodist Episcopal church, age about 67 years. Admitted a member of the traveling connexion in 1807, served 35 years. Mr. Watt expressed a desire to be buried near his friend the late Rev. Christ'r Frye, burying ground of Methodist Episcopal Church.
Married on 6th ultimate by Rev. Mr. Shiraz, Dr. M. Overfield, of Winchester to Mary P., daughter of Richard Osburn Sen. of Loudoun.

Vol. XXVI, No. 41 – October 8, 1842
Married Tuesday last by Birkby, Jno. Weadon and Nancy Boland, both of this county.

Vol. XXVI, No. 43 – October 22, 1842
Died in Urbana, Ohio on the 10th inst., Mrs. Elizabeth Ogden, wife of David Ogden, formerly of Leesburg, aged about 50 years, left husband, large family and children. [*Urbana Citizen*]

Vol. XXVI, No. 45 – November 5, 1842
Died n the 24th ult. at age 54 years, Mrs. Eliza Smith, relict of Samuel Smith, of Fairfax Co.

Vol. XXVI, No. 46 – November 12, 1842
Died at residence near Hillsborough on Monday, October 24, Mrs. Nancy White, in 63rd year, wife of John White, member M. E. Church, left large family.

Vol. XXVI, No. 47 – November 19, 1842
Married Tuesday the 13th inst. by Wickes, George W. Ropp [*sic*] [Rupp] and Sarah Birkby of this place.

Married on the 8th inst. at Weverton, Md. by Rev. Mr. Hoover, Dr. Carleton G. Sams of Hillsboro, Ohio and Charlotte D. Wever, daughter of Casper W. Wever, of the former place.

Died at Waterford on Saturday, November 12, Jesse Gover, age 50 years, Society of Friends.

Vol. XXVI, No. 48 – November 26, 1842
Married Tuesday the 22nd inst. by Rev. Geo. Adie, Newton Michie, Esq., of Staunton and Lalla, daughter of John Gray of Leesburg.

Died in town on the 24th inst., Jno. S. Cranwell, at about 72 years.

Vol. XXVI, No. 49 – December 3, 1842
Married Tuesday, November 8, by Birkby, Lorenzo D. Walker and Elizabeth Beamondaffer [*sic*], both of this county.

Married Thursday, November 17, James Laycock and Mary Ann White, both of this county.

Died Baltimore the 26th ult., age 85 years, Hon. Robert Smith. War. Rev. at Brandywine among the volunteers from Baltimore, served Legislature of Maryland, American Navy Dept. during Jefferson Administration, State Dept. during Madison Admininstration. [obit]

Vol. XXVI, No. 51 – December 17, 1842
Married at Georgetown, DC. on Wednesday the 7th inst. by Rev. L. J. Morgan, Joseph Wilson and Mary Ann Divine, formerly of this place.

Died Wednesday, Mrs. Elizabeth Cridler of this town, wife of Mr. John Cridler.

Vol. XXVII, No. 1 – December 31, 1842
Married Wednesday, December 7, by Rev. J. T. Massey of Middleburg, Charles F. Littleton and Amanda M. Corbin, both of Clarke Co.

Married Thursday, December 15, by Rev. J. T. Massey of Middleburg, James Trahern and Miss Francis Ann Overfield, both of Loudoun.

Married Thursday, December 15, by Birkby, Charles Riticor and Susanna Moss, both of Loudoun Co.

Married Tuesday, December 27, by Gover, Charles A. Ware and Elizabeth A. Mooney, both of Loudoun Co.

Married Thursday the 29th by Gover, John Hammerly and Catharine A. Zellers, both of this town.

Died in town Sunday last in this town at advanced age, Mrs. Sarah Edmunds, relict of late Wm. Edmunds of Fauquier Co.

Vol. XXVII, No. 2 – January 7, 1843

Died at Clarksburg, Montgomery Co., Md. on the 23rd inst., Mrs. Maria C. Hening, consort of Rev. Jas. G. Hening of M. E. Episcopal Church.

Vol. XXVII, No. 3 – January 11, 1843

Died at Louisa Co. on Tuesday the 3rd inst. of fever, Newton Michie, Esq., age 29, married 6 weeks to a daughter of Mr. John Gray of this town.

Died in N.Y. on the 4th inst., Stevens Thomson Mason, late Governor of Michigan, aged 31.

Vol. XXVII, No. 4 – January 21, 1843

Married the 9th inst. by Rt. Rev. Bishop Waugh, Rev. M. G. Hamilton of Baltimore Annual Conference and Eliza P., only daughter of late John Uhler, Esq. of Baltimore.

Married the 17th inst. by Rev. Littleton Morgan, Nathan White and Eliza Jane, eldest daughter of Robert White, Esq. of Georgetown, DC.

Died in Baltimore on Wednesday the 11th inst. at residence of son Charles Howard, Esq., Francis Scott Key.

Died on Wednesday the 11th inst. of scarlet fever, James Beverly, infant son of John & Sarah Surghnor at 10 months 4 days.

Vol. XXVII, No. 6 – February 4, 1843

Died at Winchester, Monday the 23rd ult., Mrs. Miranda Collins, consort of Rev. John A. Collins of M. E. Church, in 39th year of age.

Died in town on Monday eve, John Perry, age about 57 years.

Married January 26th by Gilmore, Charles S. Churchill to Catharine E. Brown, both of Fauquier Co.

Vol. XXVII, No. 7 – February 11, 1843

Married at Providence, Clarke Co. on January 5 by Rev. J. T. Massey of Middleburg, Charles J. Brent of Frederick and Emily Amanda Ball.

Married near Hillsborough on January 26 by Rev. J. T. Massey of Middleburg, William Hough and Sarah N. Love, both of Loudoun.

Married Tuesday the 7th inst. by Rev. S. Gover, Charles M. Littleton and Mary E. Poston.

Died Monday, January 31th at residence Mountain Retreat in Warren Co., Va., John Edwards, in 47th year, member M. E. Church.

Died in this town on Saturday, February 4th William Cline, age 63 years.

Died in this town Friday last at age 14 years, Sally E., 2nd daughter of Mr. John Surghnor. [*Spirit of Democracy*, 7 Feb]

Vol. XXVII, No. 8 – February 18, 1843

Married at Exeter on Thursday the 16th inst. by Geo. Adie, John Augustine Washington, Esq. of Mount Vernon and Nelly, only daughter of Wilson C. Selden, Esq.

Married Thursday, February 9th by Wickes, Samuel Carr and Elizabeth Brown, both of Loudoun Co.

Vol. XXVII, No. 9 – February 25, 1843

Married Tuesday, February 14, by Rev. Dr. Edward C. McGuire, Stevens Thomson Mason of Selma, Loudoun Co. and Sally Inness, youngest daughter of Murray Forbes of Falmouth, Stafford Co., Va.

Married Tuesday, February 14, by Rev. Dr. Edward C. McGuire, Dr. John R. Taylor of Woodport, Middlesex Co. and Bessie Fitzgerald, 2nd daughter of Murray Forbes, Esq. of Falmouth, Stafford Co., Va.

Married Thursday, February 16th by Wickes, William S. Harrison and Catharine Whietmore [sic] both of Loudoun Co.

Vol. XXVII, No. 10 – March 4, 1843

Died in town on Wednesday, February 15th Mr. Francis S. Bogue, age 34 years, leaves wife and three young children.

Vol. XXVII, No. 11 – March 11, 1843

Married Thursday, February 2, by Birkby, Mr. Aquilla Baughman and Emily Campbell, both of this county.

Married Thursday, March 2, James White and Ann Catharine Poulton, both of this county.

Vol. XXVII, No. 12 – March 18, 1843

Married the 16th ult. by Rev. J. T. Massey of Middleburg, Ewell N. Byrne and Hannah P. Jeffries, both of Loudoun.

Married the 7th inst. at Millwood, Clarke Co. by Rev. J. T. Massey of Middleburg, Hezekiah Slusher and Mary Ann Ryan, both of Clarke Co.

Married Wednesday, March 15, by Gilmore, Jonathan Ewers and Nancy McDaniel, both of Loudoun.

Died on the 2nd inst., Thomas Hughes of Loudoun Co., member Society of Friends.

Died March 16th at Rosemont, the residence of Capt. John Rose, a colored woman named Peg, believed by the best account we have to be almost 100 years old. She has been in Capt. Rose's family 51 years and the most faithful of servants.

Vol. XXVII, No. 13 – March 25,1843

Died in this town the 12th inst., Mrs. Elizabeth Kitzmiller, widow of late Martin Kitzmiller, age 66 years, member Presbyterian Church.

Died Sunday the 12th inst. at Coton near Leesburg, Benjamin Vermillion, age about 45 years.

Died in town on Monday the 13th inst., Enos W., 17 month old infant son of Dr. P. H. W. Bronaugh.

Died in town on Monday the 20th inst., Mary Jane, infant daughter of James H. Chamblin, age 3 years.

Died at Exeter near Leesburg on Monday eve, Wilson Carey Selden, Esq., age about 50 years.

Died in county on Sunday the 19th inst., James Clowe, age about 21 years.

Married Tuesday, March 21, by Gilmore, George W. Finnell of Ohio and Margaret C. Powell of Fauquier Co.

Vol. XXVII, No. 15 – April 8, 1843

Married Tuesday, March 14th by Birkby, Thomas Hawes and Ann Tavener, both of Loudoun.

Married Thursday, March 30th by Birkby, Wm. Varney and Maria Cummings, both of Loudoun.

Married Sunday, April 2, by Gilmore, Alfred B. Powell and Hannah Smith, both of Loudoun.

Died at Leesburg on Saturday last in 75th year, Miss Elizabeth Stewart, Methodist of 1790.

Died in town on March 23 of scarlet fever, Sarah Virginia, daughter of Samuel H. & Mary E. Williams, age 2 years 10 months.

Vol. XXVII, No. 16 – April 15, 1843

Married Wednesday the 12th inst. by Rev. Geo. Adie, Col. Gabriel Vandeventer and Jane Cecelia, daughter of late Dr. James Heaton.

Died at residence in county near Gum Spring on the 6th inst., Charles Lewis, Esq. age 83 years.

Died on the 12th inst. at residence in Loudoun Co., Benjamin Jackson, age about 65 years.

Vol. XXVII, No. 17 – April 22, 1843

Married Thursday, April 6th by Birkby, David Beales and Catharine Wynkoop, both of Loudoun.

Married Tuesday, April 18th by Birkby, John W. Shipley and Susan Maria Cranwell, both of this place.

Died at Arcadia in Frederick, Md. at residence of father Griffen Taylor, Esq. on Friday in Passionweek, Miss Virginia Taylor, age 16. Buried from St. Johns Church, Frederick, service by Rev. McElroy. [*Frederick Herald*]

Died in this town on Monday the 17th inst., Ellen Bronaugh, daughter of P. H. W. Bronaugh, age 3 years 6 months 11 days.

Died near Leesburg on Monday the 17th inst., Mrs. Sally Hammerly, wife of William Hammerly, age 60 years.

Vol. XXVII, No. 18 – April 29, 1843

Died Friday the 21st ult., Duanna F., daughter of Charles Shepherd of this town, age 17 years.

Died in Georgetown, DC., Leonard Mackall, Esqr., of Treasury Dept., in 76th year. [*National Intelligencer*]

Married Tuesday the 25th inst. by Rev. R. T. Berry, Capt. Samuel Purcell of Loudoun Co. and Elizabeth Steptoe, daughter of Col. Nicholas Osborn of Georgetown, DC.

Vol. XXVII, No. 19 – May 6, 1843

Married at Georgetown on Tuesday the 25th ult. by Rev. R. T. Berry, Dr. E. Boyd Pendleton of Martinsburg, Va. and Maria Lucinda, youngest daughter of late Col. Chas. Pendleton Tutt.

Vol. XXVII, No. 20 – May 13, 1843

Married at Friends Meeting at Gunpowder on 5th day 4th inst., Benjamin Birdstall [*sic*] of Loudoun Co. and Rebecca M., daughter of Thomas Matthews, of the former place.

Died on Monday at residence in Georgetown, DC., Henry J. Grayson, Esq., age about 30 years, only child of Mrs. Mary Grayson and grandson of late John Threlkeld, Esq. [*National Intelligencer* - May 3.]

Vol. XXVII, No. 21 – May 20, 1843

Died on the 11th inst. at Bellevue, Prince George Co., Md. at residence of Lloyd M. Lowe, Esq. his father, James R. M. Lowe of Loudoun Co., age 44 years, left wife and 6 small children. [*National Intelligencer* – May 16]

No Issue Date Listed in Abstracts

Died in Washington February 16th William A. Burwell, member House of Rep. from Va.

Died at New Market of Frederick Co. Md. on February 7th, Rev. John Pitts.

Died in Philadelphia, February 13th at age 15 years, Mrs. Mary Redhair, wife of Martin Redhair.

Died February 26th Sarah Ann, infant daughter of Mr. Samuel Dailey, in the vicinity of Leesburg.

Died at Philadelphia on January 18, Mrs. Ann Maria, wife of William Troutwine (Surgeon barber) her age 99 years.

Died at Philadelphia on January 19, Mrs. Mary Smith, age 99 years.

Died at New York on January 18, Eke Low, infant son of Mary Tonnojuack, one of the Esquimaux Indians, lately exhibited in that city by Capt. Hadlock.

Died in Deerfield, Conn, January 13, Mrs. Godfrey, age 100 years.

Died in Waterloo, N. Y., January 30, Mr. David Milner, a native of England, aged 57 years.

Married Thursday, February 1st by Rev. James M. C. Hanson, Mr. Thomas H. Wey to Miss Hanah Galleher.

Married February 8th by Rev. James M. C. Hanson, Mr. John N. T. G. E. Keene to Miss Harriot Triplett, all of this county.

Married at Mobile, February 1, Dominique Salle Esqr. to Miss Nathalie Herpin.

Died in Groton, Conn, Mr. J. Heulet, aged 95 years. He was father, by one wife, of 27 children.

Died in New Orleans, September 28, 1820, Joseph B. Baird, printer, formerly editor of a newspaper in that city.

Married in Lynn, on Sunday evening, the 12th October, Mr. Thomas Swan to Miss Mary Martin. It has been said "Birds of one feather in stormy times will flock together," But now the case is tasted. See what young Cupid's art has done. Behold the Martin and the Swan. Have with each other nested.

INDEX

Rev., 43, 48
Stephen B., 35, 48, 53, 63, 82
Sylvester W., 37
Baldwin
John D., 124
Mary F., 53
Samuel, 20
Bale
Roena E., 66
Ball
Anna, 114
C. B., 71
Charles B., 26, 115
Elizabeth, 1
Emily A., 137
Fayette, 86, 106
Fayette W., 115
Frances W., 71
Henry A., 87
John B., 53
Mary T., 106
Matilda, 2
Mildred, 13
Mottrom, 135
Samuel, 72
Spencer M., 80
Susan, 59
William, 86
Wm. Lee, 30
Ballard
Samuel, 58
Ballon
William, 3
Barker
Anna, 106
Mary, 1
Barnett
Alice B., 8
Barr
Adam, 57
George, 83
Mahala, 64
Barret
Robert, 21
Barrett
Caroline M. L., 106
Eliza, 94
John, 106
John F., 50, 131
Robert, 20
Barron
Otho, 127
Barry
Catharine A., 112
Honoria A., 51
John L., 88
Bartlett
Mary, 10
Barton

Bailey, 66
Richard C., 31
Bateman
William, 5
Batson
Mahala, 55
Battson
Hannah, 42
Baughman
Aquilla, 138
Baughters
Elizabeth, 115
Bayley
Virginia, 122
Bayly
John, 25, 45, 103
Leah, 3
Lucy, 103
Margaret, 25
Mary, 45
Pierce, 45
Bayne
Sarah A., 86
Beach
Emily, 60
Orlando, 97
Beacham
Mary, 126
Beale
David, 26
Elizabeth, 48
George, 48
Helena M., 39
Robert E., 73
Sarah M., 42
Beales
Colvin F., 132
David, 139
Beall
Elizabeth C., 96
George, 120
John R., 67
Lloyd, 96
Thomas B., 12
William D., 88
Beamondaffer
Elizabeth, 136
Beans
Absolam, 92
Isaiah B., 55
Minerva, 42
Samuel, 135
Bear
Rebecca, 74
Beard
Alexander, 36
Joseph, 22
Maria, 44
Martha, 4
Matilda L., 49

Beatty
David, 3, 17, 21
Elizabeth, 17, 129
John, 29
Mary, 57
William, 10
Beaumont
Jane C., 85
Beavers
Abraham H., 75
James, 7
Rachel F., 75
Samuel, 114
Beazley
John, 14
Bedford
__, 125
Bedinger
Daniel, 99
Henrietta, 99
Henry, 117
Beech
Presly, 111
Bell
Edward, 20
Hiram O., 30
Nancy, 52
Strother, 34
William D., 130
Belt
Ann, 97
Mary E., 92
Ruthyann, 63
Benedum
James H., 129
Peter, 93
Bennet
Josiah, 104
Sydnor, 130
Thompson, 99
Bennett
Ann R., 19
Charles, 13, 19, 24, 124
Eliza S., 87
Hamilton, 57
James H., 109
Jane, 1
John H., 62
Lewis H., 135
Mary A., 109
Mary W., 124
Thomas J., 21
Benson
Ann S., 122
Benjamin B., 120
Helen E., 89
Henrietta, 116
Bent
Lemuel, 89
Bentley

Branham
  Nancy J., 71
Brashears
  M. E. L., 113
Breedin
  E. C., 90
Brent
  Charles J., 137
  Robert Y., 61
  William, 82
  Winifred, 82
Brewer
  Mary, 78
Bright
  James, 113
  Martha R., 113
Briscoe
  Harriot, 42
  John, 93
  Sarah J., 109
Britenbaugh
  Samuel, 87
Broadwater
  Ann, 61
Brocchus
  Cornelius M., 100
Brockenbough
  Arthur S., 74
Bronaugh
  Eliza M., 100
  Ellen, 139
  Enos W., 138
  John C., 134
  John W., 100
  Joseph W., 64
  P. H. W., 138, 139
Brook
  Edmund, 97
Brookes
  Elijah, 88
Brooks
  Francis, 128
  Mahuldah, 92
  Thomas W., 77
Broome
  John M., 95
Brough
  Henry, 116
Broun
  E. C., 130
  Edwin C., 110, 117
  Elizabeth, 110
Brown
  Ann, 91
  B. N., 109
  Benjamin, 34
  Catharine E., 137
  Coleman, 58
  Daniel, 37
  David, 85

David E., 9
Edith, 21
Eliza, 35
Elizabeth, 137
Emily, 9
Esther R., 135
George N., 101
Giles, 42
Hannah J., 48
Isaac, 21, 92
Issachar, 63
Joel, 64
John, 45, 61, 62, 91,
       105, 121
John H., 72
Lydia N., 59
Mary A, 111
Mary A., 107
Mary E., 104
Mary S., 51
Nancy, 2
Parmelia, 51
Pleasant H., 106
Rebecca T., 61
Richard, 100
Samuel, 104
Sarah, 76, 78, 84
Susan, 6, 21, 26
William, 48, 62
Bruerd
  George W., 125
Brundige
  Timothy, 21
Bryan
  Nicholas, 109
Buchanan
  Isabella M., 105
  John, 105
Buck
  Amelia A., 54
  Marcus C., 2
  Mary E., 80
  Mary P., 34
  Samuel, 34, 54, 79, 80
  Samuel G., 115
  William G., 79
Buckey
  Eleanor, 47
  Eve, 31
Buckhart
  D., 133
  Susan D., 133
Buckley
  A., 42
  James, 42
Buckmaster
  Corbin, 23
Bunn
  Seely, 83
Burditt

Delilah, 31
Burgess
  Elizabeth, 113
Burke
  Ann, 82
  Elizabeth A., 114
  Isreal, 76
  Josiah, 115
  Maria, 12
  William, 130
Burkhart
  Daniel, 80
  Susan D., 80
Burnett
  Harrison B., 104
  Howell B., 104
  James, 104
  John, 104
  Keturah, 104
  Richard B., 104
Burrill
  James, 13
Burson
  Cyrus, 109
  Lydia, 1
Burton
  Albert G., 104
  Hannah, 15
  John, 15, 26
Burwell
  Mary B., 112
  William A., 140
Buskirk
  John, 9
Bussard
  Milton M., 105
  P. L., 119
Butler
  Benjamin, 14
  Comfort, 7
  Delia, 7
  Elizabeth, 35
Byrd
  Thompson, 22
Byrne
  Ewell N., 138
  John, 69

Caldwell
  Eliza, 78
  Eliza M., 38
  James, 6, 64, 76
  Joseph, 8
  S. B. T., 38, 78
  Samuel B. T., 1, 29
  Virginia A., 64
Cameron
  Thomas J., 30
Campbell
  Anne, 24

Clagett
  Henry, 64, 133
  Julia, 64
  Letha M., 92
  Sarah E., 97
  Thomas, 97
  Thomas H., 70, 126
Claggett
  Dr., 32
  Henry, 19
Clair
  Peter, 84
Clapham
  Elizabeth, 71
  Samuel, 44
Clapper
  Elizabeth, 112
  Henry, 71
  Susan, 71
Clark
  Bathsheba, 8
  Melinda, 11
  Willis B., 102
Clarke
  John C., 9
Clasby
  Nimrod, 87
Claxton
  Thomas, 120
Clay
  Dorothea, 65
  Henry, 65
Clayton
  Jacob, 93
Cleaveland
  Johnson, 89
Clements
  Bartlett, 58
  Joyce T., 58
  Mary, 58
  Nancy B., 58
Clendening
  Sarah A., 108
  William, 108
Clendining
  William, 131
Clifford
  Elizabeth, 74
  Thomas, 35
Cline
  William, 137
Cloud
  Daniel, 80
  Isaac, 79
  Isaac R., 54
Clough
  Sarah, 12
Clowe
  Amanda J., 105
  James, 138

William, 4
Clues
  Lott, 21
Cochran
  Elizabeth, 30
  Nathan, 66
  Richard, 60
  Susan R., 60
  William B., 100
Cocke
  Ann M., 40
  Charles, 2
  Lucinda, 40
  Washington, 40
Cockerill
  Reuben, 80
  Susan, 29
Cockrel
  Isabella, 84
Cockrell
  Bailey D., 66
  Catharine, 54
  Sanford, 94
Cockrill
  Jeremiah, 52
Coe
  Emily J., 108
  John W., 124
  Mary, 83
  Mary E., 80
  Mary J., 122
  William, 104
Coffer
  Sarah, 24
Cohee
  Elizabeth, 15
Cole
  Lewis, 17
  Phebe, 17
  William T., 67
Coleman
  E. W., 90
  Edmund W., 102
  Julia, 101
  Thomas W., 46
  William, 101, 102
Collier
  Thomas W., 94
  William M., 122
Collins
  Benjamin, 69
  John, 24
  John A., 137
  Lucinda, 34
  Miranda, 137
  Sarah, 4
Colston
  Thomas M., 127
Combs
  Henson, 62

Joseph, 71
  Rebecca, 62
  Sarah, 1
Commerel
  Susan, 105
Comstock
  I., 40
Conine
  William C., 35
Connard
  John, 56
Conner
  David, 18
  Eleanor, 20
  Pleasant, 67
  Timothy, 67
Connor
  Mary, 84
Conrad
  Charles M., 98
  Daniel P., 4, 26
  Frederick E., 26
  Mary A., 102
Conrod
  Robert Y., 58
Contee
  Eliza, 105
  John, 105
Conwell
  Josiah, 60
  Nelly, 35
  Sarah, 10
Cook
  John, 52
  Maria, 11
  Valentine, 21
  William, 11
Cooke
  Edward E., 65
  Henry S., 45
  John E., 65
  John R., 65
Cooksey
  Edward, 16
  George, 16
  Harrison, 16
  Levi, 33
  Obadiah, 16
Cookus
  John T., 93
  Julietta, 91
Cooper
  Alexander, 33
  Eli F., 105
  Isaac, 15, 24
  J., 56
  Jane, 24
  Margaret, 56
  William, 6
Copeland

Andrew, 36
David, 89
Elizabeth, 25
Jane, 36
John, 25
Sidney, 104
Susan, 101
Zelia, 71
Copsey
John, 64
Sarah, 64
Corbin
Amanda M., 136
Cordel
Martin, 36
Cordell
Asa B., 63
Catharine, 48
Colin M., 95
George E., 20
Helen A., 84
Mary E., 63
Presley, 63, 84
Cornelle
Thomas, 126
Cornwallis
Lord, 18
Corwin
Cynthia, 43
Coryton
Ann E., 6
Cost
Catharine, 29
Elizabeth, 111
Couper
Alexander, 51
Courier
Samuel, 12
Cox
Ann, 96
Hugh, 99
James A., 114
Crab
Bartholomew, 10
Craig
Jane, 49
Malenda, 25
Craighill
William P., 30
Crain
John, 102
Craine
Emily L., 40
Cramer
Jane, 37
Samuel J., 37
Crandall
Joseph, 95
Miranda, 95
Cranwell

Jane S., 87
John N., 83
John S., 136
Susan M., 139
Craven
Edith, 59
Eleanor, 59
Euphemia H., 91
Hannah, 36
Isaac S., 96
James, 100
Malinda, 32
Miranda, 100
Sophia V., 113
William L., 59, 91
Crawell
Jane S., 87
Crider
Elizabeth Y., 40
Cridler
Andrew M., 122
Ann E., 100
Elizabeth, 136
George, 48, 112
Henry L., 112
John, 97, 136
Margaret, 112
Margaret S., 91
William L. P., 97
Crim
Charles, 33
Crissey
Frederick A., 122
Cromwell
Ellen, 108
T., 108
Crooge
Bethiab, 14
Crook
Charles, 29
Elizabeth B., 85
Crooks
Nancy, 29
Cross
Benjamin, 93
Elizabeth, 63
John, 113
Nancy, 93
Nelly, 50
Crouse
John W., 38
Cruit
William, 40
Cruthus
Nancy, 125
Cummings
Ansey, 104
Hannah H., 81
Harrison, 104
Maria, 138

Currie
Elizabeth, 12
Sarah, 23
Curry
Elizabeth, 40
John, 73
Lucinder, 27
Martha, 41
Curtis
Helen, 35
Cushing
Jonathan P., 96
Cutler
B. C., 104
Benjamin C., 104
Sarah, 104
Cutsail
Mr., 9

Dade
Townsend, 10
Dailey
Aaron, 23
Betsy, 69
Eliza, 71
Elizabeth, 15, 23, 38
Ellen, 6
Jane, 81
Jesse, 69
John, 36, 38
Joseph, 37
Margaret, 52
Samuel, 14, 140
Sarah, 3
Sarah A., 14, 140
William, 11
Daily
Aaron, 49
Julia M., 31
Dale
George, 23
Dandridge
Philip P., 116
Daniel
Eli, 14, 135
Elizabeth, 135
Hannah, 5
Mary, 70
Tacy, 69
Tacy H., 125
Thomas H. C., 100
William, 119
William D., 18
William S., 88
Danner
Mary, 51
Danniel
Hannah L., 86
Darby
Thomas L., 113

John P., 47
Gill
  Beverly T., 129
  John L., 128
Gilman
  Ezra, 15
Gilmore
  Ellen S., 67
  James, 43, 67
Gilpin
  George, 10
  Gideon, 39
Glasgow
  H., 2
Glasscock
  Alfred, 108
  Caroline, 41
  Gregory, 80
  Hannah P., 130
  John C., 108
  Mary E., 108
  Thomas, 128
Godfrey
  Mrs., 140
Goff
  Adam, 35
  Letitia, 20
Goheen
  Maybury, 120
Goin
  Margaret, 13
Gold
  Julia A., 42
Goldsborough
  Caroline F., 116
  Charles, 60, 116
  Lewis M., 70
Goodin
  Maria, 92
Goran
  Mary, 28
Gordon
  Thomas G., 84
Gore
  Amanda M., 104
  Enos, 43
  Joshua, 79
  Massa, 55
  Thomas, 1
Gossom
  John H., 93
Gouverneur
  Samuel L., 9
Gover
  Ann, 82
  Anthony P., 122
  Hannah, 68
  Jesse, 136
  Sarah, 122
  Susan P., 115

Grady
  Francis, 87
Graham
  Elizabeth, 73
  Eve, 26
  George, 61
  James, 121
  John, 11
  Mary, 72
  Sarah, 4
  William, 103
Grahame
  Lucinda, 9
Grantham
  William, 83
Gray
  Algernon S., 102
  Frances W., 81
  Harriet B., 66
  Henrietta, 85
  John, 66, 85, 136, 137
  John W., 94
  Joseph, 128
  Lalla, 136
  Robert C., 12
  Robert W., 122
  Samuel, 8
  Sarah A., 107
  William H., 59, 81, 103
  William S., 131
Grayson
  Benjamin, 39, 80, 96
  Elizabeth O., 39
  Ellen R., 132
  Henry J., 139
  Mary, 139
  Mary D., 80
  Nancy, 113
  Richard O., 131, 132
  Robert O., 129
Green
  Ann L., 75
  Duff, 75
  Edward, 111
  Jane, 115
  Jane L., 93
  John C., 93, 103
  Ruth A., 23
  Sarah, 41
  Thomas, 23, 28, 55
Greene
  General, 113
Greenlease
  Charles, 102
  James, 120
  William, 59
Gregg
  Balsora, 60
  Elenor, 56
  Elizabeth, 18, 66, 123

Elizabeth P., 56
Emily, 25
Gilford, 65
Harman J., 125
Henley H., 55
Martha L., 68
Nancy L., 55
Nathan, 56
Peter, 40
Pheobe, 103
Priscilla S., 30
Semina, 65
Susan R., 56
Susannah, 125
Thomas, 17
Wilson, 75
Griffith
  Israel T., 66
  Margaret, 63
  Philip, 63
Griggs
  Castiliana, 87
  Thomas, 87
Grigsby
  Jane, 42
  Lewis, 19
Grimes
  Henry, 100
Grubb
  Curtis, 49
  Joseph, 70
Grymes
  Benjamin, 67
  Louisa J., 67
Guest
  Elizabeth E., 69
  Job, 61, 69
  Scynthia A., 61
Gulick
  Amos, 42
  Edna, 26
  Emily, 34
  George, 34
  Helena, 42
  Huldah, 34
  Ludwell, 26
  Moses, 4
Gullatt
  Amelia, 12
  Charles, 17
Gunnell
  George W., 94
  L., 94
  William, 91

Hackinson
  Hillory, 7
Hadlock
  Capt., 140
Hagarty

Thomas, 82
Holderly
 James, 19
Hole
 Abelino, 130
 Lewis, 105
Hollingsworth
 Mary, 52
Holmes
 Elijah, 29
 Elisha, 114
 Hugh, 35
 Jane, 88
 John, 36
 Phila, 83
 Rowena, 44
 Warner, 111
Holsclaw
 John H., 4
Holtzman
 George, 96
Honey
 John W., 15
Hood
 Josiah, 3
Hooe
 John, 90
 Maria M. G., 90
 William F., 81
Hope
 John D., 111
 Joshua T., 55
 Louisa, 122
 Nancy, 81
Hopkins
 Catharine B., 130
 John, 96
 Mary H., 96
 Thomas S., 70
Hornbaker
 Mrs., 112
Horner
 Inman, 98
 John S., 91
 Mary D., 88
Horseman
 William, 77
Hoskins
 Eliza, 7
Hoskinson
 Margaret, 29
Hough
 Ann, 32
 Ann E., 7
 Armistead, 133
 B., 132
 Benjamin, 45, 131
 Bernard, 27, 91, 108
 Catharine, 1
 Cecilia, 40

Edward S., 57
Eleanor, 132
Elizabeth, 117
Harriett, 49
John, 45
Joseph, 18
Louisa, 27, 55
Louisa J., 128
Margaret, 45
Mary, 29, 129
Mary E., 92
Mary F., 132
Robert R., 55, 57
Samuel, 6, 26, 96
Sarah A. A., 55
Thomas, 27
William, 117, 137
House
 James, 92
Householder
 Daniel, 30
Houser
 Honour, 27
 Philip, 115
Howard
 Jane A., 96
 John E., 49
 Samuel, 96
Howell
 Craven, 83
 William, 1, 31
Howser
 Richard, 58
Hoyl
 Eliza A., 80
Hoyle
 Mary J., 118
Huff
 Henry, 25
Hughes
 Edward, 73
 John H., 79
 Margaret E., 73
 Thomas, 138
Hummer
 Benjamin, 120
 James W., 134
 Washington, 29
Humphrey
 Thomas M., 79
 Uree, 46
Humphreys
 George Ann, 105
 James, 54
 Thomas K., 84
Hunt
 Amor, 52
 Eli, 115
 Major, 27
 Mary, 59

Hunter
 Andrew, 92
 David, 68
 Elizabeth C., 16
 George W., 102
 John, 96
 John B., 38
 John C., 16, 26, 70, 111
 Margaret P., 70
 Mary, 68
 Sarah A., 111
 William, 101
Hunton
 Charles, 89
 Jane R., 89
 John, 118
Hurst
 Catharine G. D., 88
 John, 88
Hutchinson
 E. C., 58
 Jane, 48
 Reuben, 3, 103
 Robert P., 122
Hutchison
 Ann L., 65
 John, 45
 Lucinda, 64
 Mary A., 35
 Nelson, 1

Iden
 Mandley, 101
 Mary, 28
Inser
 John, 60
Irey
 John, 30, 110
Iron
 Deborah, 10
Ish
 Mary, 118
 Peter, 60

Jack
 John, 108
Jackson
 Asa, 28
 Benjamin, 139
 John, 6
 Judah, 100
 Julia M., 115
 Mary, 47, 50
 Richard, 115
 Samuel, 91
 Samuel A., 4
 Spencer, 88
 Thomas, 30, 113
 William, 58, 67, 79, 124
 William M., 96

Jacobs
  Catharine, 134
  Eliza E., 134
  Elizabeth, 106
  John, 27
  John M., 39
  Matilda, 2, 59
  William, 7, 134
  William H., 39
Jameison
  Malcolm, 65
James
  Ann, 104
  Hannibal, 126
  Mahlon, 104
  Mary, 131
  Mason, 109
  Matson, 106
  Robert, 131
Jamison
  John, 88
  Leonard, 88
  Mary, 88
Janney
  Amos, 41
  Anna, 25
  Anna M., 125
  Charles P., 117
  Cornelia, 71
  David, 16, 17
  Eli, 112
  Elisha, 25, 111, 117, 122
  Elizabeth, 16
  Hester B., 71
  John, 26, 41
  Jonathan, 114
  Juliana, 66
  Lydia A., 51
  Mahlon, 95
  Maria, 9
  Rachel, 95
  Sarah, 122
  Sarah A., 116
  Sarah G., 131
Janny
  Mahlon, 22
  Richard, 22
Jared
  Anna, 128
Jarvis
  Hillary, 31
Jay
  Anna, 116
  William, 116
Jeffers
  Eliza, 132
Jefferson
  Hamilton, 15
  Martha, 103
  Thomas, 85, 103

Jeffries
  Braxton B., 125
  Hannah P., 138
  Hetty, 42
Jenkins
  Charity A., 94
  Edward, 94
  Ketura, 6
  Reuben, 81
  Samuel, 55
  Thomas, 133
Jenners
  Abiel, 31, 33
  Deborah, 33
  Sarah, 31
Jennings
  Edmund, 73
  M. A. Margaret, 128
Jinkens
  Eleanor, 133
  Thomas, 133
Johnson
  Absolom, 128
  Alexander, 100
  Ann, 86
  Arminda, 25
  Col., 100
  Edward, 41
  Fenton, 120
  George W., 133
  John, 4, 127
  Mary E., 109
  Ranche, 27
  Rebecca, 124
  Sarah, 77
  Susannah, 79
  Sydnor B., 116
  Thomas R., 5
  William, 91, 109
Johnston
  Charles A., 113, 123
  Charles S., 123
  James, 121
  Mary R., 123
Joice
  Eliza, 3
Jolliffe
  John, 63
Jones
  Alexander, 88
  Alice, 28
  Ann V., 80
  Anne, 35
  Anne L., 97
  Cageby, 44
  David T., 120
  Delilah, 41
  Elizabeth, 7
  Emily M., 88
  Landon, 131

Lucinda, 73
  Mary E., 119
  Nancy, 3, 52
  Philippa, 26
  Thomas, 29
  Walter, 97, 119
  William, 116
Jordan
  Anna E., 49
  Nancy, 81
Jury
  Townshend J., 70

Kabrick
  George, 95
Kaighn
  John H., 76, 127
  Mary D., 27
Kalb
  Andrew H., 104
Kankey
  Amelia V., 92
  Zebulon, 92
Kedwell
  Zedekiah, 66
Keeble
  Edwin A., 60
Keene
  Addison, 94
  John, 134
  John N. T. G. E., 140
  John N. T.G.E., 14
Kell
  John, 81
Kelly
  Lawson, 105
Kennedy
  Isabella, 38
  John, 38, 42
Kent
  Catharine A., 126
  Harrison, 58
Keppler
  John, 115
  Mary J., 128, 129
  Octavia, 115
  Samuel, 124, 128, 129
  Virginia W., 124
Kerfoot
  John B., 85
  Mr., 35
Kerney
  Terence, 13
Key
  Charles H., 137
  Francis S., 107, 137
  John R., 107
Keyes
  Robert, 44
Kid

Mr., 8

Kilgour
  Alexander, 77

Killen
  Mary C., 21

King
  Delilah, 10
  Elizabeth, 132
  Mary A., 98
  Susan, 110
  William, 24, 69, 110

Kirk
  Elizabeth, 61
  Rebecca, 67

Kitchie
  Catharine, 91

Kittle
  James, 72

Kitzmiller
  Elizabeth, 138
  Lydia, 31
  Martin, 43, 138
  William W., 115

Klein
  Catherine, 121
  L., 103
  M. C., 71
  Mary A., 103

Kline
  John N., 105
  Maria L., 87
  Mary C., 100
  Nicholas, 37, 87

Knox
  Thomas P., 18

Koontz
  Henry, 15

Krebs
  Henry, 93

Kyser
  Martin, 54

Lacey
  Castiliana, 87
  David, 5, 87
  Diademia, 4
  Elias, 119
  Isreal, 2
  John, 80
  Joseph B., 74
  Maria, 101
  Matilda W., 119
  Robert A., 101
  Sarah, 128
  Stacey, 1

Lack
  James, 72

Lackland
  George L., 2

Lacock

Joseph, 46

Lafaber
  Rachel, 72
  Susannah, 30

Lafaver
  Henry, 21

Lafferty
  Anna, 121
  Isaac, 3, 28

Lake
  Harriot, 40
  Ludwell, 41

Lamb
  Elizabeth, 125
  William, 123

Lambaugh
  Rachael, 131

Lambe
  Elizabeth H. F., 70

Lancaster
  Elizabeth, 13
  Joseph, 13

Lander
  Margaret A., 34
  William, 34

Landis
  Eliza, 50

Lane
  Benedict M., 29
  Catharine, 44
  Frances, 111
  James, 5
  Joseph, 44
  Martha, 5

Langley
  Alexander, 39
  Harriot E., 31
  Thomas, 12

Langton
  Thomas W., 5

Lanham
  Harriet A., 123

Larmour
  Samuel B., 90

Laslie
  Caroline T., 25

Latham
  Robert, 72

Lathrum
  Martha A., 72

Latimer
  Judith S., 89

Laurens
  Mary, 68

Laval
  Jacinth, 21

Laverty
  Esther A., 111
  Henry, 111

Lawder

James, 46

Lawrence
  Alexander, 36, 44
  Cornelia M., 37
  Emily, 44
  Richard, 37
  William, 125
  William W., 26, 50

Laws
  Sarah, 41

Lay
  Hamilton, 89

Laycock
  James, 136
  Samuel, 25, 104

Leach
  J. Willet, 89

Leadbeater
  John, 98

Leak
  Joseph, 32

Lee
  Alexander, 28
  Ann B., 69
  Ann C., 44
  Archibald, 117
  Arthur, 129
  Daniel, 79
  E. I., 99
  Edmund I., 81
  Eliza, 11, 81
  Elizabeth, 85
  Ellen A., 125
  F. L., 125
  George, 48, 99
  Jesse, 15
  John, 85
  Joshua, 71
  Ludwell, 11, 45, 102, 125, 127
  Margaret A., 99
  Maria C., 48
  Mary A., 71
  Mary D., 28
  Mary R., 82
  Richard H., 28, 49, 102, 129
  Richard L., 45
  Sidney S., 94
  Thomas L., 76, 82
  William F., 76
  Winifred., 82

Legg
  Eli, 98

Leigh
  Ann, 64
  Mary, 41
  Matilda, 41

Leith
  Jemima, 37

John, 36, 44, 132
John A., 54
Mary, 132
McCoy
  John B., 130
McCrae
  Mary A., 104
McCrum
  Robert, 102
McDaniel
  Augustine, 125
  Elizabeth, 36
  James, 11
  Nancy, 43, 138
McDonough
  James, 66, 134
  John A., 132
McFarland
  Alfred, 82
  Elizabeth, 89
  Francis, 89
McFarling
  Pleasant, 40
McGarvack
  Patrick, 55
McGarvick
  Mrs., 17
  Patrick, 17
McGavack
  Mary, 66
McGeath
  James, 62
  John, 18
  Sinah, 20
McGee
  Patrick, 52
McGuire
  Hugh H., 40
  William, 13
McIlhaney
  James, 102, 131
  James M., 131
  Margaret, 102, 131
McIlhany
  James, 36, 132
  Margaret, 106, 118
  Mortimer, 118
McIntyre
  Patrick, 16
McKeldon
  John, 67
McKenna
  Anna C., 127
  Hiram, 109
  J. L., 127
  James L., 97
  Nancy F. R., 97
McKenney
  Ann, 50
  John, 47, 50

McKim
  George W., 121
  Isaac, 111
  James, 43
McKimmie
  Priscilla, 34
McKimmy
  John, 109
McKnight
  Amy, 83
  Enoch, 99
  Harmon, 69
  Mary A., 116
McLaughlin
  Susannah, 93
McLean
  Dan, 108
  Douglas, 108
McLeod
  Daniel, 68
  Hester A., 81
McMullen
  George, 59
McNall
  ___, 41
McNeil
  Daniel, 120
McNeill
  Jane, 120
McNellege
  James, 49
McPhail
  William, 99
McPherson
  Catharine, 72
  Cynthia, 40
  Daniel, 94
  Mary A., 94
  Sebastian, 40
  Wesley S., 34
McQuinn
  Mary A. R., 93
McRea
  Sarah J., 104
McSorley
  James, 22
McVeigh
  Eli, 48
  Hiram, 18, 59, 84, 93
  James H., 61
  Jane A. E., 59
  Jane E., 84
  Jesse, 93
  Mary A., 93
  Townsend, 29
McVicker
  Alfred, 16
McWard
  E., 13
Mead

Elizabeth, 5
Joseph, 83, 120
Manly, 104
Martha, 50
Mary, 77, 120
Stith, 88
William, 120
Meade
  Bishop, 79
  Richard K., 79
  Richard W., 52
  William, 13
Means
  Jane, 15
  Lewis D., 131
Megeath
  Joseph P., 30
Melvin
  Benjamin, 84
  William, 75
Mercer
  Col., 11
  Mary, 62
Merchant
  James, 71
  Martina, 121
  Mary, 135
Merrick
  William D., 48
Merryman
  Mary, 69
Michie
  Newton, 136, 137
Middleton
  Mary A., 104
Milbourn
  Humphrey, 130
Miley
  Christiania, 38
Milhollen
  Henry, 127
Millar
  Francis, 35
Millemon
  Eliza, 15
  George, 15
Miller
  Capt., 13
  Daniel, 103
  David, 91
  Jeremiah, 62
  Jesse, 20
  Margaret, 42
  Peter, 15
  Robert H., 25
  Valentine, 75
  William, 13
  William H., 13
Mills
  James, 9

Mary, 127
Milner
David, 140
Mines
Ann K., 66
Eliza, 124
F. Scott, 78
John, 7, 66, 132
Martha, 7
Rev., 124
T. J. A., 78
T. J. Addison, 110
Minister
Adie, 76, 81, 83, 85, 87,
88, 94, 96, 100, 102,
103, 109, 116, 117,
122, 129, 130, 136,
137, 139
Allemong, 106
Allen, 23
Andrews, 101
Anthony, 74
Armstrong, 53
Baker, 3, 41, 44, 49, 51,
61, 62, 91
Balch, 23, 31
Barnes, 98
Bartow, 67
Bascom, 35
Bashair, 81
Bashaw, 39
Bear, 111
Beck, 13
Berkley, 110
Berry, 139
Birkby, 11, 12, 13, 14,
15, 16, 18, 19, 20, 23,
24, 25, 26, 27, 28, 29,
30, 31, 32, 34, 35, 36,
37, 38, 39, 40, 41, 42,
43, 44, 45, 46, 49, 50,
51, 52, 54, 55, 56, 57,
59, 60, 62, 63, 65, 66,
67, 71, 72, 73, 74, 75,
76, 77, 79, 80, 81, 82,
83, 84, 85, 86, 87, 91,
92, 94, 95, 96, 100,
101, 102, 103, 104,
105, 106, 107, 108,
109, 110, 111, 113,
114, 116, 120, 121,
122, 124, 125, 126,
127, 128, 129, 131,
132, 133, 134, 135,
136, 138, 139
Bishop, 116
Bond, 80
Booten, 8, 79
Bossler, 51

Boyd, 112, 115, 117,
118, 121
Boyleston, 1
Brady, 5
Broadus, 90, 106, 119
Brooke, 86, 110
Brown, 6, 24, 40, 54, 56,
75, 82
Bryson, 90
Buck, 80, 94
Bunn, 74
Burch, 28, 29, 30, 31,
34, 35, 36, 38, 41, 42,
43, 44
Burges, 78
Burkby, 11
Butler, 65
Cadden, 130
Camden, 130
Campbell, 101, 103
Carpenter, 80
Cayler, 101
Chamberlain, 74
Chapman, 23, 30
Clark, 60, 71
Clarke, 62, 63, 64, 65,
96
Collins, 70, 107, 109,
120, 130
Converse, 114
Cookman, 123
Cornwall, 99
Coskrey, 93
Crocker, 88
Curley, 115
Cutler, 70
Dagg, 13, 17, 23
Daggy, 93
Dalvol, 94
Dana, 94, 98, 130
Davis, 35, 58, 61, 67, 76,
122
Deems, 113
Dorsey, 67, 72, 75, 78,
80, 84, 87, 93, 115,
135
Drane, 96
Duncan, 58
Dunn, 2, 5, 7, 13, 17, 20,
35, 36, 39, 47
Edwards, 74, 128
Elbert, 10
Evans, 37, 40, 95, 131,
132
Finnell, 8
Foote, 64
Fry, 77
Frye, 23, 29, 60, 66, 88
Fullerton, 47
Furlong, 85, 87

Gildea, 82
Gillis, 96
Gilliss, 132
Gillmore, 4, 6, 10, 32
Gilmore, 1, 2, 3, 4, 5, 6,
7, 8, 10, 11, 14, 15,
18, 20, 21, 23, 24, 25,
26, 27, 28, 29, 30, 32,
33, 34, 35, 36, 37, 38,
40, 41, 42, 43, 44, 45,
46, 47, 48, 49, 50, 51,
52, 53, 55, 56, 57, 58,
59, 60, 61, 62, 63, 64,
65, 66, 67, 68, 69, 70,
71, 72, 73, 74, 75, 76,
77, 78, 79, 80, 81, 83,
84, 85, 86, 93, 95, 98,
100, 101, 102, 103,
104, 105, 106, 108,
109, 110, 112, 113,
114, 115, 116, 117,
118, 119, 120, 122,
123, 125, 126, 128,
129, 130, 133, 134,
137, 138
Gold, 19
Gover, 120, 121, 122,
123, 124, 125, 126,
128, 129, 133, 134,
136, 137
Green, 30, 33, 53, 56
Griffith, 5, 6, 7, 8, 9
Guest, 58, 59, 107
Hamilton, 73, 80
Hanson, 14, 92
Hargrove, 83, 84
Harrison, 37
Hauer, 91, 93, 95, 97
Hawley, 9, 73, 97, 101,
111
Helfenstein, 15, 21
Helfinstein, 19
Henderson, 90
Henning, 70
Henshaw, 43, 96
Henson, 89
Herndon, 106, 114, 118,
128, 133
Higgins, 9
Hill, 58, 74
Hitt, 23
Hoover, 136
Humphreys, 77, 105
Hutchinson, 61
Jackson, 49, 53, 56, 59,
82, 84, 90, 94, 97
Jacobs, 64
John, 58
Johns, 9, 83, 121

Robert, 70
Thomas, 20
Willie E., 20
Newton
  Ann, 18
  Eleanor, 39
  Elizabeth, 28, 89
  Frances E., 39
  Harriet, 7
  Ignatious, 89
  James, 39
  James F., 4, 62
  John, 7
  Joseph T., 59
  Mary A., 74
  Mrs., 59
Nicewarner
  Susan, 44
Nicholas
  Wilson C., 12
Nichols
  Dolphin, 63
  Hannah, 60
  Hannah J., 96
  Henry H., 133
  Isaac G., 110
  Jacab, 75
  Jacob, 106
  Joseph, 94
  Joshua, 50
  Lydia, 73
  Mary A., 104
  Mary F., 30
  Patience, 109
  Rebecca M., 114
  Samuel, 39
  Sarah, 4
  Susan A., 133
  Thomas, 30, 42, 97
Nicholson
  Philip, 11
Nickolls
  Cecilia, 40
Nickols
  Isaac, 17
Niles
  H., 82
  Hezakiah, 43
  Hezekiah, 69
  John W., 82
  Robert D., 69
Nixon
  Ann, 62, 106, 130
  James, 91
  Joel, 95
  John, 130
  Lorenzo D., 82
  Malinda E., 95
  Samuel, 119, 125, 126
  Sarah, 91

Nolan
  Frances, 23
Noland
  Anna L., 111
  Catharine P., 100
  Dade P., 113
  Elizabeth, 124
  Elizabeth M., 71
  Emily A., 63
  Frances C., 17
  George W., 94
  Lloyd, 54, 87, 88, 111
  Peyton, 88
  Samuel, 38, 88
  Thomas, 71
  Thomas J., 40
  Thomas L., 87
  W. H., 69
  William, 17
Nolands
  Lloyd, 100
Norris
  Ignatius, 91
  James, 14
  John, 74
  Mahlon T., 38
  Mary, 91
  William, 26
North
  Gen., 52
  Miss, 52
  Nathaniel G., 96
Norton
  Alvira A., 49
  Mahala S., 46
  Nathaniel, 5
Norwood
  Elizabeth, 46
  George, 27
Nuswanger
  Christian, 37

O'Neale
  Georgiann C., 57
  Thomas, 28
  William, 57, 110
Oard
  Sarah A., 99
Oatyar
  Peter, 86
Oden
  Benjamin, 70, 126
  Christiana H., 70, 126
  Thomas, 75
Odies
  Madison, 91
Offutt
  A. D., 118
  Joseph C., 92
Ogden

David, 71, 135
Elizabeth, 135
Hezekiah, 4
Jonathan, 76
Rebecca, 71
Oldham
  Newton, 134
Opie
  Hierom L., 99
Oram
  Henry, 82
  Mary, 87
Orr
  Elizabeth, 75
  Ellen L., 56
  John D., 53, 56
  Mary A., 53
  William G., 20
Orrick
  Elizabeth C. H., 92
  George, 92
Orrison
  Abel, 1
  Anna, 1
  Arthur, 65
  Elizabeth, 45
  Hannah, 29
  Jesse, 34
  John, 92
  Jonah W., 53
  Margaret, 59
  Matthew, 34
  Presley, 72
  Sarah, 15, 55
  Sarah A., 131
Orum
  Henry, 12
Osborn
  Elizabeth S., 139
  Nicholas, 139
Osborne
  Addison, 102
  Logan, 127
  Lydia A., 102
  Margaret C., 127
Osburn
  Caroline F., 43
  Dorcas, 14
  Emily P., 62
  Hannah, 81
  Harriett, 2
  Herod, 99
  Logan, 81
  Malinda, 41
  Margaret, 61
  Mary P., 135
  Morris, 41, 61, 69, 118
  Nicholas, 43
  Norval, 35
  Phenius, 61

Ann, 19
Ebenezer, 19
Mary, 43
Potterfield
Daniel, 51
Jonathan, 45, 61
Potts
E. F., 60
Edward D., 52
Eliza, 8
Elizabeth, 35
Enos, 75
Jane A., 34
Jonas, 110
Maria, 19
Matilda I., 30
Samuel, 76
Poulson
Susan, 10
Zachariah, 10
Poulton
Alfred, 41
Ann C., 138
Harriet A., 131
William, 128
Powell
Alfred B., 138
Alfred H., 45, 56, 64,
  105, 121
Amey, 109
Burr, 19, 58, 118
Charles L., 63
Cuthbert, 37, 40, 87, 98,
  101, 103, 111
Delia, 126
Elizabeth W., 58
Ellen D., 103
Francis W., 96
George C., 70
Jane E., 103
Jane S., 87
John L., 126
Joseph, 103
Levin M., 64, 132
Louisa M., 103
Margaret A., 108
Margaret C., 138
Mary E., 37, 101
S. E., 53
Samuel, 74
Sarah E., 133
Sarah H., 19
Power
Richard W. A., 100
Robert, 60
Powers
Henry, 47
Preston
Francis, 97
William C., 97

Price
Benjamin, 19, 113
Benjemimia, 113
Elizabeth, 3
George, 17, 71
Matilda H., 73
Sarah, 19
William B., 71
Priest
Thomas, 42
Prince
Mathias, 135
Prosser
William M., 118
Protzman
Francis, 84
Purcell
Samuel, 139
Valentine, 106
Valentine V., 106
Pursel
Lot, 78
Pusey
Joshua, 84
Mary A., 84
Pyott
John, 102, 106
Sarah, 102

Quaile
Mary, 47
Quick
Armistead, 108

Race
Mary, 23
Rebecca H. L., 61
Rallings
Thomas, 10
Ramsay
Andrew, 11
John, 27
Randall
Joseph, 34
Randolph
Archibald, 58
Catharine C., 76
Harry, 76
James M., 85
Lucy B., 58
Martha, 103
Robert B., 86
Thomas J., 12, 103
Thomas M., 85
Ratcliffe
Ann M., 46
Joshua, 40
R. Meredith, 109
Rathie
Benjamin D., 130

Rattie
John B., 88
Razor
Barbara, 54
Read
Mary J., 104
Reardon
Henry B., 102
Rector
Catharine, 35
Redhair
Martin, 140
Mary, 140
Reece
Mary A., 105
Reed
Alice, 11
Anna, 5
Isaac S., 75
John, 69
Lydia C., 111
Malinda, 65
Maria, 69
Mary A., 79
Mary E., 124
Rebecca, 1
Robert, 11
Robert S., 54
Reese
Sarah E., 33
Reeves
William, 68
Reiley
John W., 56
Joshua, 43, 56
Reily
Reuben, 32
Reynolds
Cornelia, 54
Enoch, 54
Rhea
John, 75
Rhind
John, 108
Rhodes
George, 17, 33, 57, 111,
  115
Jane, 111
Joseph, 111
Mary, 55, 106
Randolph, 33, 106
Susan M., 28
Rhyne
Eliza, 11
Rian
William, 126
Rice
Bethany, 21
Samuel, 106
Sarah E., 80

William H., 111
Richards
 Alice J., 36
 Ann M., 10
 Clementina B., 17
 Edmund P., 41
 Elizabeth F., 50
 George, 17, 36, 99
 Henry, 74
 Jemina, 74
 Mary A., 4
 Thomas, 59
Richardson
 Chloe A. M., 78
 Mary A., 88
Riggs
 William, 123
Right
 William, 13
Rind
 Henry G., 94
Rine
 John, 3
Rinker
 John, 79
 Thomas S., 62
Ritchie
 Catharine, 91
 Mary, 45
Riticor
 Charles, 136
Rivers
 Aminto, 3
 Charles, 64
 Elizabeth, 106
Rixey
 Churchill, 92
 Lavinia, 92
 Penelope, 92
 Richard, 92
Roach
 Frances E., 30
 Malinda, 18
 Maria, 24
 Richard, 1
 Sarah, 75
Roane
 James, 10
Robbin
 John, 52
Roberdeau
 Isaac, 54
Roberts
 George, 50
 Mrs., 15
 Sarah, 71
 Stephen, 18
 Thomas, 50
Robinson
 Archibald, 66

Seth D., 93
Robison
 Ann, 74
Rodney
 Caesar A., 65
 Joseph B., 65
Rogers
 Ann, 49
 Anna, 46
 Arthur, 60
 Asa, 56
 Edwin, 76
 Eliza, 74
 Elizabeth, 29, 127
 Hamilton, 28, 46
 Hugh, 49, 90
 James, 63
 John, 46
 Joseph, 74
 Martha A., 79
 Mary J., 76, 90
 Nancy, 85
 Sarah, 66
 Sarah Ann, 74
 Thomas, 62, 76, 85
 William, 23, 127
 William H., 90
Rogue
 Elizabeth, 29
Rollins
 Mary E., 128
 Thomas, 1
Rollison
 Frances, 134
Romine
 Mahala, 108
 Rebekah, 71
Ropp
 George W., 136
 Mary, 66
Rose
 Anna, 120
 Charles W., 96
 Charlotte, 18
 Charlotte E., 77
 Elizabeth A., 79
 Helen G., 13
 John, 5, 13, 18, 108,
  120, 138
 Levinah, 22
 Mary, 5
Roszel
 George, 57
 Nancy, 130
 S. W., 57
 Sarah, 61
 Stephen G., 130
Roszell
 Anne, 118
 S. A., 130

Stephen C., 118
 Stephen G., 127
Roundtree
 Nancy, 83
Rouse
 James, 55
Routt
 Catherine, 18
Routzong
 Adam, 47
 Catharine, 47
Rowen
 Joseph, 112
Rowles
 George, 41
 Mary A., 41
Rowzee
 Rebecca A., 94
Royal
 Ann, 100
Royston
 Matthew W., 135
 Sarah C., 135
Rozsel
 Stephen C., 27
Rump
 Frederick, 131
Rupp
 George W., 136
Ruse
 David, 134
 Lewis, 59
 Martha A., 132
Russel
 Harrison, 65
 Joseph, 1
Russell
 Aaron, 56
 Ann A., 90
 Elizabeth, 19
 Henry, 130
 John, 95
 Jonathan, 16
 Mary, 37
 Mary A., 85
 Rachel, 18
 Sarah E., 130
 Thomas, 17, 60
Russer
 Samuel, 85
Rust
 George, 117
 Hannah E., 112
 Margaret E., 117
 Mary, 63
 Robert B., 80, 133
 Susan D., 133
Ruter
 Eleanor, 81
Rutter

Brook W., 110
Catharine, 51
Charles, 12
David, 51
Maria, 22
Sowers
Catharine, 35
Spates
Eleanor, 7
Robert N., 80
Spaulding
Bazil, 94
Spencer
Catherine, 5
Emelie, 101
James S., 101
Spense
William, 61
Spiller
Thomas, 44
Spitler
Abraham, 8
Spring
Anne, 14
Jacob, 93
Susanna, 93
Stabler
Edward, 64
Mary P., 98
Stallings
John W., 126
Stanard
John, 82
Stanbaugh
S. C., 7
Stansbury
Sarah Ann, 67
Stark
General, 30
Mattie L., 97
Robert B., 97
Stedman
Eliza, 84
Uriah, 124
Steel
Nancy, 86
Steele
David, 107
Elizabeth, 107
James, 10
Lewis, 56
Steer
Eleanor, 43
Jonah, 104
Joseph, 79
Mary, 15
Steers
Isaac, 8
Stephenson
Elizabeth J., 120

George B., 95
James, 96, 132
Martha, 123
William A., 80, 132
Sterett
Joseph, 14
Sterrett
Samuel, 31, 87
Steuart
William, 97
Stevens
Henry, 106
John, 86
Thomas H., 126
Stewart
Elizabeth, 122, 139
Stocks
Hanna, 125
Stone
Daniel, 71
Jemima, 59
Mrs., 103
Sarah, 103
William M., 110
Stoneburner
Christian, 5
Christopher, 28
Elizabeth, 20
Frances M., 65
Henry, 35
Margaret, 58
Susan, 4
Stonestreet
James E., 59
Stover
Edwin A., 29
Joseph, 8
Sarah B., 120
Stovin
John L., 44
Stowe
John, 29
Stream
Jane, 125
Streeks
Martha A., 133
Stribling
C. M., 132
Cecilia, 19
Francis, 19, 26, 27, 60
Margaret A., 77
Thomas, 26
Strickland
John, 99
Strother
James, 6
John, 82
Lucy A., 81
Stuart
John, 67

Richard, 10
Stubblefield
James, 92
Mary, 92
Stuck
Ferdinand F., 24
Peter, 37
Sarah, 37
Styles
Mary, 122
Suffron
Samuel, 42
Sullivan
Catharine E., 30
Lewis, 51
Rebecca, 54
William, 110
Summerfield
John, 37
John S., 39
William, 39
Summers
Albina, 120
Emily E., 129
John, 22
Sally, 77
Samuel, 44, 129
Simon, 22
William, 120
Sumpter
Thomas, 75
Surghnor
Betsy, 69
Cuthbert P., 37
Harriett P. H., 101
Henry C., 39
James, 37, 101, 110
James B., 137
John, 39, 69, 77, 122, 137
Mary E., 122
Sally E., 137
Sarah, 137
Valentine, 113
Surghnour
John, 15
Sutherland
Alexander, 113, 135
Ann, 113
Caleb B., 93
Mary A., 135
Swan
Thomas, 140
Swann
John, 50, 57
John T., 92
Margaret, 99
Thomas, 13, 57, 87, 99
William T., 12
Swarts

Susan, 36
Winny, 52
Tilton
  Daniel, 63
Timms
  Elizabeth, 50
  Elizabeth T., 44
  James F., 115
  Jane, 104
  Jesse, 96, 105
  Mary R., 74
  Mrs., 96
Tipton
  Thomas, 131
Todd
  Erastus, 64
  Mary, 128
  Rebecca, 10
Tolbert
  Nancy, 14
Tole
  Lucinda, 41
Toler
  Richard H., 78
Tonnojuack
  Mry, 140
Torbet
  Malinda, 19
Torreyson
  Sally A., 90
  William, 90
Torrison
  Ann, 19
  Rebecca, 114
Torryson
  William, 53
Towner
  B. T., 109
  Catharine, 69
  Clarissa, 83
  Elizabeth, 56
  Jacob, 41, 112
Towperman
  Maria, 62
Tracey
  Anna, 63
Trahern
  James, 136
Trail
  Leonard W., 78
Trayhorn
  Enos, 25
  Samuel, 26
Trenary
  William, 30
Trevilla
  John, 11
Tribby
  Ellin, 3
  Jesse, 50

Sarah, 54
Triplett
  Eleanor, 127
  Harriet, 14
  Harriett, 110
  Harriot, 140
  James, 12
  James L., 12
  James S., 98
  Margaret C., 32
  Mary E., 76
  Nimrod, 122
  Payton, 1
  Richard, 104
  Sarah, 26
  Simon, 127
  Thomas, 32
  Uriel, 85
Tripplett
  George, 17
Troutwine
  Ann M., 140
  William, 140
Trundle
  Daniel, 53
  Mary E., 53
  Otho W., 114
  Perry L., 114
Tucken
  Judge, 65
Tucker
  Henry S. G., 93
  Margaret, 119
  William, 41
Turner
  Alexander, 53
  Charlotte, 127
  Jane E., 110
  John, 6, 25, 124
  Marietta F., 70
  Nancy, 85
  Thomas, 70
Tustin
  Septimus, 35
Tuston
  Mrs., 48
Tutt
  Ann M., 41
  Charles, 41
  Charles P., 115, 139
  Maria L., 139
  Mary B., 115
  Philip, 35
  Virginia M., 112
Tyler
  Alice J., 45
  Ann M., 73
  Charles, 112
  Edmund, 36, 45, 60, 109
  James M., 73

John, 134
Nathaniel, 95
Sarah, 112
Sarah B., 134

Uhler
  Eliza P., 137
  John, 137
Ullum
  Josiah, 93
Umbrage
  Joseph, 19
Underwood
  Ellen, 41
  Samuel, 42, 69
  Tamsen, 56
Updike
  Nancy, 126
Upperman
  Harry, 23
Upshur
  Lyttleton, 77
Urton
  Phebe A., 42

Vail
  Christopher, 3
  J. E., 3
Vallendingham
  Richard, 28
Van Buren
  Abraham, 114
Van Horn
  Elizabeth, 2
  James, 127
  Mary, 127
Van Horne
  Craven O., 87
Van Pelt
  Betsey A., 80
  Elizabeth, 68
  Richard, 77
Van Sickler
  John, 40
Van Swearingen
  Thomas, 21
Vananda
  Lawson, 71
Vandevanter
  Isaac, 112
  Mary, 112
Vandeventer
  Albert, 108
  Cornelius, 38
  Dr., 34
  Duanna, 36
  Gabriel, 83, 139
  Isaac, 36, 46, 87, 118
  John, 64
  Leonah, 48

Withers
  Adelaide, 102
Wolf
  Alfred L., 74
Wolkard
  Elizabeth, 2
Wood
  Elizabeth, 33
  James, 13
  John, 79
  John W., 51
  Mark, 27, 105
  Mary, 105
  Racheal, 79
Woodard
  Julia A., 124
Wooddy
  David, 58
  Elizabeth, 55
  Emily A., 46
  Jane, 60
  William, 24, 46, 55
  William W. A., 46
Woodford
  Elizabeth, 52
Woodly
  Elizabeth, 38
Woodward
  Caroline, 123
Woody
  James, 74
  John W., 116
  Mary A. L., 121
  Ruth B., 121
  William, 121
Workman
  John, 110

Matilda, 56
Wornal
  Ann, 51
  James, 51
Wornel
  John, 18, 125
  Rachel, 125
Wornell
  Elizabeth, 102
Worrall
  Anna, 90
  John, 90
Worsley
  Jane, 83
  John, 83
Worthington
  Mary M., 96
  Robert, 63, 96
  William M., 132
Wren
  John, 72
  Mary J., 107
Wright
  Anthony, 4
  Ann, 133
  Ann R., 23
  Eliza S., 82
  Isaac, 23, 106
  J. B., 80
  Jane, 16, 33
  John, 131
  Jotham, 114
  Mahala, 130
  Margaret, 131
  Mary, 117
  Nancy, 133
  Rebecca B., 114

Susan, 73, 106
William, 2, 16, 51, 133
Wyer
  Edward, 115
Wynkoop
  Catharine, 134, 139
  Garret, 127
  John, 124
  John J., 134
  Margaret, 71
  Sarah E., 131

Yabower
  Elizabeth, 126
Yachy
  Jacob, 63
Yates
  Vurlinda, 38
Yeates
  Verlinda I., 41
Yeaton
  Joshua, 90
Yemans
  Cyrus, 112
  Laura E., 112
Young
  Adam, 57
  Andrew, 38
  Deborah, 33
  Henry, 62
  Rosanna, 57
  Samuel, 112, 113

Zellers
  Catharine A., 136

Obituary of Charles Elgin
6 April 1824 page 3, column 1

We feel a melan holy [*sic*] pleasure in announcing that the body of COLONEL CHARLES ELGIN, lost in the Potomac on the 9th ultimo was found on the first instant, about 6 miles below where he was lost. On Friday his remains were brought to town and interred with Military honours in the Presbyterian burying ground, by the company of Independent Blues, commanded by Capt. Saunders. On the arrival of the body at the church it was conveyed into the open space under the pulpit, when the Rev. Mr. Burch delivered an appropriate address from these words; "There remaineth therefore, a rest for the people of God." The rev. orator in an eloquent and impressive manner adverted to the darkness which enveloped the human mind, among the most enlightened philosophers of the Heathen world, on the immortality of the soul, and their profound ignorance of the doctrine of the Resurrection. He then dwelt on the uncertainty of this consoling doctrine as displayed in the Revelation of the gospel of Jesus Christ, and illustrated this great truth by arguments drawn from the inspired writings. His address to the bereaved family of Col. Elgin was consoling and impressive. The exercises at the church were closed with solemn prayer. The body was then conveyed to the silent grave, where with throbbing hearts and tearful eyes the honours established by military usage was paid.

We cannot omit to notice that on this occasion his honour Judge White adjourned his court as a mark of respect to the deceased; a delicate attention from a gentleman who gallantly devoted the morning of his life to the service of his country, and now fills the very honourable office of administering that wise system of laws which his personal bravery contributed to establish.

It will not be uninteresting to the numerous friends and relatives of Col. Elgin to state, that a large sum of money and every valuable paper which he had about his person have been recovered uninjured.

Obituary of Mary Monroe
26 September 1826

Died, in this town, on Monday evening, the 18th inst. Mrs. MARY MONROE, consort of Mr. John H. in the 26th year of her age. The writer of this notice, averse to a practice of the kind, shall not attempt to portray in strains of fulsome panegyric, the amiable life, and unspotted reputation of the deceased. He would rather endeavour to benefit the living, than to eulogize the dead; and shall therefore strictly confine himself in these remarks, to a few brief observations touching the Christian's hope of life and immortality, as ought to light by the gospel, and evidenced in the death of the believer. The subject of this notice, though for several years a member of the Methodist Episcopal church, had never, previous to her last illness, and until within a week of her dissolution, made any profession of the real enjoyment of religion. Prostrated for a considerable length of time upon a bed of affliction and pain, she found herself destitute of the consolation which alone can cheer the sinking spirits, and support the over burthened soul. In its sad and solemn hour of distress—Death, approached, with all his gloomy terrors and the grave yawned to receive its victim–It was then, indeed, that the strong alone could deliver the lawful captive, and vanquish the destroyer. In this awful crisis, of private woe, it pleased the divine goodness to shine into the heart of the penitent suffers; and, in the exercise of his benign influence, to manifest himself as *the Saviour,* healing the broken-hearted etc. etc.